STRATEGIC REWARD

Implementing more effective reward management

Michael Armstrong & Duncan Brown

KOGAN PAGE

London and Phi

Publisher's note

Every possible effort has been made to ensure that the information contained in this book is accurate at the time of going to press, and the publishers and authors cannot accept responsibility for any errors or omissions, however caused. No responsibility for loss or damage occasioned to any person acting, or refraining from action, as a result of the material in this publication can be accepted by the editor, the publisher or any of the authors.

First published in Great Britain and the United States in 2006 by Kogan Page Limited
First published in paperback in 2009

120 Pentonville Road
London N1 9JN
United Kingdom
www.koganpage.com

525 South 4th Street, #241
Philadelphia PA 19147
USA

ISBN 978 0 7494 5618 4

British Library Cataloguing-in-Publication Data

A CIP record for this book is available from the British Library.

Library of Congress Cataloging-in-Publication Data

Armstrong, Michael, 1928–
    Strategic reward : implementing more effective reward management / Michael Armstrong and Duncan Brown — 1st ed.
        p. cm.
    Includes bibliographical references and index.
    ISBN 978-0-7494-5618-4
    1. Compensation management. 2. Incentives in industry. 3. Employee motivation. 4. Strategic planning. I. Brown, Duncan, 1960– II. Title
    HF5549.5.C67A762 2009
    658.3'2--dc22

                                                                                    2009010648

Typeset by Digital Publishing Solutions
Printed and bound in India by Replika Press Pvt Ltd

Contents

to line managers 195; The varied reward responsibilities of line
managers 197; Ensuring the commitment and capability of line
managers 203

Introduction

Strategic reward is the process of deciding what route to take in developing and implementing appropriate reward arrangements and dealing with the issues that arise in making that journey. Implementation is the most pressing of those issues. The starting point is design but the purpose is delivery.

OUR PHILOSOPHY

When mostly North American concepts of strategic HRM and reward first entered into management thinking and practice in the UK we were some of their most ardent advocates, writing and advising individual employers on the benefits of aligning their reward systems so as to drive business performance. We helped to articulate strategic plans and visions, and to design the pay and reward changes that would secure better alignment and performance.

Some 20 years later, we are a little older and a little wiser as a result of these experiences. We remain passionate proponents of a strategic approach to reward management. But in conducting and observing this work we have seen some of the risks as well as the opportunities in pursuing the reward strategy path: of an over-focus on planning at the expense of process and practice; on design rather than delivery; on the boardroom and the HR function rather than on first and front line managers and employees; and on concept rather than communications.

At times there has been a tendency to over-ambition and optimism in terms of what could and couldn't be achieved by changing pay and reward arrangements, and how quickly real change could be delivered and business results secured. At times the focus on internal business fit led to narrow-minded reward determinism, and a lack of attention to the increasingly important external influences and constraints on reward from the shifting tax and wider legislative, economic and social environment. Sometimes the focus on designs and desires meant that the requirements and skills of line and reward managers were insufficiently diagnosed and developed.

In researching this book, our reward strategy faith has been renewed and refreshed, and we have found that strategic reward management is even more critical in these turbulent times to the increasingly intertwined dual agenda of the successful performance of organizations and the motivation and engagement of their people. There is no alternative route for effective reward management. But a somewhat different, more realistic, more varied and balanced approach to reward strategy has evolved in the UK environment as summarized below. It is this broad approach, its causes and its common components that we aim to define and profile in this book.

OUR OBSERVATIONS ON REWARD

Our philosophy, which could be described as 'the new realism' on reward strategy, has been formed by what we have observed has been happening in the UK over recent years. As set out in Figure 0.1, there has been a transformation in practice and process extending to every aspect of reward management.

While every situation is different, it is this overall shift in the concept and practice of strategic reward management over recent years that we attempt to portray in this book.

UNDERPINNING THEMES

Our joint experience in advising on reward strategies and researching how organizations undertake the demanding task of formulating and implementing strategy has identified a number of key considerations that govern our views on strategic reward and are explored throughout this book. These themes are concerned with the importance of:

▌ appreciating that a good strategy is one that works and therefore focusing on implementation programmes;

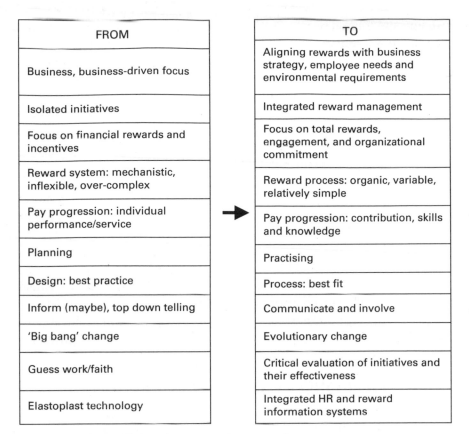

FROM	TO
Business, business-driven focus	Aligning rewards with business strategy, employee needs and environmental requirements
Isolated initiatives	Integrated reward management
Focus on financial rewards and incentives	Focus on total rewards, engagement, and organizational commitment
Reward system: mechanistic, inflexible, over-complex	Reward process: organic, variable, relatively simple
Pay progression: individual performance/service	Pay progression: contribution, skills and knowledge
Planning	Practising
Design: best practice	Process: best fit
Inform (maybe), top down telling	Communicate and involve
'Big bang' change	Evolutionary change
Guess work/faith	Critical evaluation of initiatives and their effectiveness
Elastoplast technology	Integrated HR and reward information systems

Figure 0.1 Overall developments in reward management

▎ 'planning with implementation in mind' – recognizing during the design process that plans have to be converted into reality and taking steps to anticipate the problems involved;

▎ aligning reward strategies with the business and HR strategies;

▎ ensuring that reward strategy fits the culture and characteristics of the organization, meets business needs and takes account of individual needs and preferences;

▎ being aware of good practice elsewhere but not being seduced by the notion that it is best practice, ie universally applicable and easily replicated – best fit is more important than best practice;

▎ paying more attention to using strategic reward initiatives to support the engagement and organizational commitment of people so that they are motivated and productive, rather than focusing on the mechanics of new reward 'fads';

▌ noting the following perceptive comments of Tim Fevyer Senior Manager, Compensation and Benefits, Lloyds TSB: 'It's vital that you get pay right – otherwise much damage can be done. But once it is, don't treat it like a sophisticated lever to influence motivation and empowerment. Employees place a great deal more emphasis on intangible rewards when deciding where to work and the level of commitment to give their work';

▌ bearing in mind that the development and implementation of reward strategy is an evolutionary process – it is about doing things better at a manageable pace rather than extraordinary new developments;

▌ appreciating that any reward strategy implementation programme will require a comprehensive change management programme;

▌ recognizing the importance of the part played by line managers in implementing reward strategy and the need to ensure that they are committed and have the necessary skills;

▌ paying close and continuous attention to communicating with employees and involving them in the development as well as the implementation of reward strategy;

▌ being absolutely clear about the objectives of the strategy and resolute about evaluating its effectiveness.

PLAN OF THE BOOK

In the chapters that follow we first describe the essence of strategic reward and its links to performance. We also examine how the concepts of engagement and organizational commitment can be treated strategically as an important part of a total reward programme. The second part of the book examines the context of strategic reward that explains some of the evolution in the approach – the internal and external environment, the impact of an increasingly knowledge- and service-based economy, and the broader trends in reward practices. In the third part we consider the processes involved in developing and implementing reward strategies, including looking at the roles of reward specialists and importantly, line managers, and complete it with a discussion of the vital subject of communicating the strategy to all concerned.

Part 1

The Essence of Strategic Reward

1

Strategic reward: what it means

This purpose of this chapter is to explain the meaning of strategic reward as an introduction to the various aspects of the subject contained in the rest of this book. The first part of the chapter deals with general considerations affecting the concept. It starts with a definition of strategic reward management, its aims, characteristics and rationale, and continues by reviewing the relationships between strategic reward and reward management and strategic reward and strategic management. The reality of the concept and two of the main issues affecting it (the rhetoric/reality gap and design and execution problems) are then explored. The second part of the chapter deals with the practice of strategic reward management including the development and application of a reward philosophy expressed in the form of guiding principles and the use of a total reward approach. A more detailed study of reward strategies and their content is provided in Chapter 2.

STRATEGIC REWARD MANAGEMENT DEFINED

Strategic reward management is about the development and implementation of reward strategies and the philosophies and guiding principles that underpin them. It provides answers to two basic questions: 1) where do we want our reward practices to be in a few years' time? And 2) how do we intend to get there? It therefore deals with both ends and means. As an end it describes a vision of what reward processes will look like in a few years' time. As a means, it shows how it is expected that the vision will be realized.

The foundation of strategic reward management is an understanding of the needs of the organization *and* its employees and how they can best be satisfied. It is also about developing the values of the organization on how people should be rewarded and formulating the principles that will govern how these values are enacted.

AIMS OF STRATEGIC REWARD

The overall objective of strategic reward is to develop and implement the reward policies, processes and practices required to support the achievement of the organization's business goals and meet the needs of its stakeholders. The specific aims are to:

▌ create total reward processes that are based on beliefs about what the organization values and wants to achieve;

▌ reward people for the value that they create;

▌ support the development of a performance culture;

▌ align reward practices with both business goals and employee values; as Brown (2001) emphasizes, the 'alignment of your reward practices with employee values and needs is every bit as important as alignment with business goals, and critical to the realization of the latter';

▌ reward the right things to convey the right message about what is important in terms of expected behaviours and outcomes;

▌ facilitate the attraction and retention of the skilled and competent people the organization needs, thus aiding the process of talent management and 'winning the war for talent';

▌ help in the process of motivating people and achieving high levels of engagement, positive discretionary behaviour and commitment to the organization;

▌ develop a positive employment relationship and psychological contract.

CHARACTERISTICS OF STRATEGIC REWARD

Strategic reward is a forward-looking approach to reward management that is characterized by an emphasis on integrating reward strategies with the business and HR strategies and aligning reward management processes with other key HR activities. It can be described as an attitude of mind – a belief in the need to plan ahead and make the plans happen.

Strategic reward management is visionary in the sense that it is concerned with creating and conceptualizing ideas of where the reward policies and processes of the organization should be going. But it is also empirical management that decides how in practice it is going to get there.

An important characteristic of strategic reward is that it is systematic in the sense that it is based on analyses of the organization's internal and external environment, its business needs and the needs of its stakeholders. It is conducted within a framework of articulated beliefs and values, and it is goal-oriented – the desired ends and the means of attaining them are clearly defined. Finally, it is concerned with implementation as well as design – it is about getting things done rather than just thinking about them.

STRATEGIC REWARD AND REWARD MANAGEMENT

Strategic reward is about making reward management work effectively for the organization and its people. Reward management as defined by Armstrong and Murlis (2004) deals with the formulation and implementation of strategies and policies that aim to reward people fairly, equitably and consistently in accordance with their value to the organization. It addresses issues affecting the design, implementation and maintenance of reward processes and practices that are geared to the improvement of organizational, team and individual performance. The main areas of reward management for which strategies are developed consist of processes for valuing jobs, grade and pay structures, pay adjustments, performance management, contingent and variable pay, employee benefits and recognition methods. These may be joined up and associated with other people management practices under the heading of 'total reward', as described later in this chapter.

STRATEGIC REWARD AND STRATEGIC MANAGEMENT

Strategic reward is an aspect of strategic management the purpose of which, as expressed by Kanter (1984), is to: 'elicit the present actions for the future' and become 'action vehicles – integrating and institutionalizing mechanisms for change'. Strategic management has been defined by Pearce and Robinson (1988) as 'the set of decisions and actions resulting in the formulation and implementation of strategies designed to achieve the objectives of an organization'. It has been described by Burns (1992) as being primarily concerned with:

▌ the full scope of an organization's activities, including corporate objectives and organizational boundaries;

▌ matching the activities of an organization to the environment in which it operates;

▌ ensuring that its internal structures, practices and procedures enable the organization to achieve its objectives;

▌ matching the activities of an organization to its resource capability, assessing the extent to which sufficient resources can be provided to take advantage of opportunities or to avoid threats in the organization's environment;

▌ acquiring, divesting and reallocating resources;

▌ translating the complex and dynamic set of external and internal variables an organization faces into a structured set of clear future objectives which can then be implemented on a day-to-day basis.

The emphasis is on identifying the organization's mission and strategies, but attention is also given to the resource base required to make it succeed. Managers who think strategically will have a broad and long-term view of where they are going. However, they will also be aware that they are responsible first, for planning how to allocate resources to opportunities that contribute to the implementation of strategy, and secondly, for managing these opportunities in ways that will add value to the results achieved by the firm. Strategic reward management is an important aspect of strategic management because it is concerned with the key resource in organizations, ie their human capital.

THE RATIONALE FOR STRATEGIC REWARD

In the words of Brown (2001) strategic reward 'is ultimately a way of thinking that you can apply to any reward issue arising in your organization, to see how you can create value from it'. More specifically, there are four arguments for adopting a strategic approach to reward management:

1. You must have some idea where you are going, or how do you know how to get there, and how do you know that you have arrived (if you ever do)?

2. As Cox and Purcell (1998) explain, 'the real benefit in reward strategies lies in complex linkages with other human resource management policies and practices'. Isn't this a good reason for developing a reward strategic framework that indicates how reward processes will be aligned to HR processes so that they are coherent and mutually supportive?

3. Pay costs in most organizations are by far the largest item of expense – they can be 60 per cent and often much more in labour-intensive organizations – so doesn't it make sense to think about how they should be managed and invested in the longer term?

4. There can be a positive relationship between rewards, in the broadest sense, and performance, so shouldn't we think about how we can strengthen that link?

THE REALITY OF STRATEGIC REWARD

Strategic reward in reality is not necessarily a formal, well-articulated and linear process that flows logically from the business strategy. Strategies may be formulated as they are used, and Mintzberg (1987) has emphasized that strategies emerge over time in response to evolving situations. Tyson (1997) points out that:

▌ strategy is emergent and flexible – it is always 'about to be', it never exists at the present time;

▌ strategy is not only realized by formal statements but also comes about by actions and reactions;

▌ strategy is a description of a future-oriented action which is always directed towards change;

▌ the management process itself conditions the strategies that emerge.

It has been suggested by Mintzberg et al (1988) that strategy can have a number of meanings other than that of being 'a plan, or something equivalent – a direction, a guide, a course of action'. Strategy can also be a pattern, that is, consistency in behaviour over time, or a perspective, an organization's fundamental way of doing things. Quinn (1980) produced the concept of 'logical incrementalism', which states that strategy evolves in several steps rather than being perceived as whole. Strategy, according to Mintzberg (1987), is best regarded as a 'pattern in a stream of activities'. Kay (1999), writing about 'strategy and the illusions of grand designs' also refers to the evolutionary nature of strategy. He comments that there is often little 'intentionality' in firms and that it was frequently the market rather than the visionary executive which chose the strategic match that was most effective.

Purcell (2001) draws attention to the implications of the concept of HRM strategy, which includes reward strategy, as an emerging rather than a deliberate process:

> Big strategies in HRM are most unlikely to come, *ex cathedra*, from the board as a fully formed, written strategy or planning paper. Strategy is much more intuitive and often only 'visible' after the event seen as 'emerging patterns of action'. This is especially the case when most of the strategy, as in HRM, is to do with internal implementation and performance strategies, not exclusively to do with external market ploys. As Murlis (1996) points out: 'Reward strategy will be characterized by diversity and conditioned both by the legacy of the past and the realities of the future'. All reward strategies are different just as all organizations are different. Of course, similar aspects of reward will be covered in the strategies of different organizations but they will be treated differently in accordance with variations between organizations in their contexts, business strategies and cultures.

To conclude, the reality of strategic reward is that it is not such a clear-cut process as some believe. It evolves, it changes and it has sometimes to be reactive rather than proactive.

STRATEGIC REWARD ISSUES

The rhetoric/reality gap

Stephen Bevan (2005), Director of Research, The Work Foundation, takes the view that reward management can be described as the field of HRM that boasts the widest gap between rhetoric and reality. All too often, strategic reward underpins grand plans for business improvement or cultural transformation, only to collapse into under-performance or PR disaster. He asks a number of pertinent questions:

1. To what can we attribute this spectacular and almost uniform record of under-delivery?

2. Is it that the concept of reward strategy is too grand, or is it conceptually flawed?

3. Is it that employers fail to make a sufficiently explicit link between business strategy and reward strategy?

4. Does effective reward strategy design tend to collapse once it comes to be implemented on the ground?

He suggests that failure to align each aspect of HR policy and practice – such as reward, training and development, recruitment and leadership style – with each other and with the overall business strategy was partly to blame. He examines two examples of how a choice between two competitive strategies – one innovation led, and one cost-reduction led – might lead to significantly different choices of reward structure and process. An innovation-led approach would, for example, focus on employee creativity, collaborative behaviour, a mix of individual and collective reward, broadly defined job roles and high investment in learning and development. A cost-reduction strategy, on the other hand, would have a short-term focus, narrowly defined jobs, a focus on individual reward, and limited opportunities for progression and development.

He suggests that practitioners should ask four key questions:

1. How does our reward strategy inhibit or facilitate organizational effectiveness?

2. How does our approach to reward reinforce or contradict other messages we send about performance, values and behaviour?

3. Are line managers advocates of the pay system or apologists for it?

4. How much managerial 'band-width' is taken up with pay-related issues?

Design and execution problems

Peter Reilly (2005a), Director HR Research & Consultancy, Institute for Employment Studies, considers that many types of reward are difficult to design (hence the poor take up of, say, team-based pay) and often harder still to implement – which is where most systems seem to fail. Better attention needs to be paid to:

∎ understanding the link between business strategy and reward;

∎ securing high-level understanding of the process of decision making;

∎ where possible, using a process of involving stakeholders in design;

∎ choosing design following an assessment of stakeholder needs, not preceding it;

∎ leaving lots of time for implementation, including training, communication and guidance;

∎ monitoring and evaluating the outcome and learning from the results.

A reward model for the 21st century, in his view, would probably give more attention to how to support the engagement of staff so they are motivated and productive. The problems associated with using concepts of 'new' and strategic reward are generally associated with the process, both in the design of reward schemes and in the execution. The starting point for the reward change is too often chosen without regard to the alignment with the business and HR strategies in place in the organization.

These comments and the previous ones made by Stephen Bevan pose a number of serious challenges to reward specialists. Our aim in this book is to respond to them by illustrating approaches now being taken that are in line with the themes we set out in our Introduction. Increasingly, organizations are recognizing the need to align reward strategies with business and HR strategies and employee needs; focusing on execution as well as design; allowing plenty of time for implementation, promoting organizational effectiveness and reinforcing values, performance, values and behaviour; involving stakeholders and evaluating outcomes. We include a number of case studies that suggest that Bevan's belief in 'a uniform record of under-delivery' in reward strategy is not universally applicable, and also comment in more detail on performance issues in Chapter 3.

THE PRACTICE OF STRATEGIC REWARD MANAGEMENT

Strategic reward management in practice involves:

▌ analysing the internal and external environment (see Chapters 5 to 8), existing reward arrangements and the needs of the business in order to assess the level of alignment, diagnose issues and problems and determine reward priorities (see Chapters 9 and 10);

▌ understanding the individual needs and preferences of employees (see Chapters 4, 10 and 13);

▌ formulating a reward philosophy expressed in guiding principles that inform the development and implementation of reward strategies (see pages 15 to 21 in this chapter and Chapter 2);

▌ creating a 'total reward' approach that ensures that the different elements of financial and non-financial reward are brought together (see pages 21 to 30 in this chapter);

▌ developing the detailed components and changes required in reward strategies, ensuring they support the business strategy and integrating them with other HR strategies (see Chapters 2 and 9);

▌ planning and then delivering successful implementation (Chapters 10 to 13).

The relationships between these activities are illustrated in Figure 1.1. Note the distinction between analysis and diagnosis (concepts which are often confused). Analysis is the process of finding out *what* is happening; diagnosis is the process of finding out *why* it is happening. These are related but separate activities.

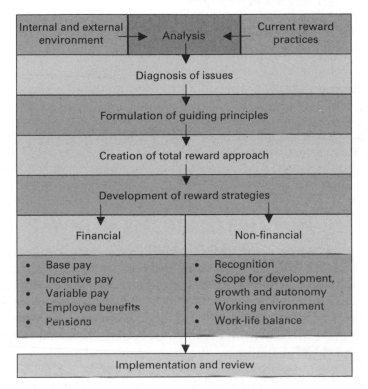

Figure 1.1   Strategic reward management activities

REWARD PHILOSOPHY AND GUIDING PRINCIPLES

Strategic reward management is based on a well-articulated philosophy – a set of beliefs and guiding principles that are consistent with the values of the organization and help to enact them. These include beliefs in the need to achieve fairness, equity, consistency and transparency in operating the reward system. The philosophy recognizes that if HRM is about investing in human capital from which a reasonable return is required, then it is proper to reward people differentially according to their contribution (ie the return on investment they generate).The reward philosophy of the organization is expressed in the form of guiding principles that define the approach an organization takes to dealing with reward. They are the basis for reward policies and provide guidelines for the actions contained in the reward strategy.

Members of the organization should be involved in the definition of guiding principles that can then be communicated to everyone to increase understanding of what underpins reward policies and practices. However, employees will suspend their judgement of the principles until they experience how they are applied. What matters to them are not the philosophies themselves but the pay practices emanating from them and the messages about the employment 'deal' that they receive as a consequence. It is the reality that is important, not the rhetoric.

Fundamental values

Guiding principles should incorporate or be influenced by general beliefs about fairness, equity, consistency and transparency. Reward strategies in the past have sometimes focused exclusively on business needs and alignment. Yet unless employees see and experience fairness and equity in their rewards, the strategy is unlikely to be delivered in practice.

Fairness

A fair reward system is one in which people are treated justly in accordance with what is due to them – their value to the organization. Fairness means that reward management processes operate in accordance with the principles of distributive and procedural justice. The concept of fairness was formulated by Jaques (1961) as the 'felt-fair' principle. This states that pay systems will be fair if they are felt to be fair. The assumptions underpinning the theory are that:

▌ there is an unrecognized standard of fair payment for any level of work;

▌ unconscious knowledge of the standard is shared among the population at work;

▌ to be equitable, pay must be felt to match the level of work and the capacity of the individual to do it;

▌ people should not receive less pay than they deserve by comparison with their fellow workers.

This felt-fair principle has passed into the common language of those concerned with reward management. It is often used as the final arbiter of how a job should be graded, sometimes overriding the conclusions reached by an analytical job evaluation exercise (the so called 'felt-fair test'). However, such tests are in danger of simply reproducing existing prejudices about relative job values.

Equity

Equity is achieved when people are rewarded appropriately in relation to others within the organization. Equitable reward processes ensure that relativities between jobs are measured as objectively as possible and that equal pay is provided for work of equal value.

Consistency

A consistent approach to the provision of rewards means that decisions on pay do not vary arbitrarily and without due cause between different people or at different times. They do not deviate from what would be generally regarded as fair and equitable.

Transparency

Transparency means that people understand how reward processes operate and how they are affected by them. The reasons for pay decisions are explained to them at the time they are made. Employees have a voice in the development of reward policies and practices and have the right to be given explanations of decisions and to comment on how they are made.

Specific guiding principles

Reward guiding principles may be concerned with such specific matters as:

▌ developing reward policies and practices that support the achievement of business goals;

▌ providing rewards that attract, retain and motivate staff and help to develop a high performance culture;

▌ maintaining competitive rates of pay;

▌ rewarding people according to their contribution;

▌ recognizing the value of everyone who is making an effective contribution, not just the exceptional performers;

▌ allowing a reasonable degree of flexibility in the operation of reward processes and in the choice of benefits by employees;

▌ devolving more responsibility for reward decisions to line managers.

Table 1.1   B&Q's reward philosophy and principles

Reward philosophy	Principles
• We will provide an innovative reward package that is valued by our staff and communicated brilliantly to reinforce the benefits of working for B&Q plc.	• Innovative and differentiated policies and benefits.
• Reward investment will be linked to company performance so that staff share in the success they create and, by going the extra mile, receive above average reward compared to local competitors.	• Basic salaries will be competitive. • Total compensation will be upper quartile. • We share the success of B&Q with all employees. • Increase variable pay as a percentage of overall to drive company performance. • Pay for performance. • Performance objectives must have line of sight for individuals/team.
• All parts of the total reward investment will add value to the business and reinforce our core purpose, goals and values.	• Non-cash recognition is a powerful driver of business performance. • Pay can grow without promotion. • Rewards are flexible around individual aspirations. • We will not discriminate on anything other than performance.

Examples of reward philosophies and guiding principles

B&Q

The reward philosophy and principles at retailer B&Q are shown in Table 1.1.

Elements of reward at BT

The five key principles of the new reward framework at BT are:

1. *Clarity* – the new reward framework brings transparency to the way people are rewarded for their contribution to the business. The same role profiles (within the same job families) now apply right across BT, and command the same published salary ranges. People know exactly where they stand.

2. *External focus* – the way we reward and recognize people must conform to the market in which we operate. Under the new reward framework, salary ranges are now aligned with the going rate for equivalent jobs across a range of comparable organizations, geographies and skill sets. This will ensure we remain competitive, and are able to recruit and retain the people we need.

3. *Focus on roles* – a person's place in the organization should be valued by the work they do – not by where they sit in a hierarchy. The new reward framework has replaced grades with job families, which represent a group of similar roles in a similar field of activity. A large number of operational managers from across the business have helped to define a structure that reflects the roles individuals actually do, not historical grades.

4. *Reward for performance* – people who perform well will earn higher rewards than people who don't. Reward decisions are now based on capability in role and proven contribution through achievement of objectives. People should be clear about why they earn what they do.

5. *Choice* – not all BT managers currently have a choice over how they receive their rewards. In keeping with BT's position as a highly innovative company and employer, the new framework will offer an increased choice over the benefits people receive as part of their total reward package. This approach ensures that everyone knows exactly where he or she stands in relation to the market, and in relation to his or her performance.

COLT Telecom

COLT's reward philosophy states that:

▌ COLT believes that talented and motivated people make a difference; talented people put us ahead of the competition and deliver the results on which the success of COLT is built. COLT seeks to offer a compensation and benefits package that rewards people for their contribution to the success of the company and ensures that external market competitiveness and internal relativities are taken into account.

▌ The *reward mix* is designed to promote a performance culture that underpins the company business strategy. Reward is geared to driving exceptional effort through the variable elements of the total package whilst maintaining flexibility, simplicity and equity within the guiding principles of driving discretionary effort, rewarding employee contribution and encouraging employees to behave like owners.

▌ The *compensation package* includes cash and non-cash payments as well as fixed and variable elements. The ability to have an impact on shareholder value influences the mix of the total reward package, with a greater emphasis on variable pay (bonus, share incentive and share ownership schemes) for those at the senior level within the company.

▌ *Base salaries* are benchmarked regularly across Europe against other telecommunication operators, the high-tech sector and other appropriate industries.

▌ The *performance management* system ensures that performance is assessed and used to differentiate achievement among employees at all levels, thus driving discretionary effort. The bonus scheme rewards individual performance against a mix of company and individual objectives and contribution to overall company performance.

▌ The company believes in encouraging an ownership mindset, so *share option* schemes offer employees a stake in the organization, which will allow them to share in the company's success over the medium and long term. COLT offers voluntary, all-employee share participation schemes in the countries where it is possible to do so. Management can participate in performance-related option schemes, and it is expected that those with greater opportunities to influence directly the success of the business will have a larger proportion of shareholding within their total reward package.

▌ *Benefits* are designed to be market competitive whilst protecting both employees and the company. They comply with local legislation, are tax effective and take into account social security benefits in all the countries within which COLT operates.

Lloyds TSB

The guiding reward strategy principles at Lloyds TSB are:

▌ Basic pay is linked to the market.

▌ Benefits are market driven and individually focused.

▌ Pay decisions are devolved to line managers.

▌ Pay reflects individual contribution in a high performance organization.

▌ Comply with equal pay principles.

▌ Variable pay is linked to performance.

▐ Wealth creation and share ownership are encouraged.

▐ Reward and HR practices are managed in an integrated way.

Tesco

The guiding principles here are:

▐ We will provide an innovative reward package that is valued by our staff and communicated brilliantly to reinforce the benefits of working for Tesco.

▐ Reward investment will be linked to company performance so that staff share in the success they create and, by going the extra mile, receive above average reward compared to local competitors.

▐ All parts of the total reward investment will add value to the business and reinforce our core purpose, goals and values.

TOTAL REWARD

An important component of what we characterize as the 'new' approach to strategic reward is the development of a total reward concept. There was a time when an organization's reward package was more or less straightforward. But this era in which reward was just about cash and benefits is gone forever. Increasingly, the emphasis in leading organizations is on total reward, including in addition to financial rewards more intangible rewards like the work environment and quality of life considerations, the opportunity for advancement and recognition, and flexible working – everything from telecommuting to variable hours. The CIPD 2005 reward survey found that 28 per cent of respondents were using a total reward approach (CIPD, 2005a).

When formulating a reward strategy it is necessary to rethink what is and what is not reward. The strategy needs to encompass all aspects of reward if it is to add real value, enhance employee engagement and commitment to the organization and minimize the loss of the best people. While there is little doubt that the financial aspects of reward remain a key element of the modern working relationship, they are not on their own sufficient to reinforce desired discretionary behaviour or support the kind of performance breakthroughs so many organizations seek today. The holistic approach of total reward provides for the integration with reward of a number of HR policies and practices such as employee development, resourcing, life-work balance, recognition schemes, work design and participation. It is about creating a truly and totally rewarding experience for people at work.

Total reward defined

As defined by Manus and Graham (2003), total reward 'includes all types of rewards – indirect as well as direct, and intrinsic as well as extrinsic'. Each aspect of reward, namely base pay, contingent pay, employee benefits and non-financial rewards, which include intrinsic rewards from the work itself, are linked together and treated as an integrated and coherent whole. Total reward combines the impact of the two major categories of reward as defined below and illustrated in Figure 1.2: *transactional rewards* – tangible rewards arising from transactions between the employer and employees concerning pay and benefits; and *relational rewards* – intangible rewards concerned with learning and development and the work experience.

A total reward approach is holistic: reliance is not placed on one or two reward mechanisms operating in isolation, and account is taken of every way in which people can be rewarded and obtain satisfaction through their work. The aim is to maximize the combined impact of a wide range of reward initiatives on motivation, job engagement and organizational commitment. As O'Neal (1998) has explained: 'Total reward embraces everything that employees value in the employment relationship.' An equally wide definition of total reward is offered by WorldatWork (2000) who state that total rewards are 'all of the employer's available tools that may be used to attract, retain, motivate and satisfy employees'.

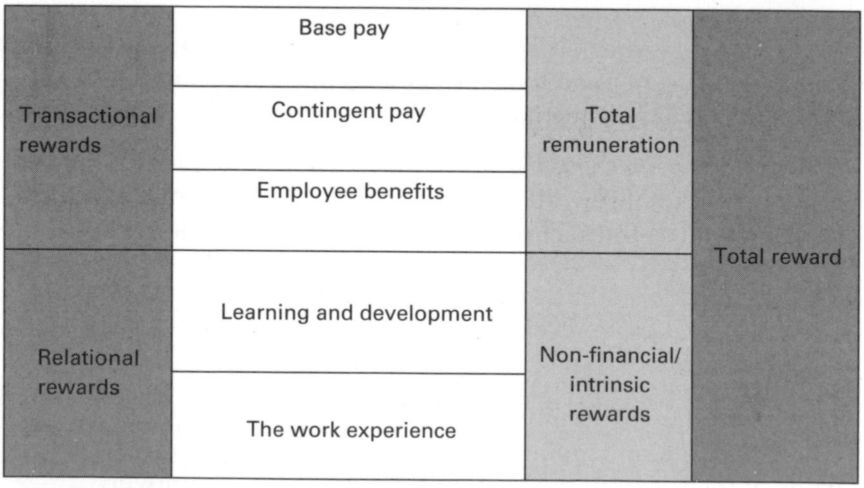

Transactional rewards	Base pay	Total remuneration	Total reward
	Contingent pay		
	Employee benefits		
Relational rewards	Learning and development	Non-financial/ intrinsic rewards	
	The work experience		

Figure 1.2   The components of total reward

The conceptual basis of total rewards is that of configuration or 'bundling', so that different reward processes are interrelated, complementary and mutually reinforcing. Total reward strategies are vertically integrated with business strategies, but they are also horizontally integrated with other HR strategies to achieve internal consistency.

The significance of total reward

Essentially, the notion of total reward says that there is more to rewarding people than throwing money at them. For O'Neal (1998), a total reward strategy is critical to addressing the issues created by recruitment and re-tention as well as providing a means of influencing behaviour:

> It can help create a work experience that meets the needs of employees and encourages them to contribute extra effort, by developing a deal that addresses a broad range of issues and by spending reward dollars where they will be most effective in addressing workers' shifting values.

Perhaps the most powerful argument for a total rewards approach was produced by Pfeffer (1998):

> Creating a fun, challenging, and empowered work environment in which in-dividuals are able to use their abilities to do meaningful jobs for which they are shown appreciation is likely to be a more certain way to enhance motiva-tion and performance – even though creating such an environment may be more difficult and take more time than simply turning the reward lever.

The benefits of a total reward approach are:

▌ *Greater impact* – the combined effect of the different types of rewards will make a deeper and longer-lasting impact on the motivation, com-mitment and engagement of people.

▌ *Enhancing the employment relationship* – the employment relationship created by a total reward approach makes the maximum use of rela-tional as well as transactional rewards and will therefore appeal more to people.

▌ *Enhancing cost-effectiveness* – research shows that many employees undervalue the true cost of their reward package, and that different employees place a different value on the various aspects of the package. Total reward involves more effectively communicating the value of the whole package, and giving employees choices to enhance the perceived value of their own package at no extra cost to the employer.

▮ *Flexibility to meet individual needs* – as pointed out by Bloom and Milkovich (1998): 'Relational rewards may bind individuals more strongly to the organization because they can answer those special individual needs.'

▮ *Winning the war for talent* – relational rewards help talent management by delivering a positive psychological contract and enhancing organizational commitment. This can serve as a differentiator in the recruitment market because relational reward processes are more difficult to replicate than individual pay practices. The organization can become 'a great place to work' thus being an 'employer of choice' and attracting and retaining the talented people it needs.

The Towers Perrin model of total reward

A model of total reward developed by Towers Perrin is shown in Figure 1.3.

The upper two quadrants – pay and benefits – represent *transactional rewards*. These are financial in nature and are essential to recruit and retain staff but can be easily copied by competitors. By contrast, the *relational (non-financial) rewards* produced by the lower two quadrants are essential to enhancing the value of the upper two quadrants. The real power, as Thompson (2002) states, comes when organizations combine relational and transactional rewards.

APPROACHES TO TOTAL REWARD

Bristol-Myers Squibb

The company states that 'reward is much wider than just paying its staff a competitive salary'. It has designed its total reward package knowing that everyone works for the company for different reasons and that everyone places a different emphasis on the importance of each of the elements of total reward – there is no one-size-fits-all. It has also set out to use total reward to 'elevate and differentiate' Bristol-Myers Squibb from other companies, both in the same industry and beyond.

The three elements of total reward are:

1. *Compensation* – salary, performance-based bonus and stock options.

2. *Benefits* – non-contributory pension, life cover, private healthcare, perks and cars.

3. *Work experience* – defined as: 'All the elements which contribute to providing you with an environment that enables you to optimize your

Figure 1.3   The Towers Perrin model of total reward

contribution to the company and achieve your full potential, whilst maintaining a balance between your personal and professional life.' These include:

- acknowledgement, appreciation and recognition;
- balance of work and life;
- culture of Bristol-Myers Squibb;
- employee development;
- the working environment.

Centrica

For Centrica employees, the total reward approach integrates many diverse elements: *financial rewards* like base pay, contingent or variable pay, share ownership and employee benefits; and *non-financial rewards* such as the work environment, including recognition, quality of working life considerations, the opportunity to learn and develop skills and work-life policies.

It concentrates overall on developing reward management as a strategic, innovative and integrative process that is designed to meet the evolving needs of the organization and the people it employs.

The company believes that a total reward programme offers substantial benefits. These include:

▌ improving employees' perception of the value of their reward package;

▌ increased organizational performance through greater workforce commitment and motivation;

▌ improved recruitment, arising from a quantified total employment package;

▌ supporting the objective of becoming an 'employer of choice';

▌ promoting flexibility in pay delivery;

▌ reallocating reward to match individual employee needs;

▌ helping manage costs and maximize the return on the investment in HR;

▌ mixing extrinsic and intrinsic rewards to encourage employees' discretionary effort.

However, Centrica was aware that there were formidable stumbling blocks in delivering its reward strategy that it had to overcome, including:

▌ developing total reward is time-consuming – it took 10 months to plan and implement;

▌ it is easier to believe that total reward strategy is a good thing than to put it into practice;

▌ implementation and management requires full support from the management team – it is not something done by HR to the business;

▌ the cost of some intangible rewards are not quantifiable, hence it is difficult to make a business case.

Financial Services Authority (FSA)

Total reward policy at the FSA emphasizes the rewards that arise from the intrinsic interest and importance of the work itself and the opportunities for development it provides. It comprises:

▌ a unique insight into the full breadth of financial services;

▌ the chance to contribute first hand to the financial well-being of millions of UK consumers and to the health of our financial markets;

▌ outstanding technical and business skills development;

▌ access to a range of career development opportunities, including the ability to specialize or do a broad range of interesting jobs;

▌ a competitive overall remuneration package including a market-leading flexible benefits system.

The FSA was one of the first organizations in the UK public sector to adopt a total reward approach. It helped the organization to integrate the very different terms and conditions that existed in its many predecessor regulatory bodies and offers considerable choice in benefits to employees.

GlaxoSmithKline (GSK)

'TotalReward' at GSK consists of three elements:

1. *Total Cash* (base salary and bonus, plus long-term incentives for managers and executives).
2. *Lifestyle Benefits* (healthcare, employee assistance, family support, dental care).
3. *Savings Choices* (pension plan, *ShareSave, ShareReward*).

The complete package, the concept of which is based on employees understanding the total value of all the rewards they receive, not just the individual elements, is designed to attract, retain, motivate and develop the best talent. The proposition for employees is that 'TotalReward' gives them the opportunity to share in the company's success, makes it easier to balance home and working life, and helps them to take care of themselves and their families.

Lands' End

At Lands' End the focus is on total reward rather than just pay. The company tries to help people understand the value of their entire reward package – both financial and non-financial rewards. This is because, says Mark Harris, the Employee Services Director, 'although pay is important it is not decisive in motivating people to continuously improve their performance' and, 'no one ever left a good job because a competitor was offering an extra day's holiday'. Instead, Lands' End concentrates on rewards that recognize the whole person, namely the experience of being appreciated and valued. Everyone wants to be great, Mark Harris says, and 'it is our job to make that happen'. The total reward strategy consists of seven key strands:

1. *Financial rewards*. Traditional rewards – such as base pay and benefits – remain important fundamentals that companies must get right in order to compete for and retain key talent. Pay rates are pitched at or slightly above the median for the location and benefits are more generous than its rivals.

2. *Career development*. There is a strong emphasis on developing all employees at Lands' End. Many people now high in the ranks of the organization have worked their way up from some of the lowest-level jobs. The whole ethos is to encourage everyone to develop as far as they are able using on-the-job training and cross training.

3. *Pride*. This is one of the key elements of how Lands' End motivates its staff. The company seeks to engender a strong sense of pride in employees as to what the business stands for and the extent to which it delivers. Whether it succeeds or not is measured by the company's score in the *Great Place to Work survey*. The thinking behind why the company wants to inspire staff is straightforward: employees' willingness to do that little bit extra is the difference between a good experience for customers and a poor one. Lands' End reckons that the reason its staff are willing to go the extra mile is because of their sense of pride in what the organization stands for: quality, service and value.

4. *Appreciation*. Lands' End favours the term 'appreciation' to 'recognition', since it thinks the latter suggests something tangible. It prefers to look for any and every opportunity to demonstrate its real appreciation of what staff do. The company tries to show its appreciation by promoting six dimensions of employee well-being: physical, emotional, intellectual, social, spiritual and occupational.

5. *Make work challenging and fun*. Where jobs are repetitive or less challenging, it is particularly important to provide some challenge and fun. Lands' End believes that if it isn't possible to give people a choice as to the type of work they do, they can be given a choice as to how they do it.

6. *Leader relations*. For Lands' End the quality of the relationship between manager and employee is the biggest motivational factor at work, and has more influence on job satisfaction than anything else.

7. *Involvement*. Mark Harris believes that: 'Involvement shows respect for others, it adds emphasis to our view that everyone is important and there are few motivational things better than being able to influence and shape the way in which you do your own job or how the company operates.'

Lloyds TSB

At Lloyds TSB the emphasis is on creating a 'compelling employment offer' – one that is individually focused, tailored to employees' needs and interests, and more in tune with the expectations of a diverse workforce. By concentrating on monetary rewards it is all too easy to overlook ways of succeeding that rivals cannot readily copy. With competitive pressures so strong, the need for Lloyds TSB to differentiate its reward package from other financial services employers has never been more intense. The bank decided that what really gives an employer the edge as it struggles to woo and retain scarce talent is appealing to the beliefs, personal values and lifestyle choices of today's employees. Its total reward package, replete with one of the biggest flexible benefits schemes in the UK and a new share incentive plan, seeks to integrate all aspects of the work experience so that prominence is given not only to remuneration but also less tangible rewards.

Nationwide

Paul Bissell, Senior Manager, Rewards at Nationwide, defines its approach to total reward as follows:

> A mixture of pay elements, with a defined cash value, benefits which have an intrinsic value, a positive and enjoyable work environment and opportunities for learning and development, all designed to make Nationwide an employer of choice.

Nationwide is the highest rated large employer in the *Sunday Times* Best Company to Work For listing of 2005.

Norwich Union Insurance

'Progression, Performance and Pay' is the name given to Norwich Union Insurance's total reward strategy. It comprises four main elements:

1. *Reward* – salary and benefits, variable pay, all-employee share option plan and incentive awards.

2. *Career framework* – meaningful job content and career opportunities.

3. *Performance* – challenging work; recognition and brand supporting behaviours.

4. *Development* – learning opportunities and personal development.

Royal Bank of Scotland

The Royal Bank of Scotland states that:

> Our approach to total reward focuses on the overall content and value of the pay and benefits package and how this supports the needs of our staff and the Group as a whole. Put another way, it's the value of everything staff get in return for working for the bank.

Pay is just one element of the RBS reward package, and the compensation team is keen to ensure that the staff understand that it is their total package that is significant rather than individual elements within it. The concept is sold at a series of events and a desk calendar given to each staff member (see below) identifies one or more significant total reward events in nine of the 12 months.

An important element of the RBS approach to total reward is the use of a concept that the bank calls *ValueAccount*, which is made up of basic pay for non-managerial staff and basic plus benefits funding for managers. This distinction is made because managerial pay is market driven and includes entitlement to a company car and private medical insurance. The benefits element has been turned into a fixed percentage whereby salary is 90.9 per cent of the *ValueAccount* and the benefits spend is 10 per cent of 90.9 per cent, that is, 9.09 per cent. Pensions, profit-share payments, bonuses and so on are all based on the basic pay element rather than the *ValueAccount*.

Each June staff receive a personal reward statement. This sets out the value of the key elements of the total reward package and the available flexible benefits. Staff are also given a total reward desk calendar to reinforce the message about the unique employment offer.

2

Reward strategy: purpose and content

Strategic reward management was described in Chapter 1 as the process of formulating and implementing integrated reward strategies in accordance with defined guiding principles and a total reward policy. In this chapter there is a more detailed examination of reward strategy in terms of what it is, what is happening to it, its aims and structure, what it contains, and the criteria for effectiveness. Examples are provided of actual reward strategies. Approaches to developing and implementing reward strategy are dealt with in Chapters 7 and 8.

WHAT IS REWARD STRATEGY?

Reward strategy is a declaration of intent. It defines what an organization wants to do in the longer term to address critical reward issues and to develop and implement reward policies, practices and processes that will further the achievement of its business goals and meet the needs of its stakeholders. It starts from where the reward practices of the business are now and goes on to describe what they should become.

Reward strategy provides a sense of purpose and direction, a pathway that links the needs of the business and its people with the reward policies and practices of the organization and thereby communicates and explains these practices. It constitutes a framework for developing and putting into effect reward policies, practices and processes which ensure that people are rewarded for doing the things that increase the likelihood of the organization's business goals being achieved.

Reward strategy is underpinned by a reward philosophy. It is concerned not only with what should be done but *how* it should be done; with implementation as well as planning. It is based on an understanding of the culture of the organization and an appreciation of its needs and those of its people within the context in which the organization operates. This provides the basis upon which cultural fit is achieved and needs satisfied.

It is necessary to distinguish between reward strategy and the other elements of reward management, namely:

▌ *Reward policy*, which sets guidelines for decision making and action; for example, an organization may have a strategy to maintain competitive rates of pay and a policy which sets the levels of pay in the organization compared with median market rates.

▌ *Reward practice*, which comprises the techniques, structures, systems and procedures used to implement reward strategy and policy; for example, the policy on pay levels will lead to the practice of collecting and analysing market rate data, and making pay adjustments that reflect market rates of increase.

▌ *Reward process*, which describes the ways in which policies are implemented and practices carried out; for example, how the outcomes of surveys are applied and how managers manage the pay adjustment and review process.

WHAT'S HAPPENING TO REWARD STRATEGY?

The CIPD (2005a) annual reward management survey of 477 organizations revealed that 45 per cent of employers have developed, or are in the process of developing, a written reward strategy, aligned to their business and human resource strategies. The survey showed that as firms grow they take, or are forced to take, a more strategic approach to their reward practices and processes. Just under one-fifth (17 per cent) of organizations with fewer than 50 staff had a reward strategy, compared with 62 per cent of employers with 5,000 workers or more.

Respondents to the survey believe that on the whole their reward strategies are working well, as is shown in Figure 2.1.

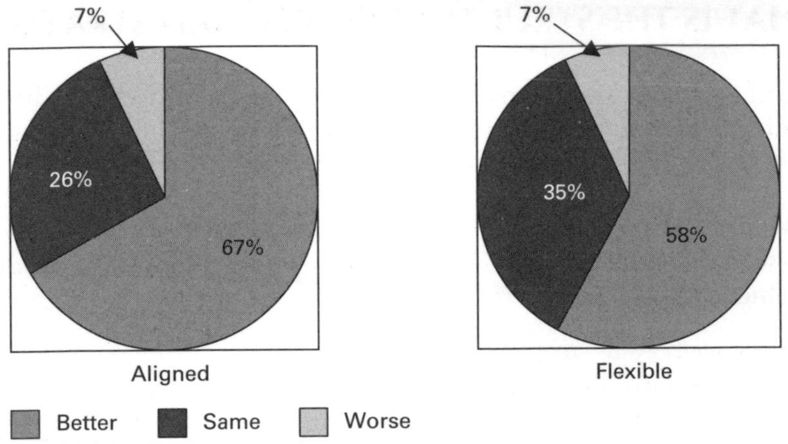
7%
26%
67%
Aligned
7%
35%
58%
Flexible
Better
Same
Worse

Figure 2.1 We think the reward strategies are working

WHAT ARE THE AIMS OF REWARD STRATEGY?

A key aim of reward strategy is to foster the development of a high performance culture, thus helping the organization to achieve its business goals. In the familiar phrase, reward strategy also aims to create policies and practices that will attract, retain and motivate high quality people. Moreover, it is concerned with enhancing job engagement and encouraging behaviours that deliver the required results and are in line with the organization's values.

Reward strategy often has to be a balancing act, because of the potentially conflicting goals. For example, it may be necessary to reconcile the competing claims of being externally competitive *and* internally equitable – paying a specialist more money to reflect market rate pressures may disrupt internal relativities.

The key reward strategy objectives revealed by the 2005 CIPD reward survey are business-related. The most frequently mentioned priority is supporting the goals of the organization, followed by rewarding, recruiting and retaining high performers. The percentages of respondents mentioning different reward strategy goals are:

Support business goals	79 per cent
Reward high performers	64 per cent
Recruit and retain high performers	62 per cent
Link pay to the market	53 per cent
Achieve/maintain market competitiveness	51 per cent
Manage pay costs	50 per cent
Ensure internal equity	41 per cent

WHAT IS THE STRUCTURE OF REWARD STRATEGY?

Reward strategies are diverse and so are the structures used by different organizations to define and present them. However, the following four headings provide some guidance on what might be included:

1. *A statement of intentions* – the future desired state of reward and the reward initiatives that it is proposed should be taken in order to achieve it.

2. *A rationale* – the reasons why the proposals are being made. The rationale makes out the business case for the proposals, indicating how they will meet business needs and setting out the costs and the benefits. It also refers to any people issues that need to be addressed and how the strategy will deal with them. It includes a clear statement of the objectives of the strategy and the criteria for success.

3. *A definition of guiding principles* – the values that it is believed should be adopted in formulating and implementing the strategy.

4. *A plan* – how, when and by whom the reward initiatives will be implemented. The plan indicates what steps have to be taken and allows for resource constraints and the need for communication, involvement and training. The priorities attached to each element of the strategy are indicated and a timetable for implementation drawn up. The plan states who will be responsible for the development and implementation of the strategy.

WHAT IS THE CONTENT OF REWARD STRATEGY?

The content of reward strategy will of course vary according to the circumstances and needs of the organization. The strategy may be expressed as an overall statement of intent that simply indicates the general direction in which it is thought reward management should go in such terms as:

▮ develop a high performance culture;

▮ promote a total reward policy;

▮ introduce a more integrated approach to reward management – encouraging continuous personal development and spelling out career opportunities;

▌ adopt a more flexible approach to reward that includes the reduction of artificial barriers as a result of over-emphasis on grading and promotion;

▌ reward people according to their contribution rather than length of time in the job;

▌ clarify what behaviours will be rewarded and why.

The overall statement may be extended into one or more particular areas of reward management, for example:

▌ the replacement of present methods of contingent pay with a pay for contribution scheme;

▌ the introduction of a new grade and pay structure, eg a broad-graded or career family structure;

▌ the replacement of an existing decayed job evaluation scheme with a computerized scheme that more clearly reflects organizational values;

▌ the improvement of performance management processes so that they provide better support for the development of a performance culture and more clearly identify development needs;

▌ the introduction of a formal recognition scheme;

▌ the development of a flexible benefits system;

▌ the conduct of equal pay reviews with the objective of ensuring that work of equal value is paid equally;

▌ communication programmes designed to inform everyone of the reward policies and practices of the organization;

▌ training, coaching and guidance programmes designed to increase line management capability.

EXAMPLES OF REWARD STRATEGIES

The following are examples of the aims of reward strategy and details of overall and specific strategies as described by a number of organizations.

Aegon UK

The aims of the reward strategy of Aegon UK, the insurance group, were to:

▌ establish an integrated approach to performance management, development and reward for all staff and ensure that this is aligned with the needs of the business;

▌ ensure that salaries and benefits remain competitive when compared with comparators within our industry sector, so that we can retain and attract staff of the highest quality;

▌ reduce the previous focus upon grades in favour of broader bands so that personal development can be encouraged; and

▌ motivate staff sufficiently so that they will ensure the company remains successful, thereby allowing for continued competitive levels of reward for superior performance.

Airbus

The objectives of the reward strategy at Airbus are to introduce an element of performance into the pay of all employees, to ensure that its rates are competitive with the external labour market, and to deal with any anomalies caused by previous rigidities, such as grade drift brought about by people having to be promoted to a higher grade to receive additional pay.

B&Q

B&Q switched from a fairly traditional pay scheme to a total reward system because of a desire for better strategic alignment of reward programmes with its business objectives in a labour market environment of increasing diversity and changing social values.

British Telecommunications (BT)

The reward strategy at BT indicates the general direction in which it is thought reward management at BT should go, with an emphasis on adopting a more holistic, total reward approach: It states:

Use the full range of rewards (salary, bonus, benefits and recognition) to recruit and retain the best people, and to encourage and reward achievement where actions and behaviours are consistent with the BT values.

Centrica

At Centrica, following the merger between British Gas and Enron, the aim of the reward strategy was to:

▌ establish a link between pay and performance;

▌ align pay with the market;

▌ boost team working and the creation of a single Centrica culture, rather than to have the two cultures of British Gas Trading and Enron;

▌ create a single Centrica Business Services employment contract instead of the two that then existed.

The Children's Society

The Children's Society defined its overarching reward strategy as follows:

> We intend to develop reward systems which will support our mission and corporate objectives. We will move towards processes which:

▌ recognize contribution;

▌ are transparent;

▌ are owned by line managers and staff;

▌ reinforce leadership, accountability, team working and innovation;

▌ are market sensitive but not market led;

▌ are flexible and fair.

COLT Telecom

The reward strategy of COLT Telecom is expressed as follows:

▌ Base salaries should be determined generally by position against median market, but always taking account of personal performance and contribution to business success.

▌ At the senior level there will be greater emphasis on the variable portion of the total package including bonus potential and the opportunity to participate in share programmes.

▌ Internal equity is sought by working to ensure that the overall compensation package reflects the value and contribution of each job, in relation to other jobs in the organization across Europe through the introduction of COLT job levels.

▌ Increases to base salary and variable pay will always be related to the company's ability to pay. Compensation must be affordable by the business in relation to its business success and equitable to its employees, customers and shareholders.

Diageo

The overall objective of the reward strategy at Diageo is to 'release the potential of every employee to deliver Diageo's performance goals'. The role of the reward strategy in Diageo comprises five key elements:

1. *Support and enable the talent agenda.* 'Our role in reward is to help to provide the talent the business needs, at the right time, in the right place and for the right price' says Nicki Demby, Diageo's Performance and Reward Director. 'This means developing reward processes and plans that will hire the best talent, keep it and develop it. We simply can't buy all the talent that we need to take the organization into its future. We need to grow our own'.

2. *Provide clear principles to enable decision-making in the business.* By developing clear principles, Diageo hopes that when line managers are faced with choices, the right decisions will be more obvious. 'Less demand will be placed on reward "experts" in the business, who can spend more of their time on value creating enhancements to our processes, plans and communications,' says Nicki Demby.

3. *Align the reward approach with Diageo business strategy.* The success of the reward strategy depends heavily on developing appropriate performance measures in incentives, the cost-effective delivery of reward and consistent processes.

4. *Enable every employee to understand why he or she gets paid what he or she gets paid.* 'We need to have a big push on communication,' admits Nicki Demby. 'People do not necessarily understand what they are paid and how we perform. The connection between performance and reward needs to become visceral. As a formal part of each business review, we are telling people the impact the performance of their business is likely to have on their pay. It helps people to make the connections between the business decisions that they make and the likely personal impact.'

5. *Have a customer service ethic that results in great execution.* The reward team's ethic is now based on a much greater orientation towards the needs of employees – its internal customers. 'This demands great planning, great communication and great execution,' says Nicki Demby.

Friends Provident

The rationale behind the development of a reward strategy at Friends Provident was the need to:

▌ match salaries directly to the market;

▌ give line managers greater accountability for staff salaries and career progression;

▌ increase the flexibility of pay arrangements at business-unit level;

▌ facilitate a real and fundamental top-down change in corporate culture;

▌ reward the best performers by paying salaries above the market rate;

▌ manage salary costs;

▌ encourage greater accountability by staff for development of their own competencies.

GlaxoSmithKline

When Glaxo Wellcome and SmithKline Beecham merged to form GlaxoSmithKline (GSK) with100,000 employees worldwide at the end of 2000, the organization adopted a new approach to reward that embodied the new GSK 'spirit' of entrepreneurship, innovation and performance. This stresses pay for performance and increases the proportion of pay 'at risk' whilst creating and emphasizing total reward.

Lloyds TSB

The emphasis at Lloyds TSB is on creating a 'compelling employment offer' – one that is more individually focused, tailored to employees' needs and interests, and more in tune with the expectations of a diverse workforce.

Nationwide

At Nationwide the organizational redesign of its reward system emerged from the company's desire to:

▌ respond to occupational and labour market pressures;

▌ encourage more flexible working practices;

▌ streamline operations;

▌ improve customer service;

▌ increase skills.

Norwich Union Insurance

The Norwich Union Insurance strategic reward framework is shown in Figure 2.2.

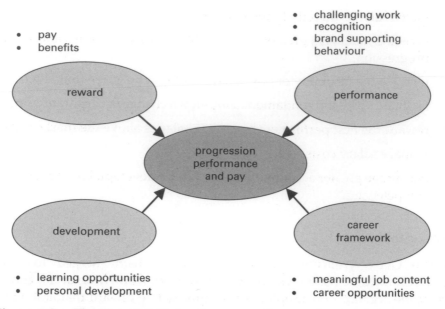

Figure 2.2 The Norwich Union Insurance Progression, Performance and Pay framework

Pricewaterhouse Coopers

Pricewaterhouse Coopers (PwC) considers itself engaged in the 'war for talent'. It recruits hundreds of graduates each year, and seeks to attract the best. The average age of the firm's employees is only 27, so its attitude to reward is pitched towards the aspirations and needs of this age group in the sense that younger workers are likely to demand fulfilling careers, excellent development and competitive pay as well as work-life balance. To meet its employees' requirements PwC has therefore adopted a total reward policy – replete with a competitive reward package, flexible benefits, genuine work-life choices, flexible working and a strong emphasis on personal development, advancement and recognition.

Tesco

Tesco's overall reward strategy is to:

▌ be on the right side of the competition on total reward, with the reward package being above the median;

▌ focus on making reward investment deliver more rather than reducing the size of the pot;

▮ reinvest to ensure that every element of reward adds value to the business and is valued by staff;

▮ build a simplified, global pay and grading system that enables mobility and flexibility and supports the values that are critical to future business growth;

▮ ensure the affordability of the reward package is sustainable, and using Tesco's buying power to deliver as much unbeatable value to staff as to customers;

▮ focus on rewarding staff for their contribution in a way that enables them to benefit directly from the success they help to create;

▮ ensure more transparency so that the reward package offered by the company is fully understood and valued.

WHAT ARE THE CRITERIA FOR AN EFFECTIVE REWARD STRATEGY?

Brown (2001) has suggested that effective reward strategies have three components:

1. They have to have clearly defined goals and a well-defined link to business objectives.

2. There have to be well-designed pay and reward programmes, tailored to the needs of the organization and its people, and consistent and integrated with one another.

3. Perhaps most important and most neglected, there needs to be effective and supportive HR and reward processes in place.

The questions to be answered when assessing the effectiveness of a reward strategy include:

▮ Is it aligned with the organization's business strategy (vertical alignment or integration) and its HR strategies (horizontal alignment or integration)?

▮ Will it support the achievement of business goals and reinforce organizational values; if so, how?

▮ Are the objectives of the reward strategy clearly defined?

▮ Is there a convincing statement of how the business needs of the organization will be met and how the needs of employees and other stakeholders will be catered for?

∎ Is it based on a thorough analysis and diagnosis of the internal and external environment of the organization and the reward issues that need to be addressed?

∎ Has a realistic assessment been made of the resources required to implement the strategy and the costs involved?

∎ Is it affordable in the sense that the benefits will exceed any costs?

∎ Have steps been taken to ensure that supporting processes such as performance management, communication and training are in place?

∎ Is the programme for implementation realistic?

∎ Have steps been taken to ensure that it is supported and understood by line managers and staff?

∎ Will HR and line managers be capable of implementing and managing the strategy in practice?

∎ Has accountability and ownership for the various reward policies and practices been clarified, defining what success looks like and how it will be measured? Are effective review mechanisms in place?

∎ Is the reward strategy flexible in adjusting to changes in the business and in the environment?

Reward strategists may have a clear idea of what needs to be done but they have to consider the views of top management and be prepared to persuade them with convincing arguments that action needs to be taken. They have to take particular account of financial considerations – the concept of 'affordability' looms large in the minds of chief executives and financial directors who will need to be convinced that an investment in rewards will pay off. They also have to convince employees and their representatives that the reward strategy will meet their needs as well as the needs of the business.

In the final analysis, a good reward strategy is one that works. It delivers its promises. The reward strategist must not create Hamlet's 'chameleon dish' and mutter 'I eat the air with promise-crammed'. And strategists should remember what was said of Lloyd George: 'Count not his broken promises a crime, he meant them, how he meant them at the time.' The same could be said of some managements, who introduce promising reward strategies with a flourish of trumpets and are left with 'a dying fall' as the promise falls apart. The danger is that reward strategy will just consist of a wish list prepared by senior management or HR, with no basis in the operating reality of the organization. This is what Purcell (2001) refers to as 'illusions in the board room'.

3

Strategic reward and performance

Great incentives should be used to drive great business performance. Great performers will always perform. Great reward programmes can help the whole organization to perform. (Nicki Demby, Performance and Reward Director, Diageo)

One of the prime objectives of strategic reward management is to create a high performance culture in order to deliver improved individual and organizational performance. In this chapter, the characteristics of such a culture and how one can be developed are considered. This is followed by an examination of the factors that help to generate high performance in organizations and the support that reward management strategy and practices can provide. Performance is also related to levels of engagement and organizational commitment, as discussed in the next chapter.

It is necessary from the outset to understand the full meaning of performance. Colloquially, performance is often regarded simply in terms of results or outputs. But it is more than that. Performance is about how things are done as well as what is done. As Brumbach (1988) explained:

Performance means both behaviours and results. Behaviours emanate from the performer and transform performance from abstraction to action. Not just the instruments for results, behaviours are also outcomes in their own right – the product of mental and physical effort applied to tasks – and can be judged apart from results.

THE CHARACTERISTICS OF A HIGH PERFORMANCE CULTURE

A high performance culture embraces a number of interrelated processes which together make an impact on the performance of the organization through its people in such areas as productivity, quality, levels of customer service, growth, profits and, ultimately, in profit-making firms, the delivery of increased shareholder value. This is achieved by 'enhancing the skills and engaging the enthusiasm of employees' (Stevens, 1998). As we detail in Chapters 6 and 7, in our more heavily service- and knowledge-based economy, employees have become the most important determinant of organizational success.

The starting point is leadership and vision to create a sense of momentum and direction. The characteristics of such a culture will be unique to any particular organization but, typically, they might comprise:

▮ the existence of a clear line of sight between the strategic aims of the organization and those of its departments and its staff at all levels;

▮ the awareness of management of what drives performance in the organization and their capacity to act accordingly;

▮ the definition by management of what is required in the shape of performance improvements, involving setting goals for success and monitoring performance to ensure that the goals are achieved;

▮ leadership from the top, which engenders a shared belief in the importance of continuous improvement;

▮ a focus on promoting positive attitudes that result in a motivated, committed and engaged workforce;

▮ the presence of performance management processes aligned to the organization's objectives to ensure that people are engaged in achieving agreed goals and standards;

▮ the development of the capacities of people through learning at all levels to support performance improvement;

▮ the provision of opportunities for people to make full use of their skills and abilities;

▮ valuing and rewarding people according to their contribution.

Lloyds TSB has produced the following definition of what it means by a high performance organization:

▌ people know what's expected of them – they are clear about their goals and accountabilities;

▌ they have the skills and competencies to achieve their goals;

▌ high performance is recognized and rewarded accordingly;

▌ people feel that their job is worth doing, and that there's a strong fit between the job and their capabilities;

▌ managers act as supportive leaders and coaches, providing regular feedback, performance reviews and development;

▌ a pool of talent ensures a continuous supply of high performers in key roles;

▌ there's a climate of trust and teamwork, aimed at delivering a distinctive service to the customer.

DEVELOPING A HIGH PERFORMANCE CULTURE

A high performance culture can be developed by taking into account the characteristics set out above and applying an integrated set of processes, of which reward is an important part. The processes will include those concerned with resourcing and talent management (ensuring that the organization has the high performing people it needs), learning and development, performance management, reward management, the enhancement of the working environment (for example, work design and work-life balance) and communication. It is necessary to take into account all of the factors that affect organizational and individual performance.

Factors affecting organizational performance

The point was made by Hamel and Prahalad (1989) that competitive advantage is obtained if a firm can obtain and develop human resources that enable it to learn faster and apply its learning more effectively than its rivals. This concept of resource-based strategy was developed by Barney (1991), who stated that sustained competitive advantage stems from the acquisition and effective use of bundles of distinctive resources that competitors cannot imitate. As Purcell et al (2003) suggest, the values and HR policies of an organization constitute an important non-imitable resource. This is achieved by ensuring that:

1. the firm has higher quality people than its competitors;

2. the unique intellectual capital possessed by the business is developed and nurtured;

3. organizational learning is encouraged; and

4. organization-specific values and a culture exist which 'bind the organization together (and) give it focus'.

The aim of a resource-based approach to strategy is to improve resource capability – achieving strategic fit between resources and opportunities and obtaining added value from the effective deployment of resources. In line with human capital theory, resource-based theory emphasizes that investment in people adds to their value to the firm. Resource-based strategy can produce what Boxall and Purcell (2003) refer to as human resource advantage. This is a fundamental aim of reward strategy as an important element in HR strategy.

The extensive research conducted by Purcell and his colleagues at the University of Bath (Purcell *et al*, 2003) indicated that the most effective organizations produced high performance by:

∥ formulating a clear vision and set of values that were 'embedded, enduring, collective, measured and managed';

∥ developing a positive psychological contract and means of increasing the motivation, commitment and engagement of employees;

∥ formulating and implementing policies that meet the needs of individuals and create 'a great place to work';

∥ providing support and advice to front line managers on their role in implementing HR policies and practices, bearing in mind that practice and implementation is the vital ingredient in linking people management to business performance, and this is primarily the task of line managers;

∥ managing change well.

Factors affecting individual performance

As described by Boxall and Purcell (2003), the level of individual performance is a function of ability, motivation and opportunity (AMO). People perform well when:

▌ they are able to do so (they *can* do the job because they have the necessary abilities and skills);

▌ they have the motivation to do so (they *will* do the job because they want to and are adequately incentivized);

▌ their work environment provides the necessary support and avenues for expression (for example, functioning technology and the opportunity to be heard when problems occur).

HOW REWARD STRATEGIES IMPACT ON PERFORMANCE

Basic considerations

There are three considerations to take into account in examining the impact of reward on organizational performance. First, it must be recognized that reward strategies will only affect performance if they work, ie they are implemented effectively by all concerned, especially front line managers.

Secondly, the extent to which reward strategies and policies on their own can make an impact may be more limited than early US exponents of the concept believed. US advocates of the 'new pay', such as Schuster and Zingheim (1992) implied that reward policies could drive cultural change. But Mark Thompson of Oxford University (1998) feels that in the UK context: 'Managing reward is often a job of short-term damage limitation, not the strategic lever for change that appears so seductive to American commentators.' Tim Fevyer, Senior Manager, Compensation and Benefits, Lloyds TSB, believes that reward processes can underpin structural and cultural change and support the achievement of business goals – but not on their own, and they do not lead change.

Thirdly, reward strategies work best if they are integrated with other HR strategies, so that there is a coherent approach with mutually supporting policies and practices. As Tim Fevyer puts it: 'Pay can support business change and consolidate key messages, but it can't drive it.' In his view, pay should be regarded as one of the instruments available to achieve transformation, working in conjunction with other instruments as part of top management's overall strategy. Importantly, he says, it must be integrated with the other key areas of business and HR strategy to reinforce the achievement of corporate goals.

As a guide to action, the following questions need to be answered on the impact of reward.

Can financial rewards make a direct impact on performance?

The answer to this question in the 1980s and 1990s was a clear 'yes', through individual performance-related pay (PRP). But PRP, although still a common practice (the e-reward 2004 survey of contingent pay found that 65 per cent of respondents had PRP), is by no means universally successful. It has often failed, particularly in the public sector, because of poor supporting processes, especially performance management, inadequate consultation with those concerned, and line managers without the commitment or capability to implement it fairly and consistently.

Research conducted by the Corporate Leadership Council in 2002 to establish the percentage impact of different strategies on individual performance found that financial incentives had a significant impact on intent to stay (19 per cent) and commitment (13 per cent) but an almost negligible impact on individual performance (2 per cent).

The lesson taught by expectancy theory (Porter and Lawler, 1968) is that extrinsic financial motivation such as a PRP or bonus scheme only works if the link between effort and reward is clear (ie, as Lawler, 1990, put it, a 'line of sight' exists) and the value of the reward is worth the effort. These are hard criteria to meet especially, in times of low inflation, the last one.

The extent to which any form of contingent pay can incentivize on its own is therefore questionable. It may do this crudely in the case of piecework or sales commission, but in most jobs today performance consists of a more complex mix of factors than job units of output or sales value. It is a bad mistake to believe that money by itself will result in sustained motivation. It can assist in the motivation process but, as Kohn (1993) points out, only in a crude, behaviourist, Pavlov's-dog type of way. People react in widely different ways to any form of motivation. The assumption that money in the form of PRP will motivate all people equally is untenable. It is a belief that has led governments, as well as managements, in the direction of making the naïve and unjustified assumption that PRP by itself can act as a lever for change and can make a direct impact on performance.

One of the problems concerning the impact of financial reward on performance is fairness or 'distributive justice'. Without it, the impact of pay may be considerably reduced, but it is difficult to achieve. Annette Cox, Lecturer in Human Resource Management at the Manchester Business School, University of Manchester, reported to the e-reward/CIPD 2005 reward symposium on her research into the effect of organizational change on pay systems. She found that issues of fairness arose in all of them.

In a building society there was a perception that men were paid more than women at senior levels, and that the appraisal process was not consistent across the organization, resulting in potentially unfair decisions on bonuses. The fairness of bonuses was an issue at another financial services organization, while benchmarking salaries to market rates was also believed by some to result in unfair pay decisions. At a telecoms company an equal pay audit identified many local-level problems and perceptions of inequities. Similar issues of the unfair distribution of bonuses, inconsistent appraisal decisions and the fairness of market rates were apparent in a cable network company, while conflicts between the job evaluation process and maintaining market parity were problematic in a large city council. There were also concerns about the fairness of reward for both lower grade and senior women in another council.

Overall the research found that:

▌ it was resource-intensive to maintain perceptions of fairness;

▌ managing market pressures was a key challenge;

▌ it was difficult to balance flexibility and transparency in pay systems;

▌ there was confusion as to whether equal pay issues should be managed centrally or locally;

▌ employers struggled to afford to be 'fair';

▌ staff were more concerned about how pay decisions were made than who got what, but across the case study sites more men than women were likely to perceive that their pay level was unfair.

Can financial rewards make an indirect impact on performance?

In the case of contingent pay schemes, the answer to this question is a qualified yes, although the impact may be small and temporary. Performance-related or contribution-related pay can deliver a message that performance or contribution is important. Such schemes, especially contribution pay, which rewards people not only for what they do but how they do it, can also spell out what behaviours are valued and will be recognized. Any process that makes people feel that they are valued according to their contribution can increase engagement if it is perceived to be operating fairly and consistently – but that is a big if.

Financial rewards also affect decisions to join or stay with an organization and in so far as people are motivated by money, rewards may improve organizational performance by helping to ensure the recruitment and retention of high quality people.

What about other approaches to reward?

The non-financial reward processes which form part of a total reward policy (see Chapter 1) can contribute to improving performance by providing intrinsic or extrinsic motivation and by making an impact on engagement. This can be done intrinsically through work and job design, giving people interest, challenge (the opportunity to achieve), variety in their work, autonomy to decide how the work should be carried out, task identity (the degree to which the job requires completion of a whole and identifiable piece of work) and task significance (contributing to a worthwhile end-result). It can also be done extrinsically by formal and informal recognition schemes and performance management processes that give positive feedback (recognition) and set the scene for growth through personal development. A focus in the organization on learning will increase commitment by providing opportunities for development and growth.

Much of the research literature on the links between HR practices and organizational performance suggests that it is not only difficult but also undesirable to try to isolate the effects of particular reward and HR practices on performance. Almost all of these studies include some elements of employee rewards, typically performance-related in some way, in their 'bundle' of high performance HR practices. But it is the interaction of these components in the hands of effective line managers that creates the desired high performing and totally rewarding work environment, rather than any single one of them.

How do we know what the impact is?

For a long time no one has been certain of what the impact of the various approaches mentioned above have been. Using them was largely a matter of faith. But human capital management activities involving the use of HR metrics are increasingly making measurement possible. Purcell (2005) says that: 'HR metrics – a tool for evidence-based HR – is a breakthrough which will enable managers to establish what works in their organization and for their employees.'

Nationwide's model of what the organization should provide in order to have an engaged and committed workforce has five elements – reward, development, environment, quality of work and leadership behaviours – and each of these has between three and eight constituent parts. Which of these is most important, and what return will Nationwide get on any investment it makes in HR practices? The tools used by Nationwide's Genome project to answer these questions are an annual employee survey, which gets a 90 per cent response rate, and the measurement of human capital. These have identified key drivers of committed employees. Employee satisfaction with these drivers is measured regularly in different business areas, which enables problems to be remedied.

The Genome project has helped to focus activity on:

▌ recruitment and retention;

▌ greater understanding of employee commitment – that is, what is the difference between those employees who want to be here, need to be here or feel they ought to be here;

▌ transparency and flexibility of reward;

▌ first line management development and coaching/mentoring to deliver the emotional as well as the task management aspects of their role;

▌ promotion of recognition and ad hoc/spontaneous rewards for employees – visible and tangible celebrations of success;

▌ development of an organizational culture where managers and employees are emotionally committed to and demonstrate the right behaviours.

However, Geoff White, Professor of HRM at the University of Greenwich Business School, reported at the 2005 e-reward/CIPD symposium on their research in seven large unionized UK organizations that had recently introduced new pay and grading systems, all of which had at least some stated, measurable objectives. In practice, none of the organizations used quantitative measures such as reduced recruitment costs, absence or employee turnover, and only some used softer measures such as the impact on staff motivation.

The reason for this was that few HR managers saw a direct correlation between changes in pay systems and business performance, and most were sceptical about the value of hard measures, given problems with linkage and 'background noise'. Some HR managers took the view that no negative reaction indicated success. Geoff White explained these findings by suggesting that managers have such a psychological investment in the changes that they would have difficulty admitting that their objectives had not been met.

It is true that the difficulty of measurement should not be underestimated. But a number of organizations such as Nationwide, Norwich Union, the Royal Bank of Scotland and Standard Chartered Bank are adopting a human capital management approach that uses metrics as a key tool to assess the effectiveness of HR policies and practices and indicate where improvements need to be made. To rely on an act of faith is insufficient. An attempt must be made to measure the impact of any aspect of reward strategy. As we see in the following chapter, regular attempts and improvements to such measures of effectiveness have allowed Nationwide to develop a sophisticated model of the effects of HR practices and employee attitudes on performance.

4

Engagement and organizational commitment strategies

The overall objectives of strategic reward are to support the achievement of organizational goals and to meet the needs of the people the organization employs. The three associated aims are:

1. to ensure that people are valued fairly and appropriately for what they do and achieve;

2. to develop a high performance culture; and

3. to help establish the organization as a 'great place to work' so that high quality people are attracted to join it and want to remain working there.

The first two chapters of this book examined how reward strategies can contribute to achieving the first aim and the third chapter looked specifically at how reward processes can improve performance. In this chapter we extend the analysis in Chapter 3 by considering the process of job engagement. We also discuss the linked concept of organizational commitment and how commitment strategies associated with engagement strategies can make an organization 'an employer of choice'.

ENGAGEMENT AND ORGANIZATIONAL COMMITMENT DEFINED

Engagement, sometimes known as 'job engagement', takes place when people are committed to their work and motivated to achieve high levels of performance. The Hay Group defines engaged performance as:

> A result that is achieved by stimulating employees' enthusiasm for their work and directing it towards organizational success. This result can only be achieved when employers offer an implied contract to their employees that elicits specific positive behaviours aligned with the organization's goals.

Organizational commitment is about identification with the goals and values of the organization, a desire to belong to the organization and a willingness to display effort on its behalf.

In a presentation to the e-reward/CIPD symposium on reward, Purcell (2005) commented that the beneficial effects of employee engagement and organizational commitment are being increasingly recognized and that encouraging these is now a priority for organizations. He has been studying the links between a range of HR practices and organizational commitment in his research for the CIPD into people and performance in 12 'excellent organizations'. Because they are excellent they have a wide range of HR policies, but his analysis showed that some policies had more impact than others across all occupational groups (namely managers, professionals and workers). These were, broadly, rewards and recognition, communication and work-life balance. Individual performance-related pay, on the other hand, did not trigger organizational commitment across the board, and had a slightly negative effect on individual commitment in these organizations.

Engagement and organizational commitment are two important concepts affecting work performance and the attraction and retention of employees provide good examples of how reward and HR strategies can be integrated. However, the two concepts are often confused and the terms used interchangeably. They are indeed closely linked – high organizational commitment can increase engagement and high engagement can increase commitment. But people can be engaged with their work even when they are not committed to the organization except in so far as it gives them the opportunity to use and develop their skills. This may be the case with some knowledge workers (see Chapter 6). For example, researchers may be more interested in the facilities for research they are given and the opportunity to make a name for themselves. They therefore join and stay with an organization only if it gives them the opportunities they seek. Combinations of engagement and organizational commitment are illustrated in Figure 4.1.

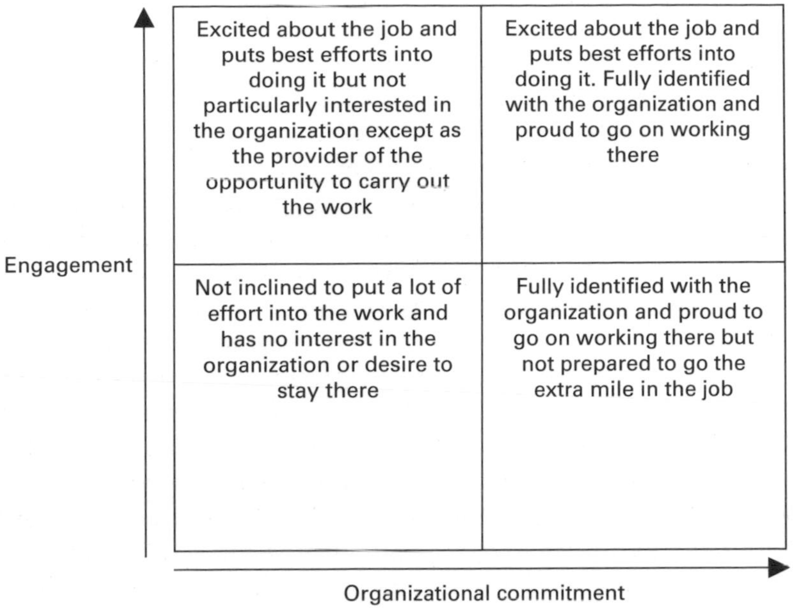

Excited about the job and puts best efforts into doing it but not particularly interested in the organization except as the provider of the opportunity to carry out the work	Excited about the job and puts best efforts into doing it. Fully identified with the organization and proud to go on working there
Not inclined to put a lot of effort into the work and has no interest in the organization or desire to stay there	Fully identified with the organization and proud to go on working there but not prepared to go the extra mile in the job

Engagement (vertical axis)

Organizational commitment (horizontal axis)

Figure 4.1 Combinations of the impact of engagement and organizational commitment

Because the concepts are different although linked, it is necessary to consider strategies that are specifically concerned with engagement and strategies that deal with organizational commitment. However, these strategies will be mutually supportive – actions to increase engagement will enhance commitment and vice versa; and reward strategies can potentially influence both.

ENGAGEMENT

Engagement is concerned with people and their work. It happens when people are caught up in and interested in, even excited, about their jobs and are therefore prepared to exert discretionary effort in getting them done.

Significance of the concept

The significance of the concept of engagement is that it is at the heart of the employment relationship. It is about what people do and how they behave in their roles and what makes them act in ways that further the achievement of the objectives of both the organization and themselves. The importance attached to the notion of engagement has intensified recently in association with the rise of total reward concepts. It is high on the strategic reward agenda of a number of leading organizations. For example, Tim Fevyer, Senior Manager, Compensation and Benefits, Lloyds TSB, comments that: 'Pay is no longer the great differentiator. The only way we are going to keep people is by engaging them.'

Trevor Blackman, Head of Reward at the Royal Bank of Scotland explains that the desire to enhance engagement underpins much of the work undertaken by Human Resources in the bank and is a key principle underlying the approach to the design of reward programmes. Quantifying the relationship between reward and engagement is one of the methods used to measure the impact of those programmes. He notes that: 'Reward done well can drive engagement throughout the organization.' Kevin Brady HR Director, Reward and Employee Relations at BT, feels the most important thing for employers to do is 'engage, engage, engage'.

Standard Chartered Bank also attaches importance to engagement. The bank measures it through its 'Q12' staff attitude survey and conducts regular reviews. The survey shows that branches with higher levels of engagement achieve greater growth in their profit margins, higher customer ratings and increased productivity.

Engagement and discretionary behaviour

There is a close link between high levels of engagement and positive discretionary behaviour. As described by Purcell *et al* (2003) discretionary behaviour refers to the choices that people at work often have on the way they do the job and the amount of effort, care, innovation and productive behaviour they display. It can be positive when people 'go the extra mile' to achieve high levels of performance. It can be negative when they exercise their discretion to slack at their work. Discretionary behaviour is hard for the employer to define and then monitor and control the amount required. But positive discretionary behaviour is more likely to happen when people are engaged with their work.

The propositions made by Purcell *et al* on discretionary behaviour as a result of their longitudinal research in association with CIPD were that:

∎ Performance-related practices only work if they positively induce discretionary behaviour, once basic staffing requirements have been met.

∎ Discretionary behaviour is more likely to occur when enough individuals have commitment to their organization and/or when they feel motivated to do so and/or when they gain high levels of job satisfaction.

▌ Commitment, motivation and job satisfaction, either together or separately, will be higher when people positively experience the application of HR policies concerned with creating an able workforce, motivating valued behaviours and providing opportunities to participate.

▌ This positive experience will be higher if the wide range of HR policies necessary to develop ability, motivation and opportunity are both in place and mutually reinforcing.

▌ The way HR and reward policies and practices are implemented by front line managers and the way top-level espoused values and organizational cultures are enacted by them will enhance or weaken the effect of HR policies in triggering discretionary behaviour by influencing attitudes.

▌ The experience of success seen in performance outcomes helps reinforce positive attitudes.

What is an engaged employee?

An answer to this question was provided by Bevan *et al* (1997) who describe an engaged employee as someone 'who is aware of business context, and works closely with colleagues to improve performance within the job for the benefit of the organization'.

A more detailed answer was given by Dilys Robinson, Principal Research Fellow, Institute of Employment Studies (IES). She presented to the 2005 e-reward/CIPD reward symposium a summary of discussions held by the IES with 46 organizations in the private and public sectors. These led to a picture of an engaged employee, who is:

▌ positive about the job;

▌ believes in, and identifies with, the organization;

▌ works actively to make things better;

▌ treats others with respect, and helps colleagues to perform more effectively;

▌ can be relied upon, and goes beyond the requirements of the job;

▌ sees the bigger picture, even sometimes at personal cost;

▌ keeps up-to-date with developments in his or her field;

▌ looks for, and is given, opportunities to improve organizational performance.

Robinson commented that the role of pay and benefits in fostering engagement is somewhat ambiguous. So far, the IES research suggests that pay is important to employees, but that improvements in pay are rarely at the top of their 'wish list'. However, getting reward wrong – for example, withdrawing benefits, failing to promote, allocating bonuses unfairly – has a huge impact and is very 'disengaging', as these aspects of working life are held as proxies of the extent to which the organization values the individual. In this sense, pay remains a 'hygiene' factor. Their research also illustrates the manner in which the emphasis on the various HR and reward policies in generating engagement varies in each organizational setting.

What are the factors that influence engagement?

Levels of engagement are influenced by four factors as discussed below and modelled in Figure 4.2.

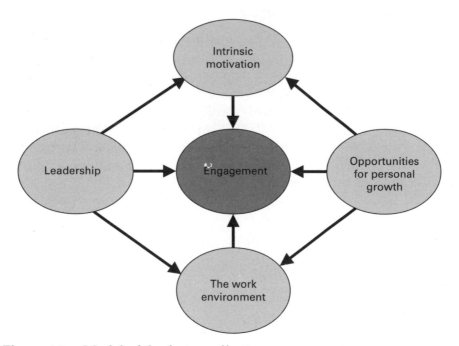

Figure 4.2   Model of the factors affecting engagement

Intrinsic motivation

In his seminal 1968 article, 'One more time: how do you motivate employees?', Herzberg launched the term 'intrinsic motivation'. This was derived from the findings recorded in his book, *The Motivation to Work* (Herzberg *et al*,1957) in which he and his colleagues identified the five key motivation factors that are intrinsic to the job: achievement, recognition for achievement, the work itself, responsibility (autonomy) and growth or advancement. This is still a relevant list of the basic factors that influence engagement. It applies particularly to roles where there is scope for discretionary behaviour, but it can apply to more routine jobs. Lands' End, the mail-order clothing company, believes that where jobs are repetitive or less challenging, it is particularly important to provide some challenge and fun. At Lands' End, if it isn't possible to give people a choice as to the type of work they do, they can be given a choice as to how they do it.

The work environment

An enabling, supportive and inspirational work environment creates experiences that impact on engagement by influencing how people regard their roles and carry them out. An enabling environment will create the conditions that encourage high performance and effective discretionary behaviour. These include work processes, equipment and facilities, and the physical conditions in which people work. A supportive environment will be one in which proper attention is paid to achieving a satisfactory work-life balance, emotional demands are not excessive, attention is paid to providing healthy and safe working conditions, job security is a major consideration and personal growth needs are taken into consideration. An inspirational environment will be where what Purcell and his colleagues (2003) refer to as 'the big idea' is present – the organization has a clear vision and a set of integrated values that are 'embedded, collective, measured and managed'.

The environment is affected by the organization's climate which, as defined by French *et al* (1985), is 'the relatively persistent set of perceptions held by organization members concerning the characteristics and quality of organizational culture'. It is also directly influenced by its work and HR practices. As Purcell (2005) points out, the way HR practices are experienced by employees is affected by organizational values and operational strategies, such as staffing policies or hours of work, as well as the way they are implemented. He also emphasizes that work climate – how people get on in the organization – and the experience of actually doing the job – pace, demand and stress – all influence the way employees experience the work environment. This has an important effect on how they react to HR and reward practices and how these influence organizational outcomes.

Employees react in a number of different ways to practices in their organization and this affects the extent to which they want to learn more, are committed and satisfied with their jobs. This, in turn, influences how well they do their jobs and whether they are prepared to contribute discretionary effort.

Leadership

The degree to which jobs provide intrinsic motivation and therefore encourage engagement and positive discretionary behaviour depends more on the way in which jobholders are led and managed than on any formal process of job design. Managers and team leaders often have considerable discretion over how they allocate work and how much they delegate and provide autonomy. They can spell out the significance of the work people do. They can give them the opportunity to achieve and develop, and provide feedback that recognizes their contribution.

Opportunities for personal growth

Most people want to get on. As Lawler put it in 2003: 'People enjoy learning – there's no doubt about it – and it touches on an important "treat people right" principle for both organizations and people: the value of continuous, ongoing training and development.' Learning is a satisfying and rewarding experience and makes a significant contribution to intrinsic motivation. Alderfer (1972) emphasized the importance of the chance to grow as a means of rewarding people. He wrote: 'Satisfaction of growth needs depends on a person finding the opportunity to be what he or she is most fully and become what he or she can.' The opportunity to grow and develop is a motivating factor that directly impacts on engagement when it is an intrinsic element of the work.

Strategies for enhancing engagement

An overall approach to improving engagement was described by Helen Murlis at the e-reward/CIPD symposium in 2005. She warned that pay, and especially variable pay, is very hard to get right and requires care in both design and implementation. But our leaders in both the public and private sectors 'buy' and like the idea of 'pay at risk' and reward for performance, since it matches values and beliefs they have or aspire to. 'There are still people around who believe that pay systems can be used to manage people – from the shop floor to the boardroom.' If everyone was only interested in wealth creation, variable pay would make more sense, but people go to work for a wide range of reasons, which arise from their personalities, preferences and stage of life as well as their role in the organization. This means that they have 'diverse engagement factors'. If you do not take account of these, you are unlikely to get high performance with any reward mechanism that you introduce.

Total reward is therefore an important consideration. The experience of being at work is 'multi-faceted'. Hay Group's Engaged Performance Model captures the most important of these, which are:

- tangible rewards;

- quality of work;

- work-life balance;

- inspiration and values;

- enabling environment;

- future growth opportunity.

All of these elements will be important to some staff, but they will not all be equally important. Hay's own research found that inspiration and values – especially quality of leadership – is most important to staff, followed by opportunities for career advancement and learning as well as development, with tangible rewards typically coming third on a list of important issues.

Specific engagement strategies

Specifically, engagement strategies can be developed under the headings of the four factors affecting engagement set out above.

1. Intrinsic motivation

Intrinsic motivation depends basically on the way in which work or jobs are designed. Three characteristics have been distinguished by Lawler (1969) as being required in jobs if they are to be intrinsically motivating:

- *Feedback* – individuals must receive meaningful feedback about their performance, preferably by evaluating their own performance and defining the feedback. This implies that they should ideally work on a complete product/process/service, or a significant part of it that can be seen as a whole.

- *Use of abilities* – the job must be perceived by individuals as requiring them to use abilities they value in order to perform the job effectively.

∎ *Self-control (autonomy)* – individuals must feel that they have a high degree of self-control over setting their own goals and over defining the paths to these goals.

The approaches to motivation through job design suggested by Robertson and Smith (1985) are to influence:

∎ skill variety by providing opportunities for people to do several tasks and combining tasks;

∎ task identity by combining tasks and forming natural work units;

∎ task significance by informing people of the importance of their work;

∎ autonomy by giving people responsibility for determining their own working systems; and

∎ feedback by establishing good relationships and opening feedback channels.

These approaches may be used when setting up new work systems or jobs and the intrinsic motivation strategy should include provision for guidance and advice along these lines to those responsible for such developments. But the greatest impact on the design of work systems or jobs is made by line managers on a day-to-day basis. The strategy should therefore include arrangements for educating them as part of a leadership development programme in the importance of good work and job design and what they can do to improve intrinsic motivation. Performance management, with its emphasis on agreeing role expectations, is a useful means of doing this.

2. The work environment

A strategy for increasing engagement through the work environment will be generally concerned with developing a culture that encourages positive attitudes to work, promoting interest and excitement in the jobs people do and reducing stress. Lands' End believes that staff who are enjoying themselves, who are being supported and developed and who feel fulfilled and respected at work, will provide the best service to customers. The thinking behind why the company wants to inspire staff is straightforward – employees' willingness to do that little bit extra arises from their sense of pride in what the organization stands for, ie: quality, service and value. It makes the difference between a good experience for customers and a poor one.

The strategy also needs to consider particular aspects of the work environment, especially communication, involvement, work-life balance and working conditions. It can include the formulation and application of 'talent relationship management' policies that are concerned with building effective relationships with people in their roles, treating individual employees fairly, recognizing their value, giving them a voice and providing opportunities for growth.

3. Leadership

The leadership strategy should concentrate on what line managers have to do if they are going to exercise leadership in order to play their vital and immediate part in increasing levels of engagement. This will include the implementation of learning programmes that help them to understand what they are expected to do and the skills they need to use. The programmes can include formal training (especially for potential managers or those in their first leadership role) but more impact will be made by 'blending' various learning methods such as e-learning, coaching and mentoring.

It should also be recognized that a performance management process can provide line managers with a useful framework in which they can deploy their skills in improving performance through increased engagement. This applies particularly to the performance management activities of role definition, performance improvement planning, joint involvement in monitoring performance and feedback. The strategy should therefore include the steps required to make performance management more effective by increasing the commitment of managers to it and developing the skills they require.

4. Opportunities for personal growth

A strategy for providing development and growth opportunities should be based on the creation of a learning culture. This is one that promotes learning because it is recognized by top management, line managers and employees generally as an essential organizational process to which they are committed and in which they engage continuously. Reynolds (2004) describes a learning culture as a 'growth medium' that will 'encourage employees to commit to a range of positive discretionary behaviours, including learning' and which has the following characteristics: empowerment not supervision, self-managed learning not instruction, long-term capacity building not short-term fixes. It will encourage discretionary learning, which Sloman (2003) believes takes place when individuals actively seek to acquire the knowledge and skills that promote the organization's objectives.

It is suggested by Reynolds (2004) that to create a learning culture it is necessary to develop organizational practices that raise commitment amongst employees and 'give employees a sense of purpose in the workplace, grant employees opportunities to act upon their commitment, and offer practical support to learning'. He proposes the following steps to establishing a learning culture:

1. Develop and share the vision – the belief in a desired and emerging future.

2. Empower employees – provide 'supported autonomy'; freedom for employees to manage their work within certain boundaries (policies and expected behaviours) but with support available as required.

3. Adopt a facilitative style of management in which responsibility for decision making is ceded as far as possible to employees.

4. Provide employees with a supportive learning environment where learning capabilities can be discovered and applied, eg peer networks, supportive policies and systems, protected time for learning.

5. Use coaching techniques to draw out the talents of others by encouraging employees to identify options and seek their own solutions to problems.

6. Guide employees through their work challenges and provide them with time, resources and, crucially, feedback.

7. Recognize the importance of managers acting as role models.

8. Encourage networks – communities of practice.

9. Align systems to vision – get rid of bureaucratic systems that produce problems rather than facilitate work.

Specifically, the strategy should define the steps required to ensure that people have the opportunity and are given the encouragement to learn and grow in their roles. This includes the use of talent management policies that focus on role flexibility – giving people the chance to develop their roles by making better and extended use of their talents. Talent management is not just about developing high flyers; it is also about developing the abilities of the core people on whom the organization depends. The philosophy should be that everyone has the ability to succeed and the aim should be to 'achieve extraordinary results with ordinary people'. It includes using performance management primarily as a developmental process with an emphasis on personal development planning.

The strategy should also cover career development opportunities and how they can be provided, by giving individuals the guidance, support and encouragement they need if they are to fulfil their potential and achieve a successful career with the organization in tune with their talents and aspirations. The strategy should include the actions required to provide men and women of promise with a sequence of learning activities and experiences that will equip them for whatever level of responsibility they have the ability to reach.

An 'opportunities for growth' strategy can be closely associated with another aspect of total reward strategy, namely the establishment of career family grade structures, as discussed in Chapter 8. These describe the levels of knowledge and skills required in families of jobs that are related through the activities they carry out at those different levels. They therefore define career paths within families that can be extended into other families for which similar level definitions exist. The paths can be used to identify growth opportunities and plan the acquisition of the knowledge and skills required.

Measuring the impact of engagement

The effectiveness of engagement strategies needs to be evaluated by measuring their impact and therefore indicating any areas for improvement. An example of how this can be done was provided by Paul Bissell, Senior Rewards Manager, Nationwide Building Society, who described at the 2005 reward symposium their project Genome as 'the process of identifying, characterizing, and mapping the key drivers (or corporate DNA) of employee engagement in our business to establish their effect on and importance to member commitment and business performance'.

For example, the Genome business simulator predicts that if Nationwide increases the average length of service of employees from 10.2 to 11.2 years, then this will increase customer commitment by almost 1 per cent, which will improve mortgage completions against target by almost 2 per cent, bringing in an additional £5.6 million in revenue. Similarly, a 1 per cent increase in employees' perceptions of coaching leads to almost a 1 per cent increase in personal loan sales against target. Nationwide says that it uses the information from the Genome project to 'improve the characteristics of our employee brand proposition, to increase employee engagement and in so doing improve the value our members derive from doing business with us'.

ORGANIZATIONAL COMMITMENT

People are committed to their organization when they are proud of it and want to go on working there. As Purcell *et al* (2003) explain, if people feel committed they are more likely to engage in discretionary behaviour to help the organization be successful. They suggest that successful organizations are able to meet people's needs both for a good job and to work 'in a great place'. In this way they become an 'employer of choice'. People will want to work there because their individual needs are met – for a worthwhile job with prospects.

Factors affecting organizational commitment

The factors affecting the level of organizational commitment have been defined by Kochan and Dyer (1993) as follows:

1. *Strategic level* – supportive business strategies, top management value commitment and effective voice for HR in strategy making and governance.

2. *Functional (human resource policy) level* – staffing based on employment stabilization, investment in training and development and contingent compensation that reinforces cooperation, participation and contribution.

3. *Workplace level* – selection based on high standards, broad task design and teamwork, employee involvement, and a climate of cooperation and trust.

Developing an organizational commitment strategy

An organizational commitment strategy will cover what needs to be done to:

▮ communicate the values and aims of management and the achievements of the organization, so that employees are more likely to identify with it as one they are proud to work for;

▮ demonstrate to employees that management is committed to them by recognizing their contribution as stakeholders and by striving to maximize job security;

▮ develop a climate of trust by ensuring that management is honest with people, treats them fairly, justly and consistently, keeps its word and shows willingness to listen to the comments and suggestions made by employees during processes of consultation and participation;

▮ create a positive psychological contract by treating people as stake-holders, relying on consensus and cooperation rather than control and coercion, and focusing on the provision of opportunities for learning, development and career progression;

▮ establish performance management processes that provide for the alignment of organizational and individual objectives;

▮ help to increase employee identification with the organization through rewards related to organizational performance (profit sharing or gain-sharing) or employee share ownership schemes;

▮ overall, establish and maintain a working environment that makes the organization an 'employer of choice' because it is 'a great place to work'.

The criteria used by the *Sunday Times* in identifying the 100 Best Companies to Work For, 2005 were:

▮ leadership at senior management level;

▮ 'my manager' – local management on a day-to-day basis;

▮ personal growth – opportunities to learn, grow and be challenged;

▮ well-being – balanced work-life issues;

▮ my team – immediate colleagues;

▮ giving something back – to society and the local community;

▮ my company – the way it treats staff;

▮ fair deal – pay and benefits.

Creating a great place to work starts with developing the image of the organization so that it is recognized as one that achieves results, delivers quality products and services, behaves ethically and provides good conditions of employment. Organizations with a clear vision and a set of integrated and enacted values are likely to project themselves as being well worth working for. The aim is to create an employee value proposition which, in order to attract and retain high quality people, recognizes that they will be looking for strong values and expecting to be well managed, to have freedom and autonomy, high job challenge and career opportunities. One way of doing this is to establish an 'employer brand' that presents a coherent picture to prospective employees of what the organization has to offer them. Rewards are a visible and vital element of such a brand.

Alan Reed, Founder and Chief Executive of Reed Executive plc, suggested (Reed, 2001) the following methods of developing an employer brand:

▌ analyse what ideal candidates need and want and take this into account in deciding what should be offered and how it should be offered;

▌ establish how far the core values of the organization support the creation of an attractive brand and ensure that these are incorporated in the presentation of the brand as long as they are 'values in use' (lived by members of the organization) rather than simply espoused;

▌ define the features of the brand on the basis of an examination and review of each of the areas that affect the perceptions of people about the organization as 'a great place to work' – the way people are treated, the provision of a fair deal, opportunities for growth, work-life balance, leadership, the quality of management, involvement with colleagues and how and why the organization is successful;

▌ benchmark the approaches of other organizations (the *Sunday Times* list of the 100 Best Companies to Work For is useful) to obtain ideas about what can be done to enhance the brand;

▌ be honest and realistic.

We comment in more detail on using communication to build an employer brand in Chapter 13.

Developing the employment brand at B&Q

B&Q recognized that it faced a daunting challenge if it was to present itself as an employer of choice. The findings of internal and external research on B&Q as an employer had told senior managers something very important about what employees and potential employees actually thought of the employment relationship at B&Q. They realized that its 'employment brand' had to change. Work was carried out with consultants TMP on developing a clearly defined employment brand proposition. The stated aims of the exercise were to:

▌ create high awareness of the B&Q brand;

▌ change the negative misconceptions of B&Q as an employer;

▌ raise awareness of the company's positive employment attributes both internally and externally;

▌ attract and select the right kind of people to deliver great service.

The 'employment value proposition' is the name given to B&Q's approach to a distinct employer brand. According to the company, the employment value proposition 'sits behind the entire relationship that B&Q has with our employees throughout the entire life cycle of their employment'. In essence, it is a way of determining what drives people to join B&Q, stay in the company and be motivated to higher levels of performance.

But as Will Astill, B&Q's Reward Manager explains, it was not just about trying to sell B&Q as an employer to potential recruits: 'B&Q wanted to be the type of employer with the systems and practices actually in place. We needed to formulate strategy and plans, so the reality is similar to perception before we sell the vision externally'. By assembling and marketing a compelling employment offer that will attract, engage and retain the people needed for organizational success, B&Q was confident that a good brand would create a competitive advantage. Says Astill: 'Engaged employees will go beyond the strict boundaries of the job and offer better service. This means customers become more loyal and increase their overall spend, thereby boosting profits.'

Engagement and commitment: the new reward fads?

Cynics may say that engagement and organizational commitment are just a modern 'gloss' and terminology for the traditional concepts of motivation and incentive. However, we hope we have demonstrated that this is not the case, although they are related, and that total rewards play a vital part in developing both attributes amongst employees in an organization.

The strong focus in early reward strategy work was on business alignment, sometimes without due consideration for employee needs and motivations. The new focus we have profiled on engagement and organizational commitment has at the very least served to place employees, and the importance of their motivation and performance, right back at the centre of reward work. This is where it needs to be if the potential benefits of reward strategies are to be realized in practice. It constitutes a major aspect of what we refer to as the 'new realism' in reward strategy.

Part 2

The Context of Strategic Reward

5

The reward environment

Strategic reward takes place within the context of the internal and external environment of the organization. Variations in these environments explain why the approach to reward between organizations often differs so much. One of the recurring themes in this book is the importance of best fit rather than best practice. Best fit is what organizations have to strive for when formulating reward strategies, although to a degree, 'fit' can be forced upon them by the circumstances in which they operate and the type of people they employ.

There are some key aspects of the external environment that may influence a number of organizations in broadly similar ways, and traditional models of reward strategy, in asserting the driving influence of an organization's business strategy, have often underplayed the importance of these contextual issues. One instance is the rate of price and wage inflation, which generally affects policies on pay progression. Underpinning this is the rate of growth in the economy. It is no coincidence that the years after 2001 saw public sector pay rates generally closing the gap with the private sector, in a period of sustained government investment in health and education, while the private sector experienced a weak stock market, shaky consumer demand and intensifying international competition.

Another instance is the existence of new approaches to reward that have been popularized as best practice (although it can be argued that there is no such thing as 'best practice' in the sense of something that is universally applicable, only 'good practice', which may or may not be appropriate). The danger is in adopting 'flavours of the month' such as performance-related pay and broad-banding unthinkingly without exploring what they mean for the organization and the problems and consequences of introducing them. However, current developments in reward as applied in the country or countries in which the organization is based will exert influence and need to be considered as part of the external environment.

This chapter gives an overview of the factors that need to be taken into account in developing a reward strategy within the internal and external environment and the patterns and trends in UK reward practices that they are helping to drive. In the following three chapters we detail the impact of some of the most important economic and reward trends on contemporary reward strategies.

THE INTERNAL ENVIRONMENT

The internal environment consists of the corporate culture, especially the organization's core values, the business of the organization, its technology, the type of people it employs and its business strategy.

Corporate culture

The corporate culture of an organization has often somewhat crudely been expressed as 'the way we do things around here'. There is more to it than that, but at least this definition focuses attention on the organization's core values and behavioural norms. Organizations may consciously develop core values or the values may simply have evolved over time and have never been expressed formally, in which case they are more like behavioural norms. Core values may be espoused as in the examples set out below. The issue is the extent to which they become 'values in use'. One approach to help ensure that people in the organization 'live the values', as at Standard Chartered Bank, is to build the performance management scheme around the values so that the degree to which they are followed becomes part of the assessment and reward processes.

Tesco has a widespread recognition scheme applying to all staff, including the directors. *Values Awards* are designed to recognize staff for living the 'Tesco values', which are:

▮ No one tries harder for customers.

▮ Understand customers better than anyone.

▮ Be energetic, be innovative and be first for customers.

▮ Use our strengths to deliver unbeatable value to our customers.

❙ Look after our people so they can look after our customers.

❙ Treat people how we like to be treated.

❙ There's one Tesco Team.

❙ Trust and respect each other.

❙ Strive to do our very best.

❙ Give support to each other and praise more than criticize.

❙ Ask more than tell and share knowledge so that it can be used.

❙ Enjoy work, celebrate success and learn from experience.

The awards are non-financial, taking the form of a blue badge for anyone who receives four *Values Awards* and a gold badge for anyone with seven awards. Thus these non-financial rewards are being used as part of a clear strategy to inculcate the corporate values and culture that create the context for high performance in the organization.

The B&Q 'work ethic' is set out in Table 5.1.

The four core values at Centrica are:

1. think team;

2. have respect;

3. listen and share; and

4. deliver results.

Its reward system is designed to set a clear line of sight from business strategy to individual objectives using a balanced scorecard approach. The focus is on what is expected – 'delivering results', and how it is delivered – the ability to understand and manage behaviour within the context of the organization.

The Progression, Performance and Pay framework at Norwich Union Insurance is underpinned by its brand values: Progressive, Shared benefit and Integrity.

Xansa's exceptional recognition scheme aims to recognize and celebrate exceptional achievement that demonstrates the company's values in operation.

The business of the organization

The business of the organization – manufacturing, profit-making services, not-for-profit services, public sector services and education – will govern

Table 5.1 The B&Q 'work ethic'

We work hard	• Winning through hard work
	• We're well rewarded
	• A job worth doing…
	• Real job satisfaction
The B&Q family	• Belonging
	• Supporting and encouraging each other
	• Real teamwork
	• Fun to be with
Total involvement	• Know where B&Q is heading
	• Know where I fit in
	• My voice is heard
	• My contribution is valued
	• I can grow
Proud to be here	• Proud of B&Q
	• Proud of our success
	• Proud of my store
	• Pride in my team
	• Pride in my personal growth
	• Proud of my career
	• Proud to be a professional in my current job and future career
	• Proud to grow, to be well rewarded and recognised and to make an impact
We can do	• Drive energy and passion
	• Focused on achieving
	• Individual and team rewards
	• Lead and not follow

its ethos and therefore core values. It will influence the type of people it employs and the degree to which it is subject to turbulence and change. All these factors will contribute to the reward strategy. For example, in the public and voluntary sector the tradition of paying service-related increments rather than progressing pay according to performance or contribution dies hard, although successive governments have driven the latter forward to now make it predominant practice in the Civil Service.

Changes in the dynamics of the business may also lead to changes in market practice. For example, the industry-wide tradition of paying sales staff on a low basic, high commission package in the life and pensions industry was challenged in the 1990s by a series of mis-selling scandals and company fines. Higher base pay levels and customer service-focused incentives resulted. More recently the employment of direct sales staff has declined significantly as selling takes place online and through call centres, presenting a new set of strategic challenges for rewarding staff in these activities.

Technology

The technology of a business exerts a major influence on the internal environment – how work is organized, managed and carried out. The introduction of new technology may result in considerable changes to systems and processes. Different skills are required, new methods of working and therefore rewards are developed. The result may be an extension of the skills base of the organization and its employees, including multi-skilling (ensuring that people have a range of skills that enable them to work flexibly on a variety of tasks, often within a teamworking environment). Traditional piecework pay systems in manufacturing industry have been replaced by higher fixed pay and rewards focused on quality, employee teamwork and, as at Volvo's Belgian car plant, up- and multi-skilling. But it could also result in de-skilling and a reduction in the number of jobs (downsizing).

New technology can therefore present a considerable threat to employees. The world of work has changed in many ways. Knowledge workers are employed in computerized offices and laboratories, and technicians work in computer integrated manufacturing systems. They have to be managed and rewarded differently from the clerks or machine operators they displace (see Chapter 6). The service industries have become predominant and manufacturing is in decline so that rewarding those involved in customer service becomes a major preoccupation (see Chapter 7).

People

As mentioned above, the type of people employed and therefore the approach to reward will largely depend on the type of business and its technology. But what has become increasingly recognized by management is that 'people make the difference' and that unique competitive advantage is achieved by having better people who are capable of doing better things than those in other businesses. The aim is to acquire, develop, motivate and retain people who possess distinctive capabilities (competencies) that arise from the nature of the firm's activities and relationships. As Nicki Demby, Director of Reward at Diageo observes:

> It is our people who deliver our performance, which is why *release the potential of every employee* is at the heart of our growth strategy. Alongside what

we deliver, every bit as important is how we deliver. Our people are judged against global leadership capabilities: edge, emotional energy, ideas, people performance, and living the values.

The employment value proposition in a tight labour market

Clearly, reward strategy can play a part in achieving this aim and this can be joined up with what has recently emerged as an important item on the HR agenda: the development of an 'employment value proposition'. With competition in the employment marketplace remaining tough and demand for skilled people outstripping supply, more and more organizations are having to think harder about how to obtain and hold on to talented people who contribute to business success – and also ensure that they are productive. As detailed later in this chapter, 85 per cent of employers in the CIPD's latest recruitment and retention survey (CIPD, 2005b) said they were experiencing recruitment problems, largely due to staff and skill shortages.

The need for organizations to be recognized as an 'employer of choice' has been intensified by this situation. Earning recognition is a necessity not an option in a marketplace driven by the search for competitive success. It can help foster an emotional connection between employees and the organization, thereby enhancing employee loyalty and performance.

This is a resourcing issue but it is also a good example of how reward strategy can and should be integrated with other key aspects of HR strategy, as is illustrated in Lloyds TSB.

Responding to people imperatives at Lloyds TSB

Lloyds TSB is operating in a rapidly changing business environment, with ever-increasing consumerism and the harsh challenges of a competitive world market. Customers have a multitude of choices in today's financial services industry. The company is perpetually under pressure to improve quality, keep a lid on costs and reduce process times to meet customers' expectations and keep the organization ahead of the competition. Lloyds TSB needs to offer the highest standards of service if it is to remain customers' first choice. To achieve this, the bank realizes it must offer employment policies that will attract and retain the best people from the widest possible pool of applicants.

In the past, the 'big four' banks dominated the financial services sector. This meant that employees could generally be sure of a job for life, and there was little or no turnover of staff. People were sometimes paid (and promoted) according to their grade and length of service, rather than ability or performance. Today, the marketplace is full of competition from new entrants, and all financial services companies are competing for good quality staff.

Lloyds TSB recognizes that it is people – rather than finance or technology – that make the difference. Operating in a vastly different employment environment in which there is intense competition for a pool of increasingly skilled people, employees really are the primary sustainable source of competitive advantage in the modern service-based economy. Compensation and benefits not only account for about half of the bank's £3.5 billion per annum operating costs, but for better or worse, it is people – their intellects, creativity, scarce skills, commitment and leadership – who are central to business success.

A key question emerging from the new strategic orientation to reward at Lloyds TSB concerned the need to redefine the organization's performance culture. Put simply, what would this low inflation environment mean for the pay for performance system introduced in 1989? Was it sustainable? Lloyds TSB decided it most certainly was not.

Salary budgets of around 3 per cent or at most 4 per cent offer little or no opportunity to differentiate between high flyers and poor performers. Moreover, with almost a third of Lloyds TSB employees already paid above the market rate, the company was faced with the prospect of informing some employees that they were unlikely to receive a pay rise during forthcoming annual reviews.

As Tim Fevyer, Senior Manager, Compensation and Benefits, Lloyds TSB, points out, this required a complete change of mindset amongst employees. In essence, managing this process was about changing employees' expectations. Rather than a focus on movements in the cost of living, Lloyds TSB's emphasis is now very much on the market. 'If the market has not moved, our market indicators might not move,' says Tim Fevyer. This represented a far-reaching cultural change for Lloyds TSB. If an employee's salary is going to increase, it is either because they are growing in terms of competencies, skills and performance or because the market has changed. Tim Fevyer sums it up:

> Previously the deal was, 'I've been here so I'll get an increase' or, 'I've been here and I've done a good job so I'll get a good increase.' Actually, now our philosophy is that you are paid to do a good job, and if you are paid the right rate, you only get more if you are contributing more or because the market has moved. Otherwise you are being paid the right price.

Business strategy

Where the business is going – the business strategy – determines where reward should go – the reward strategy. Integrating reward and business strategies means combining them as a whole so they contribute effectively to achieving the mission or purpose of the organization. The process of linking strategies is the best way of achieving integration, or 'internal fit', in the sense that business and reward strategies are in harmony. It is necessary to see that reward goals are aligned with business goals and reward strategies are defined in a way that spells out how they will contribute to the achievement of the business plan.

Business strategies change and as Nicki Demby, Diageo's Performance and Reward Director remarked: 'This is a key issue. This changes reward strategy.' Put simply, she said:

> Your organization's fundamental purpose may be revised. Major long-term goals in terms of outcomes and achievement of performance objectives may change. As a result, what your organization has to be good at doing to fulfil its mission and achieve its strategic goals will need refining.

Nicky Demby pointed out to e-reward that:

> Whenever you change your business strategy and/or your HR strategy, your reward strategy may need to respond. We are just getting to grips with the profound and detailed implications of a shift in our business strategy in the last two or three years. What Diageo calls its 'Organization and People Strategy' has also necessarily been given greater clarity. It provides direction to our talent, operational effectiveness and performance and reward agendas.

The company's underlying thinking here is that the people strategy is not for the human resource function to own but is the responsibility of the whole organization, hence the title, 'Organization and People Strategy'.

Clive Wright of Mercer HR Consulting describes the case of an engineering company which restructured into three global lines of business following a strategic review, to become better aligned with global customers. This led it for the first time to consider and articulate a formal reward strategy in order to better support and align with the new business strategy. Key components included a move to more sector- and line-of-business-specific reward practices, rather than a uniform across-company approach; stronger-performance related rewards, but rewarding the behaviours required as well as the results achieved, and team as well as individual performance; and stronger reinforcement through rewards for the group values of openness, teamwork and achievement.

THE EXTERNAL ENVIRONMENT

It has been suggested by Ulrich (1997) that environmental and contextual changes present a number of competitive challenges to organizations, which mean that HR has to be involved in helping to build new capabilities. Some of the main contextual factors that influence HR and reward policies and practices are competitive pressures, globalization and changes in demographics and employment. We describe these briefly here to illustrate their importance, and then describe the key economic and reward trends and their impact in the following three chapters.

Competitive pressures

Customers are demanding more as intense international competition is simultaneously driving quality up and cost and prices down. The public sector is not immune from the trend, with overseas companies winning out in the bids to set up new treatment centres for the National Health Service, for example. Organizations are reacting to this competition by becoming 'customer-focused', speeding up response times, emphasizing quality and continuous improvement, accelerating the introduction of new technology, operating more flexibly and 'losing cost', and taking advantage of increasingly international supply chains. With customer service assistants available at £1,300 per annum in China and £800 in India, the pressure for 'off-shoring' activity is intense.

The pressure has therefore been for businesses to become 'lean and mean', downsizing and cutting out layers of management and supervision, which has helped to explain the move to flatter grade structures and broadbands. They are often reducing permanent staff to a core of essential workers and increasing the use of peripheral workers (sub-contractors and temporary staff). Some are 'outsourcing' work to external service providers and overseas, thus reducing employment costs and enabling the enterprise more easily to increase or reduce the numbers available for work, in response to fluctuations in the level of business activity.

They become 'flexible firms'. The ultimate development of this process is the 'virtual firm', where through the extensive use of information technology a high proportion of marketing and professional staff mainly work from home, only coming into the office on special occasions to occupy their 'hot desks', and spending more time with their customers or clients.

All these factors can influence reward strategy by, for example, introducing more flexibility into the reward system and variations within and between business units, as at BT; or by requiring greater tailoring of reward practices to suit the particular needs of certain key categories of employees such as knowledge workers or customer service staff, as in some of the job family approaches described in Chapter 7; or by influencing the grading structures and pay differentials in an organization.

A Nottingham University study suggests that cost-cutting by moving activities to overseas locations has also affected pay rates in the UK and has contributed to increasing pay differentials between managerial/professional and unskilled work. These wider differentials are evident now in the pay structures of many large employers and have helped to drive pay structure reform, for example in the UK Senior Civil Service's adoption of wider, market-related pay bands. Illustrating the complex interplay of these external influences and trends, demographic and legislative pressures such as the National Minimum Wage (which we describe in the next section) have encouraged employers such as Tesco to reduce the pay differentials between lower graded staff.

Traditional pay bargaining has taken on a new twist as staff and unions realize that simply escalating pay costs may have a negative effect on employment levels if work is instead sourced from cheaper overseas locations. The pay and employment practices at Ireland-based airline Ryanair have attracted some external criticism, yet the low cost base this provides has enabled the company to expand rapidly and become Europe's largest airline by market value.

Correspondingly, companies have to consider the impact that overseas sourcing can have on their corporate reputation, with Nike suffering after publicity of the poor treatment of workers in some of its Asian suppliers' factories. The National Health Service has recently reached an agreement with certain developing countries not to 'poach' medical and nursing staff to meet the growth in service provision in the UK; while the relative pay and employment conditions in the NHS's new private treatment centres and more independent foundation hospitals also present complex employment and reward issues to deal with, going well beyond the simplistic stereotypes of typical public and private sector reward practices. These are novel and sensitive issues for the specialists in reward strategy to respond to by designing and delivering modifications to their policies and practices.

Globalization

Global competition in mature production and service sectors is increasing. This is assisted by easily transferable technology and reductions in international trade barriers. As Ulrich (1997) has pointed out, globalization requires organizations to move people, ideas, products and information around the world to meet local needs. New and important ingredients must be added to the mix when making strategy: volatile political situations, contentious global trade issues, fluctuating exchange rates and unfamiliar cultures.

With greater international business competition comes greater competition for staff. Over a fifth of the FTSE 100 companies in the UK have a non-UK national on their board, and the UK company which lost its head of research to a much higher offer from one of its US competitors probably wishes it had given greater consideration to the reward implications of these international trends. The high proportion of overseas football players and massive wage bills in the UK Premier League may be an extreme manifestation of the global war for talent, but the same trends are affecting many areas of the economy.

Attracting key talent has become not just a corporate but also a matter of national concern, with countries from Australia to Scotland putting together attractive relocation propositions to attract workers in high demand and high skill occupations, and also to avoid the dreaded 'brain drain'.

Firms are being forced to react to these issues in their international resourcing and reward approaches. A survey by Cendant Mobility (2002) showed a majority of organizations with operations in more than one country planning to move more staff between locations, to meet their increasingly global business's needs and to transfer relevant knowledge and skills. Yet a growing number also reported increasing difficulty in actually achieving this, with factors such as the growth of dual career couples and political instability contributing to an apparent greater reluctance to move overseas.

Traditionally, discussions of international reward strategies and practices have tended to focus on an elite of expatriate workers, sourced from headquarter locations and rewarded in isolation from local country staff. Their package is typically established through the balance sheet method, which builds on the basis of their home country package to compensate them for the disruption of being overseas.

Today, as Managing Director of consultancy ORC UK, Siobhan Cummins, explains, we are seeing a far more diverse and complex pattern emerging, requiring a much more strategic approach than simply copying the near-universal practice of other multinationals. While expatriates on long-term assignments and the balance sheet approach remain the commonest means of sourcing internationally mobile staff, we are seeing:

▌ the emergence of more mixed expatriate populations from different geographies, a trend towards greater use of local managers at senior levels, and faster localization of expatriate staff, with 'sundown' provisions on their allowances after three to five years;

▌ a wider variety of staffing patterns, with over half of the companies in the Cendant study making greater use of short-term and 'virtual' assignments, extended business travel and international commutes, as well as more localized transfers;

▌ cost pressures in particular leading to a challenge to the balance sheet reward approach, which in some cases may not be applied to all international staff in all locations, but might be restricted to key/senior staff in the most difficult locations; host country, net to net, and international or regional pay scales are also now in evidence;

▌ greater attention to the needs of the 'trailing spouse': while some of the traditional expatriate family benefits such as international schooling costs are being scaled back because of their cost, over three-quarters of ORC's clients now offer formal spouse assistance to address this common cause of assignment rejection and failure, which can include job search assistance and language training, as well as cash allowances.

As Perkins (2006) explains, achieving an appropriate 'global/local' balance in international staffing and rewards has therefore become a much more strategic, that is important and challenging, issue for HR and reward managers to address. Major organizations such as BP and The World Bank have overhauled their policies in recent years to better address their key strategic reward goals of mobility and affordability in this more demanding global context.

Seija Vuori from Nokia for example, explained at a recent conference in Stockholm the 'mid-Atlantic' remuneration philosophy that his company now employs, an approach that involves 'thinking globally but acting locally'. Helped by an integrated e-HR system, this has involved a move to more commonality in approach, with global incentive and stock plans and common job levels and market and performance-related pay review methodologies. But flexibility and personalization within a total rewards framework are also key principles of the approach.

In the USA, Nokia's changes have involved greater attention to team-working from a traditionally individualistic culture, while at headquarters in Finland the movement has been towards greater individual differentiation. In making a success of the changes, Vuori emphasizes those factors we have highlighted as being key to the new and emerging approach to reward strategy: senior and line management commitment and support; project and change management skills; and a positive and flexible approach to implementation, with heavy communication and involvement of managers and staff.

Employment and demographic trends

Employment patterns and practices have changed significantly in the last decade, with some of the most influential trends including:

▌ a rising demand for skills and qualifications, which is particularly marked for managerial and professional workers, knowledge workers, customer service staff, technical and office staff and skilled manual workers;

▌ an apparent growth in job insecurity, more so for men than for women;

▌ historically low levels of unemployment that are serving to create skills shortages in areas way beyond the traditional 'gold-collar' occupations such as IT and financial services work, for example for transport drivers and catering staff;

▌ an increase in the number of part-time and female workers – the expansion of women's work has been almost entirely an expansion of part-time work;

▌ a greater emphasis on flexible working to provide for rapid response;

▌ an associated increase in the number of workers on non-standard contracts (part-time, short-term and the use of self-employed sub-contract workers);

▌ a reduction in career prospects through promotion as a result of the rise of the flatter organization;

▌ a reduction in the power of the trade unions, partly because of legislation, but more significantly in numerical terms for structural reasons, with the decline of large-scale manufacturing and the rise of the service industries;

▌ associated with the decline in the significance of the trade unions, a move towards individualizing the employment relationship with less reliance on collective bargaining.

These trends have all impacted on the nature of reward practices that organizations employ. One of the most important factors helping to explain them, which reward and HR strategies have to address for the future, is that of demographic change. It is no use having a business strategy the organization does not have enough staff of the right calibre to implement. Yet demographic trends are placing enormous pressures on traditional staff resourcing and reward approaches, which require responses way beyond the simple 'tweaking' of a few market supplements.

Birth rates throughout the developed world have been falling in recent decades, and this has been paralleled by declining mortality rates and increasing longevity. In 2006 there are more people in the 55–64 age range in the UK than are aged 16–24, and the trends are set to continue across Europe, with the average age of the population by 2050 estimated to reach almost 50 years, and a 12 per cent forecast reduction in the UK's working-age population.

Just as traditional labour pools are shrinking, traditional reward practices and mindsets have been encouraging a further reduction in employment, with early retirement through defined benefit pensions arrangements in the 1990s helping to explain falls in the average age of retirement for both men and women. The UK faces a long-term pensions 'crisis' as the ratio of the working to the retired population decreases. In individual companies such as British Airways and BAe Systems, this has produced major deficits in traditional defined benefits pension plans, which represent a significant proportion of the market value of the firm. Industrial action in public and private sectors has resulted from employers trying to change pension arrangements to address these deficits.

Resourcing and reward strategies that are heavily focused on either recruiting young 'dynamic' staff and getting rid of 'old' employees at a fixed retirement date or before, or the opportunistic poaching of staff with the requisite skills and experience from competitors, are therefore becoming increasingly outdated and undesirable from both an employer and national perspective. One European bank estimates that over the next five years, the traditional pool of high calibre graduates and MBAs, which has historically been its main source of future executive talent, will decline by a fifth, while significantly more employers will be chasing them. No wonder chief executives across Europe rated the attraction and retention of talented staff as their number one concern, according in a recent Conference Board study, and over 80 per cent of UK employers reported recruitment and retention difficulties in the CIPD's annual survey.

Employment legislation and fair reward

The issue has also been a matter of concern for politicians in the UK, with the then Secretary of State for Trade and Industry Patricia Hewitt telling delegates at the CIPD's annual employment law conference of the importance of addressing labour market 'dysfunctionalities', such as the low employment rates of ethnic minorities, the 18 per cent pay gap between average female and male earnings, and declining employment rates of the over-60s.

The Labour government has passed a raft of employment legislation in its quest for both social justice and economic efficiency. Under previous Conservative administrations the need for rewards strategies to be legally compliant was generally unspoken, and often easier to achieve with a general reduction in employment legislation and in trade union powers. Reward strategy thinking from free-market North America generally paid little direct attention to legislation in favour of considerations of internal business fit.

Today it is critical that the reward strategies respond to, and better anticipate, employment regulations. Legislation that has been passed since the Labour government was elected in 1997 includes:

▌ the national minimum wage and working time regulations;

▌ the right to request flexible working and a range of measures to encourage family-friendly policies and improve maternity and paternity provisions;

▌ a number of pieces of legislation on diversity, including protection from discrimination against the disabled and on the basis of religious beliefs and sexual orientation, soon to be followed by age and the formation of a new Commission of Equality and Human Rights;

▌ a number of pieces of pensions legislation, as well as enquiries and guidelines on executive remuneration and equal pay.

There is no doubt that this legislative and political context has pushed factors such as equality and equal pay up the reward strategy agenda. The £4.2 million that UK employers paid out in 2003 as a result of losing cases for unlawful discrimination at work has undoubtedly focused attention on the issue in boardrooms. But as Patricia Hewitt said, employers and reward managers should not need legislation to compel them to realize that resourcing and reward strategies need to change to recognize and exploit these changing employment and labour market realities. Common responses revealed by the CIPD's annual recruitment and retention survey go well beyond increasing pay levels, throwing 'golden hello' payments at new recruits and overseas recruitment. They include:

▌ advertising vacancies outside the traditional 'mainstream' media and deliberately targeting non-traditional labour pools, by half of those making policy changes;

▌ improving training and development, by 66 per cent, and appointing flexibly on the basis of potential, rather than exact fit with the job specification;

▌ offering more flexible and family-friendly working hours and rewards, by 43 per cent.

Brett (2005) notes that:

Expectations of both reward and diversity functions have shifted in the past decade to become more strategic. The gender pay gap has become a hot topic not because of recent legislation – the Equal Pay Act has been in place for 30 years – but because of the under-utilization of the skills and talents of a significant part of the workforce.

Building society Nationwide provides a good example of a strategic and integrated response to these trends in its resourcing and reward strategies. Changes have included:

▮ moving to a more affordable but still good career average pension plan from the previous defined benefits scheme;

▮ removing a fixed date of retirement and encouraging the employment of older workers;

▮ increasing the diversity of the make up of branch staff to better reflect the diversity of the customer population – the increased employment in particular of older workers has led to reductions in employee turnover and training costs;

▮ analysing the ratio of female to male earnings in its different pay bands, and encouraging the employment of women at senior levels.

Online bank First Direct discovered that only 12 per cent of its employees were over 45 years old, and just five per cent under 21. Resulting initiatives have included coffee mornings and adverts on Saga radio to attract older workers and targeting local universities for potential student recruits.

The Co-Operative Group meanwhile is considering responding to the declining numbers of young people by replacing its graduate recruitment programme with a general entry talent programme. It already targets universities with a high proportion of part-time, mature students.

Barclays has developed a 'Success through Inclusion' charter, documenting its aspirations for the next 10 years, and recognizing that by the end of that period it will have a different sort of employee, and a different sort of customer. This followed a survey of 10,000 of the bank's staff. It has been signed off by the bank's executive committee members, and all customer facing, recruitment and training staff are trained in its core principles. The introduction of the bank's flexible 'Afterwork' pension and raising of the retirement age has resulted in the retention of hundreds of knowledgeable staff, and it is now recruiting staff over 60 years of age. According to Diversity Manager Charlotte Sweeney, as quoted by the CIPD (2003a): 'If you want to have a business in the future, you just have to do this.'

Retailer Asda has gone way beyond the government's requirements in offering a wide range of flexible working conditions, including Benidorm and adoption leave. The anticipated savings to the firm from reduced attrition are estimated by Director of People, David Smith, at over £4 million.

In the public sector, Phil Badley, Assistant Chief Executive of Stockport Borough Council, explains that:

> It is difficult to attract young people into local government. In Stockport around 5 per cent of our workforce is under 25. We are working to make our offer to young people more attractive. At the other end of the spectrum we have a healthy proportion of employees over 45. We have been looking at a range of strategies to maintain and develop the skills base in older workers. This is leading to better appraisal and development processes to improve employees' skills for the future. (CIPD, 2003a)

REWARD STRATEGY AS MULTI-DIMENSIONAL ALIGNMENT

Reward strategy today is therefore a much more complex process than just addressing the alignment with business strategy, having to take account also of the broader economic context and legislative environment as well as, in a 'sellers' labour market, the needs and motivations of an increasingly diverse workforce. Balancing these requirements in an appropriate future direction for practice is perhaps the touchstone of success for contemporary reward strategies. In the following chapters in this part of the book we consider in more detail the impact of an increasingly knowledge- and service-dominated economy on reward, and the effects of these external and internal contextual factors in driving some of the commonest current trends in UK reward practice.

6

Reward strategies in a knowledge economy

The Western literature on business, HR and reward strategies has traditionally focused on individuals making free choices in order to engineer unique approaches that can deliver competitive advantage to their organization. The selected business strategy has been positioned as the primary driver of the reward strategy, with reward practices aligned so as to encourage actions by employees that support the delivery of business goals and recognize their achievement (see Lawler, 1990, for example).

In reality, influences and constraints from outside the organization are always going to be evident, and a successful reward strategy has to anticipate, react and adapt to these factors. Major trends in executive compensation over the past 20 years, for example, can very largely be explained by changes in the tax and regulatory environment rather than individual company choice.

Yet perhaps the most influential factor on our work and lives over this period has been the evolution towards a post-industrial, heavily knowledge- and service-based economy. In this and the following chapter, after showing the evidence for this shift, we consider the reward implications for the increasing numbers employed in information-, knowledge- and service-based occupations and jobs.

Much has been written, particularly during the period of the dot com 'bubble', about how an elite of IT and knowledge workers are and should be rewarded. The advice, though, is at times confusing and contradictory, even on such basic issues as how important money is for their motivation.

We draw out the common themes and trends from research in the field in this chapter.

Much less attention has been devoted to those in the increasingly numerous and often low paid, front line customer service roles and how their reward arrangements can help or hinder the delivery of customer service strategies. The coffee shop assistant, the courier and delivery driver, the hairdresser, the teaching and healthcare assistant, community support officer, aromatherapist and the leisure club trainer are at least as much a part of the 'new economy' as the IT consultant, hedge fund manager and highly paid sports star.

In the following chapter, we argue that predominant reward arrangements for service staff are still often based on an outdated, industrial, cost-reduction model. We show powerful research evidence to demonstrate that appropriate reward and HR policies can have a major positive effect on the levels of service that such staff deliver to customers, and thereby on financial performance, the ultimate aim of any reward strategy.

THE RISE OF THE POST-INDUSTRIAL ECONOMY

US HR expert Dave Ulrich defines the first tenet of his 'HR value proposition' as 'knowing (the) external realities' (Ulrich and Brockbank, 2005a). Throughout the developed world, the reality is that our economies are now ever more heavily knowledge and service based. An estimated 70 per cent of total GDP growth in the European Union derives from the services sector. Intangible assets and human capital are becoming a more important component of economic and stock market performance, representing up to three-quarters of growth in the value of major corporations (Scarborough, 2003). Customer service and innovation are seen as being key to national economic success and to the business strategies of most of our major companies today. Sixty-nine per cent of over 4,000 business leaders surveyed by consultancy DDI ranked improving customer service as a top business priority, two-thirds improving quality and 43 per cent developing new technology and innovation (DDI, 2005).

Economist Diane Coyle draws out the implications of these economic changes for the world of work:

> The economy is becoming increasingly weightless: what is valuable is not the material stuff that goes into making goods... we pay for the characteristics of the people providing the service. The burgeoning professional and managerial classes are spending their time acquiring information and presenting it in a performance for co-workers or customers. The more the economy is made up of services, the more of us will be performing. (Coyle, 2001)

Table 6.1 Occupational employment trends and projections, UK 1982–2012

	1982		2002		2012	
	000s	%share	000s	%share	000s	%share
Managers & Senior officials	2698	10.7	4349	14.9	4934	16.2
Professional Occupations	2003	8.0	3305	11.3	4008	12.9
Associate Professional & Technical	2406	9.6	4121	14.0	4895	16.0
Administrative, Clerical & Secretarial	3895	15.5	3857	13.2	3434	13.7
Skilled Trades	4289	17.0	3341	11.4	3062	8.1
Personal Service	952	3.7	2147	7.3	2894	9.4
Sales & Customer Service	1527	6.1	2334	7.9	2732	9.0
Transport and Machine Operatives	2981	11.8	2473	8.4	2225	7.2
Elementary Occupations	4463	17.6	3409	11.6	2735	8.9

Source: *Working Futures: National Report 2003–4*, Institute of Employment Research/Sector Skills Development Agency, 2004

Former US Labour Secretary Robert Reich (2004) additionally highlights the impact of market globalization on jobs, so that 'every task that's repetitive... is no longer going to be done by Americans at American wages'. He identifies two main categories of employment growth in developed economies. The first are knowledge workers, 'identifying and solving new problems, analysing, manipulating and communicating... working alone or in small teams'. Second are personal service jobs which 'computers can't do because they require human beings, their value comes from human touch, care and attentiveness'.

UK labour market trends and projections very much support Reich's analysis – see Table 6.1. By 2012 the 'knowledge elite' in managerial, professional and technical work will have increased from roughly a quarter of all jobs 20 years ago to almost a half. In the year to March 2005, 90,000 new jobs were created in the UK in both finance/business services, and education/health/public administration sectors.

But the growth of the 'cappuccino' and the 'upstairs-downstairs' economy is also evident, with the numbers in personal service occupations almost trebling since 1982. Bars and restaurants, for example, now provide over a million jobs in the UK, sport and leisure over 400,000, exceeding the numbers in most sectors of manufacturing, which lost another 86,000 jobs in 2005. The decline in jobs in administrative and clerical occupations is also evident.

Many still common reward practices today were developed in a very different era and environment: productivity-driven incentive plans for the cottage weaver and on the factory floor; job evaluation and graded pay structures for the massed ranks of US government clerks; and defined benefit pension plans in the Victorian civil service and amongst the railway companies at that time.

So just what are the most appropriate reward strategies and techniques to use for employees in our high-technology, high-touch economy? How important is cash versus more intrinsic rewards? Does performance-related pay help or hinder in these settings, and should it be individually or team focused? And ultimately, do pay and reward practices for knowledge and service workers have much effect on organizational performance, or are other aspects of people management more important?

REWARDING KNOWLEDGE WORKERS: THE THEORIES TESTED

'In order to generate extraordinary value a company has to learn and apply knowledge through its businesses faster and more widely than its competitors.' These sentiments of Lord Browne, Chief Executive of BP, would be echoed by the majority of business leaders today. But the reward packages required to recruit, retain and motivate the workers developing and applying this knowledge have been an area of considerable debate and disagreement.

According to Chris Patten, Chancellor of Oxford University, a major cause of Europe's declining competitiveness is that our 'research systems remain structurally ill-adapted to the challenges of the coming decades... it is difficult to attract the best young brains into science and technology – career structures are rigid and financial rewards better elsewhere' (Patten, 2005). Florida (2005) agrees that for the broader 'creative class' of workers, existing arrangements are creating a 'talent deficit'.

But is it just a question of money? 'Do not rely on pay, a different set of rewards needs to be available,' recommends Peter Reilly at the Institute of Employment Studies (Reilly, 2005a). Richard Reeves and John Knell agree that in a 'post-scarcity' knowledge economy, 'money is losing its lustre... the reward equation needs to be rewritten' (Reeves and Knell, 2001). The image of the work-obsessed 'techie', profiled so well in Tracey Kidder's Pulitzer prize winning book about the foundation of Digital Equipment, working 'thankless hours for not a lot of pay' but at the technological 'cutting-edge', there for 'the intellectual challenge, the teamwork, the pride of achievement', remains popular today (Kidder, 1981).

Anyone who has watched the bonus determination process in an investment bank might question the general applicability of such advice. Coyle (2001) instead foresees 'more winner-takes-all earnings patterns... a star system in pay' spreading to wider areas of the economy. Lawler agrees that the 'amount of money matters' in the new, knowledge-driven economy. He believes that we are likely to see more individualization of employment contracts and a growth in pay differentials within and between different groups of workers (Lawler, 2002).

Bronson's (1999) review of working life in Silicon Valley profiles street-wise IT workers fully aware of their own value to skill-short employers, regularly job-hopping to improve their rewards package and career prospects. They are 'no longer nerds in the backroom: they want owner-ship, they want money'.

Lawler also recommends a move away from job-based pay to rewarding on the basis of the market value of someone's skills and knowledge, reflecting Drucker's original definition of a knowledge worker as someone 'who knows more about his or her work than anyone else in the organi-zation'. At the height of the 1990s stock market and technology boom, skills and competency-related pay were hailed by a number of influential con-sultants and practitioners as the way tomorrow's organizations would pay their knowledge workers.

Key drivers were seen as the moves to flatter, more fluid organization and job structures; the motivations of knowledge workers; the difficulty of measuring their value and contribution in terms of traditional perfor-mance 'outputs'; and the inflexibility of traditional job-based pay struc-tures to reflect personal growth and market value (see Risher, 2002, for example). Yet as well as competency and skills-related base pay, unlike many writers on the subject, Lawler (2000) also advocates 'an intense focus on paying for performance' using cash bonuses and share schemes.

Performance pay for knowledge workers is one of the most hotly debated subjects. Gupta and Shaw (1998) found non-financial recognition and a trusting environment, 'not money as the prime motivators for sci-entists'. Yet Katzell's research (cited in Koning, 1993) revealed positive associations between the performance and satisfaction of knowledge workers in the pharmaceutical and IT sectors and the use of individual merit pay. No wonder Nancy Leonard concludes that the field is replete with 'splintered and perplexing theories of motivation that only create conceptual clutter for researchers and confusion amongst practitioners' (Leonard et al, 1999).

An overview of UK reward practices and trends in the CIPD's Annual Reward Management Survey (2005a) suggests that the reality is not match-ing the predictions in a number of areas. Job evaluation remains common and is increasing in incidence (used by 51 per cent of employers), even if the external market is also becoming a more influential determinant of pay (in 75 per cent of the CIPD's sample).

Though a trend towards more flexible pay structures with wider differentials continues (36 per cent use broad-bands), along with a greater use of bonus plans (in 52 per cent), this is a gradual evolution. Analysis of data from the UK's Annual Survey of Hours and Earnings shows that the dispersion ratio between the lowest 10 per cent of earners and the highest 10 per cent nationally of 3.6 in 2004 was virtually unchanged since 1998 (Dobbs, 2005). Also, the incidence of all-employee share plans has actually declined marginally in recent years.

Pure skills and competency-related pay approaches remain rare, at just 6 per cent of the 500 organizations surveyed by CIPD, and they appear to be more common for administrative and manual staff rather than high-level professionals. An example is British Sugar, where administrative staff can progressively move through three pay grades having achieved three skill 'blocks' in each (Incomes Data Services, 2005a). Research evidence suggests that over-complexity and practical difficulties in measuring the application of skills and the value and impact of higher competence have limited the spread of such approaches (Brown and Armstrong, 1999).

REWARDING KNOWLEDGE WORKERS: THE EMERGING PRACTICE

So where does that leave practitioners wondering how best to pay their knowledge workers, other than in Leonard's state of confusion? While much of the dot com hype has evaporated, there does nonetheless appear to be broad agreement that the switch to a knowledge-based economy with more knowledge workers has some common implications for employers, and these chime with many of the key themes we have been focusing on in this book. With such a wide variety of types of workers and settings being lumped together under the knowledge worker heading, it is not surprising that there are contradictory findings and, as we describe in the rest of this book, no universally successful approaches.

However, these common themes have received a reasonable degree of support from the extensive research on the links between people management and performance carried out for the CIPD by researchers at Bath University (Purcell *et al*, 2003; Swart and Kinnie, 2004; Swart *et al*, 2003). This research profiled practices in 12 major organizations and six small knowledge-intensive firms, mostly engaged in software development. As we saw in previous chapters, the research highlighted the critical contribution of employees' discretionary commitment to high performance in a

Table 6.2 Association between human resource and reward policies and the attitudes of professional knowledge workers

HR policy	Organizational commitment	Job satisfaction	Employee motivation
Performance appraisal		+	+
Career opportunities	+	+	+
Teamworking			+
Work-life balance	+	+	
Rewards and recognition	+		
Involvement		+	
Relationship with line manager	+	+	
Job security			−
Effort	+		

+ positive association
− negative association
n = 769
Source: Bath University survey of 18 companies, Purcell *et al* (2003)

knowledge- and service-based economy. Good people and reward management really can have a major influence on organizational performance.

The study also draws out the common factors that are most strongly associated with the commitment and motivation of professional and knowledge workers – see Table 6.2. Employee's views on rewards and recognition, in regard to their absolute and relative level of pay, reward for their performance and the adequacy of non-pay rewards, have a strong correlation with their level of commitment. But the table also shows that other, less tangible aspects of reward and the environment have a similarly powerful influence on these workers' motivation and commitment.

Taking these common themes, we consider in turn:

▌ the use of distinct reward schemes for knowledge workers, versus the introduction of more flexible arrangements for all staff;

▌ the emphasis on learning and career development opportunities for knowledge workers;

▌ flexible rewards and working;

▌ the broader work context and line management relationship.

EMERGING PRACTICE: FLEXIBILITY IN A FRAMEWORK

Perhaps the key decision for anyone responsible for managing and rewarding groups of knowledge workers is whether or not to differentiate them from the practices applying to other employees in the organization. Distinct reward and HR practices are not new for various types of knowledge workers, for example: the distinction between front and back office staff in firms in the City; distinct pay structures and career ladders for research and development staff in a number of large pharmaceutical companies; and for IT staff more generally – at Barclays for example.

However, the CIPD's data suggest that such outright differentiation is not on the increase, and the 'mass customization' of individual contracts forecast by writers such as Coyle has not yet spread significantly, though we have seen individuals such as Richard Granger, the NHS's IT Director, and Bob Kiley, the commissioner at Transport for London, hired in on distinctly high and highly bonus-oriented packages in the public sector in recent years. The modestly paid journeyman footballer is still more representative of the 'performers' Coyle describes in the new economy than is someone like David Beckham.

Complete differentiation of terms and conditions is being restrained by a number of factors including, most notably, the growing numbers of knowledge and professional workers throughout UK organizations; the drive to encourage innovation in a wide range of cross-functional activities rather than just in the R&D lab; and the increasing pressures to display equitable and consistent pay approaches to comply with equality legislation.

Rather, more typically we are seeing the growth of 'flexibility within a framework', with a common architecture of reward arrangements across the organization, but the flexibility to vary and tailor arrangements to suit the specific needs of particular groups of knowledge and professional workers and the individuals within those groups. A number of techniques are being employed to achieve this.

First is the incorporation of skills and competencies into traditional job evaluation factor plans, as described in more detail by Armstrong and Baron (1995). For example, the JESP system used for jobs in the Senior Civil Service has five measurement factors, one of which is level of professional competence that is applied when appropriate, for example for top policy roles with no management responsibilities. In the new system being applied to over 1 million employees in the National Health Service there are 16 measurement factors, but the knowledge, skills and experience factor accounts for almost a quarter of the total points weighting. The scheme acknowledges the explicit bias towards knowledge in an organization with huge numbers of professional workers (Rees, 2005).

Second, we are seeing the increasing use of job and career family structures. In some cases these may employ totally separate pay structures for different families of jobs, as at Norwich Union Insurance. But a fifth of the organizations in the CIPD's annual reward survey (2005a) operate with a common structure of broad pay bands, but overlay on to this career families, allowing them to reflect different market and work demands for specific groups of staff. Examples include Nationwide, Tesco and Abbey, where there are common bands or levels of job, but many market-related pay points and ranges within them to reflect the different skills and values of different types of knowledge worker.

At BAT there are salary ranges for each grade and job family, with varying market anchor points. We describe the approach in the NHS and at Vertex below, and look at this trend more widely in Chapter 8.

Third, while pure competency and skills-related pay adjustment is still rare, two-thirds of employers in the CIPD 2005 reward management survey claim now to relate pay reviews to personal contribution, a combination of individual performance and competence, for at least some of their staff. This combination of the 'what' of objectives and results achieved, and the 'how' of competence displayed and skills applied seems to work particularly well for knowledge workers.

Salary progression at BAT, for example, is linked to individual development and individual performance. Suffolk County Council has implemented the national Local Government Single Status Agreement but developed its own system of job families (Incomes Data Services, 2005a). Pay progression up to grade mid-points depends on the achievement of personal objectives and business results. Occupational competencies contribute to employee's movement over the mid-point bar.

While the existence of performance pay systems in organizations in the Bath University research was not positively or negatively associated with levels of staff commitment, the perception of some link between pay and performance at the individual or collective level was strongly correlated with commitment. So within organizations such as Barclays and Prudential we are increasingly seeing a mix of variable, performance-related reward schemes and measurement criteria (as recommended by both Reilly and Lawler) including short-term project bonuses to motivate goal achievement; annual profit sharing to reinforce collective performance and identity; and share schemes to reward long-term performance and retention. At Prudential UK, as well as an employee share incentive plan, there is a general employee bonus scheme that reflects a scorecard of six key performance indicators, including an index of customer, people and regulatory performance, as well as profitability.

A competency underpinning for many of these approaches is evident, and not surprising perhaps for organizations and workers whose role, as Coyle (2001) and Reich (2004) describe, is to add value by importing and applying knowledge and information. The pure career and competency-based approach described by Risher (2002) at Dow Chemical, in which pay ranges and progression are wholly related to employees' personal career stages and growth, may be rare, but the sorts of more blended, job family, market and contribution-related approach of IBM also described in his article looks like it is becoming the norm for today's knowledge-dependent organizations.

EMERGING PRACTICE: LEARNING AND A REWARDING CAREER

Whether it is instead of or alongside financial rewards, the learning opportunities and career development offered do appear to be a critical determinant of the motivation and retention of knowledge workers. As Reich (2004) explains, 'in a knowledge based economy, the new coin of the realm is learning. The brightest and the best want an intellectual challenge and the chance to keep learning'.

Rather than the provision of lots of training courses, Martyn Sloman's research illustrates how there is a marked shift away from programmed off-the-job training to more informal forms of learning that are strongly influenced by the individual learner, such as mentoring, coaching and on-the-job development (Sloman and Philpott, 2005). As he explains, in the new economy, 'both discretionary work effort and discretionary learning raise the ability of organizations to generate knowledge and share information that add value to their products and services and satisfy customer requirements'.

The Bath University research in knowledge-intensive firms demonstrated significant attention to providing these learning opportunities (Swart *et al*, 2003). Group and team learning and project reviews were pervasive, with assignment staffing reflecting people's desire to learn new skills as well as existing expertise. Senior managers devoted considerable time to mentoring and coaching staff. Dedicated time was provided for experimentation and learning, and in a number of cases the opportunity to acquire new knowledge was given as a reward for high performance, for example by attending a work-related conference abroad.

The researchers contrast the levels of commitment and satisfaction of staff resulting from the different approaches to reward and career management in two similar sized software companies. An employee in FinSoft explains:

> it's a great place to work... the people I work with are brilliant, the work is quite challenging. There are plenty of opportunities and the pay is good...

people feel valued and there is scope for advancement. They encourage you
to make more of your skills.

The bespoke projects the company focuses on provide such development
opportunities and differentiate them from their competitors.

Correspondingly in DataWare, commitment levels are much lower. As
an employee complains, 'the work is not challenging or stretching. I know
how to engineer things but I get ignored'. Managers devote much less time
to performance management and coaching their staff. The company's
business strategy is to deliver standard systems at a competitive cost, and
less investment is made in the staff and their careers.

This study also highlights the importance of professional affiliation,
development and recognition as drivers of the commitment and motivation of knowledge workers. Describing the open-sourced development of
the Linux operating system, Coyle (2001) explains that, 'skilled program-
mers don't seem to fret about getting enough money. The more highly
valued reward, because it is so much harder to come by, is the esteem in
which they are held by their peer group'.

Swart and Kinnie (2004) illustrate the apparent paradox that those software firms that concentrated on giving their staff the opportunities to
develop the most transferable skills and to communicate and interact most
freely right across the company and with external peers, were also those
in which staff displayed the highest levels of loyalty and commitment to
the organization. FinSoft had a deliberate policy of recruiting straight from
university and 'growing their own' while encouraging staff to maintain
their external contacts so as to import new knowledge effectively. Staff
there felt recognized but as part of 'a big team', whereas at Dataware, 'there
is no collaboration; we are a collection of individuals'. Reeves and Knell
(2001) similarly recommend, based on their experience, that employers
should 'support employees in identifying career opportunities inside and
outside the company'.

At Norwich Union Insurance, its job family initiative started out as a
means of improving career development, and was only subsequently used
for pay management purposes. But perhaps the largest illustration of the
fusion of career and reward management designed to improve the recruitment, retention and motivation of hundreds of thousands of knowledge
workers and professionals is the Agenda for Change exercise within the
NHS. As Workforce Director Andrew Foster explained to a CIPD HR
Leaders Network meeting in July 2005, this project involves a £3 billion
investment as over a million employees have their jobs evaluated and
placed within an integrated structure of nine pay bands. But the reforms
are driven by the concept of the skills ladder, and meeting the growth in
future staffing needs by providing career opportunities and paths for all
staff up through this structure – see Figure 6.1. Progression through bands

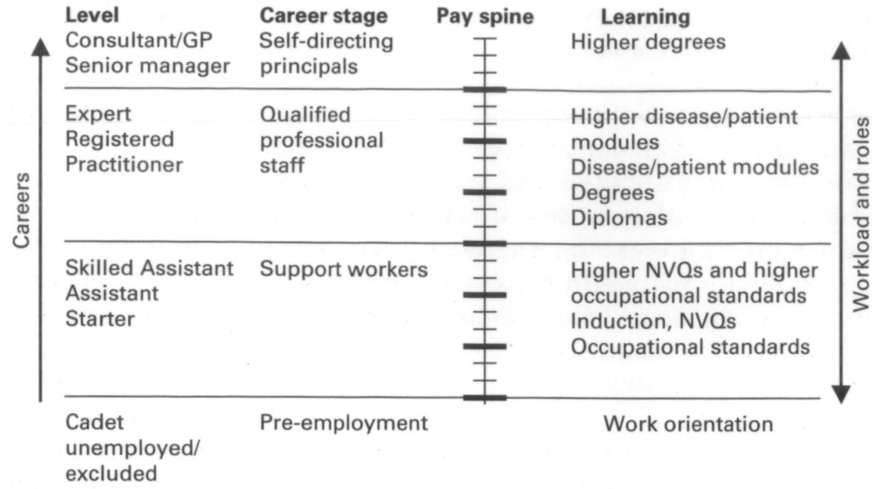

Level	Career stage	Pay spine	Learning
Consultant/GP Senior manager	Self-directing principals		Higher degrees
Expert Registered Practitioner	Qualified professional staff		Higher disease/patient modules Disease/patient modules Degrees Diplomas
Skilled Assistant Assistant Starter	Support workers		Higher NVQs and higher occupational standards Induction, NVQs Occupational standards
Cadet unemployed/ excluded	Pre-employment		Work orientation

(left axis label: Careers; right axis label: Workload and roles)

Figure 6.1 The NHS skills ladder

and personal development will be supported by a knowledge and skills framework for the various occupational categories, giving all staff clear objectives, helping them to apply their knowledge and skills to their current role and identify and address the skills and knowledge needed for career progression.

So in a knowledge economy, the traditional divide in responsibilities in HR functions between the work of reward and of training and development professionals cannot be allowed to prevent the development of an intrinsically and extrinsically rewarding environment for staff, addressing personal and professional development, as well as pay.

EMERGING PRACTICE: FLEXIBLE REWARDS AND WORKING

Rather than tailoring reward arrangements to fit the needs of particular groups of knowledge workers, flexible benefits and rewards packages allow employees not just to tailor their package to suit their work interests and career stage, but also their domestic circumstances, age, personal motivations and leisure interests. In the CIPD's Annual Reward Survey, private sector service firms had the highest incidence of fully flexible (12 per cent) and voluntary benefits (31 per cent), with many more offering at least some level of choice to staff. A key aspect of flexibility brought out by the research on knowledge workers, and as shown in Table 6.2 (see page 97), are flexible working arrangements.

Encouraged by the 2003 legislation providing the right for employees in the UK to request flexible working, a survey of 500 organizations by CIPD in 2005 illustrated the rapid growth in arrangements such as job sharing (evident in 63 per cent), term-time working schedules (38 per cent) and regular working from home (55 per cent) (CIPD, 2005c).

It is no coincidence that professional services firms such as Linklaters and PwC, which traditionally have been some of the most demanding in terms of the hours required from employees and with strongly chargeable hours-based pay systems, have been in the vanguard of the growth of flexible working arrangements and work-life balance programmes.

For reasonably well-paid and busy people, free time is an extremely valuable resource; and for employers facing major staff and skill shortages, recruiting and retaining from groups other than their traditional worka-holic male target population is essential. A number of studies, including the Bath University research, show that particularly for women, work-life balance considerations are critical when deciding to join and stay with an employer, and the CIPD survey demonstrates that improving recruitment and retention is the prime employer motivation. Forty per cent of employ-ers offer flexible working arrangements to all their staff, beyond the statutory requirements. Many public sector organizations have been enhancing their traditional strengths in this area recently, with the High-ways Agency, for example, moving to 15 days paid paternity leave.

As well as the ability to have and 'buy' more free time, the freedom to choose one's own schedule and location of work appears to be an impor-tant motivator in its own right for knowledge workers. Back at FinSoft, 'We organize our own working day. You can organize your own time with nobody looking over your shoulder.' Autonomy appears to be a key non-financial reward that many knowledge workers value highly.

REWARDING KNOWLEDGE WORKERS: CREATING THE CONTEXT

The CIPD's research into people management and organizational perfor-mance shows that pay and reward policies influence the organizational context in which employees are motivated and commit to delivering high performance, and that these policies cannot be considered, designed or operated independently of that context. This brief overview of the reward practices which are associated with the successful management and motivation of knowledge workers very much reinforces this analysis.

There are no universally effective or ineffective reward practices for these workers: they are too diverse a population operating in highly varied organizations and settings for this to be the case. The debate over perfor-mance-related pay proves to be a largely irrelevant one, when the 'how' of operating and managing schemes is so much more important than the 'what' of design.

Ryan *et al's* (1983) research investigated the relationship of financial, extrinsic forms of motivation and intrinsic rewards. The research found that in an environment of tight managerial control and limited communication, the two were inversely related; that is, the stronger the emphasis placed on financial rewards like performance pay, the lower the intrinsic motivation to work. Yet in an open, high-communication culture, both intrinsic and extrinsic motivation increased together. Context is key.

We have seen that certain sets of reward arrangements based on a very broad definition of 'reward' appear to be more generally appropriate for knowledge workers – those that financially reward the growth in competence and contribution of the employee, that provide challenging work and personal and career development opportunities, that offer flexible benefits and work and time sovereignty. Often, changes to introduce these types of scheme are progressed as part of an integrated strategy.

Kevin Brady, Reward and Employee Relations Director for BT Group, which has a significant proportion of knowledge workers, explained to the CIPD's Annual Reward Conference in 2005 the reward strategy it has been implementing over the past two years for its 28,000 management and professional staff. This was designed to produce a focus on roles and skills rather than hierarchical position; a clearer link between pay and performance and pay and the external market, with wider pay differentials; more variable pay; and more employee choice. The changes have involved a new structure of 18 job families, such as Customer Service and Network Engineering; the 300 new job roles are placed within these families and each has its own market-related salary range; a new salary management process; and the introduction of total rewards statements and flexible benefits.

Whatever the role of money – and increasing pay differentials between and within different categories of staff does seem an inescapable conclusion of current economic trends (even if it is taking longer to emerge than many had predicted) – this analysis has highlighted the growing importance of the 'softer', broader and more informal parts of the employment contract to the recruitment and motivation of staff in a knowledge economy. Reeves and Knell (2001) spell out the implications of these findings for reward managers:

> Much of the effort currently being devoted to the construction of fiercely complicated pay systems may be better devoted to the recruitment and development of front line managers who can create appropriate reward 'spaces' for their staff.

This is a theme we develop further in Chapter 11 of this book.

7

Reward strategies in a service-based economy

Considerable attention has been devoted to the reward and motivation of knowledge workers, but much less advice and research is evident for the rapidly expanding and larger population of front line customer service staff. Although the job of answering the phones in a call centre may be less complex and well paid than that of developing the software and on-screen systems that support them, the CIPD's research in this area draws some very similar conclusions to those just made for knowledge workers.

While writers such as Coyle (2001) foresaw a new elite of knowledge workers and pay superstars emerging from economic and technological changes, it is easy to ignore the democratic and down-skilling effects of technology, which Tomkins (2005) describes as 'the debunking of expertise... the rise of the common expert'. The NHS skills ladder is designed to facilitate the passing of skilled work down the ladder, for example for Healthcare Assistants to take your blood pressure instead of doctors or nurses, as well as the career movement of staff up it. As Professor Julian Burkinshaw of London Business School says, 'when you ask in a large organization today who is responsible for new ideas... you need to get everyone alert to them' (Tyrrell, 2005).

Similarly, the rise of the service economy has seen the emergence of flatter structures and large numbers of front line customer service staff who are critical to the delivery of organizations' customer-focused business strategies. This is the core objective of the Gershon reforms underway across UK government, and it is why business leaders today emphasize the requirement to meet customer and employee needs. As

William Purves, former chair of HSBC puts it, 'we think the customer is first, the staff second and the shareholders third; if you get the first two right, the third will come right as well' (Lascelles, 2005).

Johnstone's research work (2004) highlights that for ever more discerning and less loyal customers, it is the immediate employee-customer interface, and staff being seen to go 'the extra mile', displaying discretionary commitment and paying attention to 'the little things', that characterize their perceptions of high levels of service.

Satisfied customers served by motivated and committed front-line staff means repeat business and higher sales. More and more companies are repeating the finding of a service-profit chain at Sears, the US retailer, where research demonstrated that a 5 per cent increase in general employee satisfaction was associated with a 1.25 per cent increase in customer satisfaction and a 0.5 per cent increase in sales.

Standard Chartered Bank has found that its consumer banking branches with higher levels of staff engagement have above-average levels of customer satisfaction, higher revenue growth and higher profit margins (CIPD, 2005d). Nationwide Building Society's extensive research has shown that its 15,000 employees' perceptions of various HR policies, including pay, correlate with employee commitment and retention, which in turn are associated with higher levels of customer commitment and higher sales. West *et al* (2002) demonstrated correlations between the use of various HR practices for hospital staff and mortality rates in the National Health Service.

REWARDING CUSTOMER SERVICE?

Yet the popular impression of typical reward and HR arrangements for front line customer service staff would seem to belie such a vital, valuable and valued role. Low pay, low skills, high levels of staff turnover and absence, poor selling and mis-selling; these are the images that regularly appear in the media when the employment of staff in shops, call centres and similar front line settings is profiled. A TUC report (2001) on the UK call centre industry found wages 40 per cent below the national average and highlighted 'sweatshop' conditions. Concern has been expressed recently that new electronic tagging technology might be applied to monitor the movement of retail staff, as well as goods.

Worldwide, staff turnover in call centres rose to 23 per cent in 2004, while investment in staff training and development declined (Merchants, 2005). The CIPD's annual recruitment, retention and turnover survey (2005b) found that private sector service firms had an average annual labour turnover of 21.4 per cent, with a 31 per cent average in retail businesses and

65 per cent in hotels, catering and leisure. Lack of development and career opportunities (42 per cent) and level of pay (37 per cent) were seen as major causes of turnover.

The UK's poor reputation and performance in service industries has been an issue of government concern, highlighted in a report commissioned by the Department of Trade and Industry from Harvard professor Michael Porter (Porter and Ketels, 2003). It helps to explain the introduction in the UK of the national minimum wage in 1999 and the relatively high levels of annual increase made to it (7.1 per cent in 2003 and 7.8 per cent in 2004), which has had a major effect on the pay of customer service and sales staff in sectors such as retailing. IDS reported, for example, that minimum pay levels at HSBC were recently raised by 22.5 per cent, with other large increases at Marks & Spencer and Tesco (Incomes Data Services, 2004).

Some UK business leaders have complained at the resulting cost increases. Yet many of them share the government's concern at poor service levels, and the need to improve customer service and relationships was regarded as the most significant business issue by the UK executives in DDI's international leadership study (DDI, 2005).

REWARDING CUSTOMER SERVICE: THE RESEARCH

In a globalizing and intensely competitive environment, just what are the best strategies for managing and rewarding staff to deliver high levels of customer service on the front line? The CIPD in conjunction with the Institute of Customer Service commissioned Professor Michael West and a team from Aston University to investigate these issues (West *et al*, 2005).

West's research project took 18 months and encompassed 15 organizations and 22 customer service locations. They represented a variety of industries and sectors – banks, building societies and insurance companies, utilities, telecoms firms and retailers, local and central government departments and services. The service staff employed in each location varied from 37 to over 1,000.

The researchers gathered information on reward and HR policies, interviewed managers and also surveyed employees' views and experiences. The jobs they were carrying out were both face-to-face and telephone-based in a wide range of settings, including call centre customer service agents and technical support roles; charity workers; financial advisers and branch staff; hotel receptionists, restaurant and bar staff; as well as employees in leisure centres and libraries.

The 580 staff involved illustrated that front line customer service workers do not all conform to the young/female/fleeting image: 70 per cent were women but their average age was 34 years and average length of service six years; 80 per cent were employed on a full-time basis and just 9 per cent on temporary contracts.

Nor did their working environment and conditions reflect the stereo-typical 'sweatshop' image. While the HR and reward practices varied, working conditions were generally good and staff rated their supervisors' skills, as well as their colleagues and the level of teamworking. Staff benefits such as company pension plans and sick pay schemes were the norm, as were various training courses.

The pattern of pay practices used by these 15 organizations for front line staff and their first line managers is shown in Table 7.1. Base pay levels were generally competitive for the location and sector, and a number mentioned the effect of the national minimum wage.

IDS noted that opticians Dolland and Aitchison had similarly increased the pay of its shop staff by between 8 and 11 per cent in 1994 in order to be 'sufficiently above the statutory level ... (to) not keep returning to the issue of uprating year after year' (Incomes Data Services, 2004). Thus pay levels per se did not emerge as a significant driver of customer service performance from the Aston research.

Most employees in the researched organizations had the opportunity to progress their base pay on the basis of their performance or competence, either through a range, or up a pay spine, or between grades/levels of job. Such arrangements have generally supplanted 'spot' pay rates for service roles in call centres and retail shops. At Boots the Chemists for example, shop staff can progress up through a number of pay points according to their level of performance and skill – from entry level, to experienced, to advanced, to expert/specialist (IDS, 2005b). At House of Fraser, employees are allocated to one of four competency bands – training, bronze, silver and gold, with staff assessed for a 'promotion' every six months.

Low base pay, high commission arrangements were rare amongst the 15 organizations, but most of them operated variable performance-related pay schemes of some type, which again has become the norm for service staff today in these contexts, at least in the private sector. Tesco and John Lewis staff for example, received company-wide profit sharing payments in 2004 of 3.6 per cent of basic pay and 12 per cent respectively; British Gas uses a company-wide balanced scorecard bonus scheme; while Homebase, Asda and Marks & Spencer use team, store-based schemes. A number of the organizations used multiple plans; for example, Royal Bank of Scotland has a profit sharing scheme to reward corporate achievement and pays bonuses to reward good and exceptional individual performance.

As well as analysing reward policies and staff attitudes, the Aston researchers also studied the performance of the 15 organizations in the study. They specifically focused on measures of customer service levels

Table 7.1 The pattern of pay practices in the Aston research organizations

Pay structure	Managers	Customer service staff
Grades	6	6
Broad-bands	3	3
Individual ranges	4	4
Pay spine	2	2
Pay progression and bonus		
Individual performance-related pay	4	5
Skills/competency pay	2	2
Contribution pay	3	3
Individual bonus	5	6
Team bonus	4	6
Commission	0	1
Profit sharing	2	2

and quality, and supplemented this data with personal observations of a sample of employee-customer interactions.

Using these indices, they found that five organizations were superior to the others in terms of their customer satisfaction and service performance levels. So what differentiated Scottish Water, Torfaen and Kent County councils, Impulse Leisure and the Unite Group from their often larger and better-known comparators? The study shows a distinctive pattern of reward and management practices in these five, which, together with the views of their staff on these practices, differentiated them from the other 10 and underpinned their outstanding customer service delivery – see Table 7.2.

Table 7.2 Significant differences in the reward arrangements of the highest performing organizations in the Aston research

Reward practice	Top 5	Other 10
Individual performance-related pay	60%	29%
Team/collective bonus scheme(s)	60%	12%
Team and individual recognition	100%	12%
Company pension	100%	71%
Restaurant	100%	53%

(Figures are percentage of organizations with each practice.)

REWARDING CUSTOMER SERVICE: EFFECTIVE PRACTICE

All forms of performance-related pay and recognition schemes were utilized more frequently and more extensively by the highest performing organizations in the research than amongst the other participants and by UK organizations as a whole. They were twice as likely as other UK organizations to use individual performance-related pay and various forms of individual and team non-financial recognition schemes, and five times as likely to use some form of team/collective bonus scheme as the remaining organizations in the study.

The issue for the top performing organizations appeared to be not whether to but how to best reward performance, and most used multiple approaches. At student accommodation provider the Unite Group, performance was rewarded using individual and team bonuses, gifts, 'thank you' letters from managers, and an annual 'Oscars' ceremony. While the value of cash bonuses or non-cash awards was typically not huge, there was a strong focus on recognizing and reinforcing outstanding performance swiftly and strongly.

A member of the Torfaen Council customer service centre team observed of their annual awards ceremony, 'I know everyone who has gone has enjoyed that they have been nominated and noticed... recognized for the work they do.' According to a manager in Kent County Council's service centre:

> If you want to acknowledge something straight away, it's easy to get a bunch of flowers or take them out for a meal. It's the little things, but things that are in control of the manager, so that it happens instantaneously and everyone knows why.

But these organizations were not necessarily just 'easy' and 'fun' places to work. The relentless and overwhelming focus of the performance pay and other reward and management processes in these five organizations was on the customer and serving them well. The wisdom of the old adage, that what gets measured and rewarded gets done, is well illustrated. While the remaining participants were more likely to employ performance pay measures of staff 'output' and productivity, all of the highest performers focused on measures of customer satisfaction and service quality.

According to Lorna Mapson, a manager at Impulse Leisure:

> The quality of customer service has been strategically allied to our reward and recognition strategy. Staff are aware that their customer service is continually assessed through a variety of methods. All of these are fed into the performance pay scheme.

The business strategy at the company, according to Mapson, is that we, 'listen to customer's opinions and act on them to give us a competitive edge.'

Similarly, through regular performance management meetings with their immediate manager, Shane Speirs explained that at the Unite Group, 'everyone has targets which are linked to our company strategy, which drive the bonuses.' Similar motivations presumably led Boots to introduce a bonus scheme in its shops, which is based on assessments by a 'mystery shopper' of factors such as shop layout and staff helpfulness, rather than just sales volume.

Another area of difference in reward practices between the high performers and the rest of the research participants, perhaps more surprisingly, was employee benefits. They were more likely to provide a wider range of financial and on-site benefits, such as a company pension and staff restaurant. But the most statistically significant factor was the lack of differentiation in rewards between managers and staff in the locations studied, with single status benefits and harmonized pay arrangements.

The researchers calculated an overall score for each organization based on the commonality of reward policies between managers and front line staff. While there were of course differences in pay levels, the top organizations for customer service performance scored notably higher than the remainder, with an average 88 per cent harmonization score for pay policies, and 84 per cent for benefits.

Carol Sharpe at Kent County Council explained, 'our managers would feel strange and uncomfortable about receiving different and better benefits packages.' At Unite, 'we used to have differences for managers – in holiday allowances and so on – but we realized, as everyone is working hard to improve customer performance, we should all have the same benefits.' The impression, context and culture that this reward practice helped support was what mattered, rather than just the benefits scheme per se.

The most successful organizations were not employing universally successful pay and benefits schemes, and indeed the other organizations in the research generally used some of them. But the top five recognized that they needed to use these schemes as part of an overall strategic approach to reward and people management that focused on meeting their employees', as well as their customers', specific needs.

As the manager at Scottish Water's customer service centre observed in explaining its high levels of staff commitment and customer satisfaction: 'It's not just about what you do, but how you do it.' The company was created by the merger of a number of different water authorities, so the harmonization of pay, terms and conditions represented a complex and at times contentious exercise. He explained the process of doing so as 'intentional and time-intensive', with extensive 'involvement with unions and staff representatives' to create the necessary trust and mutual accommodation. 'The hard work has paid off' he felt, in terms of the positive employee relations it created, and the resulting centre performance.

REWARDING CUSTOMER SERVICE: CREATING THE CONTEXT FOR COMMITMENT

At Unite Group, Shane Speirs echoed HSBC's ex-chair in describing the company strategy as being 'around customers, people and shareholders... in that order'. For front line customer service staff in today's flatter and customer facing organizations, every bit as much as for higher paid and skilled knowledge workers, however close the management and supervision is, an employer cannot enforce high performance. Purcell's 'discretionary commitment' from employees is essential. That smile and concern for the customer has to be genuine, that staff member has to want to go the 'extra mile' – like the Kent County Council employee Carole Sharpe described, who voluntarily visited a customer on his way home from work to fix their computer.

Reward policies in the research study did not of themselves create high customer service performance. They operated through the medium of staff perceptions and in a general work and management context that encouraged positive perceptions and high levels of staff commitment – see Figure 7.1. The best organizations recognize that when it comes to delivering outstanding service, staff perceptions and management practice, rather than fancy reward and HR strategy statements, plans and policies are what matters and make the difference.

The Aston research with the service staff themselves revealed wide variations in expressed levels of commitment, and in satisfaction with their pay and reward practices, which was strongly associated with it. The more committed staff in the higher performing organizations believed that their employer, at all levels, was genuinely committed to delivering high customer service, a factor that also correlated with high commitment in a recent IES study in the National Health Service. Customer service was not a set of targets imposed from above, but something everyone in the organization bought into, applying to all. These staff were also more satisfied with the rewards and recognition they received, and believed that the organization rewarded them fairly and generally looked after employees.

The best five organizations displayed the type of positive psychological contract that Guest (2004) describes, with a strong sense of fairness, trust and reciprocity between managers and staff that the Scottish Water manager referred to. Hence the importance of common reward arrangements in environments where employees have become far less tolerant of

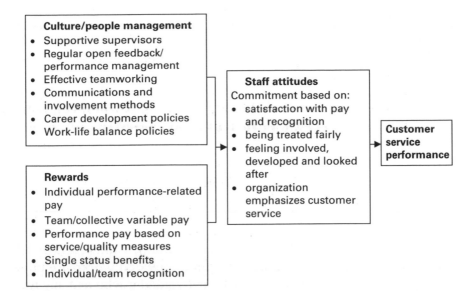

Figure 7.1 A summary of the relationships between HR and reward practices, employee attitudes and customer service performance

arbitrary, status-based differences in how they are treated; and of employers avoiding the 'say/do' gap, when they talk about customer service in their mission and policy statements, but reward staff according to their volume of transactions in bonus plans; or talk about the importance of teamwork but reward only individual sales.

As for the knowledge workers discussed in the first half of this chapter, three other types of HR and broadly defined 'reward' policies were associated with high levels of staff commitment and customer performance, by supporting that positive psychological contract and work context.

First, the concern for employees was demonstrated by devoting considerable effort to meeting the personal and career development needs of staff. There was no assumption of 'dead-end' jobs or a lack of staff interest in developing themselves and progressing.

Common practices included a considerable investment in training staff at all levels, often with opportunities to acquire nationally recognized vocational qualifications; the use of bespoke competency frameworks for development and reward purposes; a staffing strategy that emphasized internal promotions rather than external recruitment, particularly for filling first line supervisory roles; and a pay and career structure that provided a number of levels of customer service jobs, meaning that everyone had the chance to develop their competence and move up into more specialized or multi-skilled roles.

In a number of companies, the structure mirrored that of Vertex, the outsourced call centre provider. As IDS (2005a) describes, there are six generic levels in their 'pathways' structure. Staff in the call centre operations job family can move progressively from scripted call centre jobs for one client, up to higher paid multi-client and multi-skilled roles, and then into more technically complex positions.

This approach to career and reward management may help to explain the surprisingly lengthy average service profile of employees in the Aston study. Attention to the needs of a predominantly female workforce with an average age over 30 years was also evident in another area of HR practice.

Second, evident in all the top five organizations but less commonly provided by the remainder, despite the notoriously stressful nature of some customer service and call centre roles (and again displaying these employers' commitment to meeting employees' as well as customer needs), was the provision of work-life balance policies and practices. All of them had such policies in place and three provided workplace nurseries/crèches, compared to just three of the remainder who had any type of work-life balance policy in place.

Typical practices amongst the five organizations included career break schemes and term-time working arrangements; the opportunity for employees to switch hours and contracts, for example from full to part-time working, as their domestic circumstances changed; flexible working hours and start and finish times; and the provision of family-friendly benefits such as crèches and tax efficient childcare vouchers.

A number of studies show that women still play the primary role in looking after children, despite the increasing incidence of dual careers. They strongly value these aspects of flexibility and support and hence the relationship with reward satisfaction and commitment in the Aston research. A visitor to an early on-site factory nursery school at the New Lanark Mills in Scotland in 1818, also observed on the link with performance: 'This baby school is of great consequence for it enables the mothers to attend to their duties in the factory without concern for their families' (New Lanark Conservation Trust, 2004).

Rather than just the benefits schemes, however, it appears that the way in which these policies were operated – balancing business and employee needs, with fairness and consistency in application, and with a strong sense of reciprocal 'give and take' between managers and staff at the informal level – really made the difference to employee attitudes and performance in these five organizations.

However wonderful a bonus plan may look on paper, if employees who suggest improvements to the measures included are ignored by their supervisor, then it will not have the intended impact on performance.

So the third area of importance was involvement and communication practices. Committed staff in the high performing organizations felt involved in decision making, received regular, open feedback from supportive supervisors and contributed themselves in a genuinely two-way process of performance management. Great attention was paid to communicating with and involving staff, not just through performance management but also through a wide variety of processes. These included regular team and staff meetings, director briefings, online message boards, quality and performance improvement groups, suggestion schemes and 360-degree appraisal mechanisms, as well as social events for all staff.

Perhaps surprisingly, given the wealth of research evidence from all eras and types of organization and staff that employee involvement correlates with satisfaction and performance (see Mayo, 1933, for example), across the whole sample of the Aston research companies, employees generally gave low ratings to the extent to which they were involved in decision making. The temptation, particularly in a call centre context, is to be encouraged by the masses of available statistics to adopt a 'performance-push', top-down management approach, as evidenced in the TUC's research (2001). Opportunities to learn from staff about how to improve customer service performance are being wasted as a result.

The Scottish Water customer service centre manager on the other hand told the researchers that formal discussions with staff representatives and informal staff briefings took time, but, 'involving people is key... because to have that customer responsiveness, you have to trust people to respond.'

Gloria Evans at Torfaen Council emphasized its team briefing and upward feedback mechanism, whereby:

> Through their teams, all staff have input into our customer service plan, allowing them to take ownership of it. The weekly team meetings are an open communication process and all staff suggestions are considered.

Since these processes were introduced, the number of lost calls in the Council's service centre has fallen by 62 per cent and staff turnover is down to negligible levels. The association of these two sets of performance variables was recognized in the council's receipt of the Institute of Customer Service's Frontline Team of the Year award.

We are indebted to Stephen Taylor of Stanton Marris (2005) for providing us with perhaps the ultimate illustration of crafting this highly rewarding and involving, employee-focused approach to delivering high levels of customer service. The Nordstrom Shoe Company employee handbook begins as follows:

> Welcome to Nordstrom. We're glad to have you with our company. Our number one goal is to provide outstanding customer service... We have great confidence in your ability to achieve (it). Nordstrom Rules: Rule 1. Use your good judgement in all situations. There will be no additional rules. Please feel free to ask your store manager any questions at any time.

The organizations in the Aston study were perhaps less ambitious in their goals, but through a deliberate strategy of using their reward and HR policies, in practice, to build a context of high employee engagement, they too are achieving outstanding levels of customer service.

STRATEGIES FOR REWARDING KNOWLEDGE AND CUSTOMER SERVICE

Professor Clark Gilbert at the Harvard Business School believes that the best innovations occur as a result of learning from your external environment (Tyrrell, 2005). Of course, your reward strategy should reflect and be driven by the needs of your business and its strategic goals. But as Gilbert shows, effective business strategies combine the internal resources and core capabilities of the organization with an excellent understanding of the external environment, the key trends and influences within it and the opportunities it presents. The same is true of reward strategies.

A major external trend affecting reward and people management in all UK organizations is the growth of the service and knowledge-based economy, and the increasing numbers of workers who manipulate information and serve customers. Reward managers have been directly experiencing this phenomenon through having to respond to significant skill shortages and market pay pressures for these high-demand, high-tech, high-touch roles.

However, our analysis in the previous chapter of effective reward approaches for knowledge workers, and the comprehensive Aston University study on rewarding customer service staff profiled in this chapter, have demonstrated that much more is required of a truly strategic reward approach in this emerging economy than simply recruiting sufficient headcount and keeping base pay levels competitive.

Although apparently very different types of job and employee, with their stereotypical images of research 'boffins', IT 'geeks' and service 'Mcjobs', the reality is that because of technological advances and labour market shortages, these sorts of roles are becoming increasingly widespread and intermixed throughout contemporary organizations. These two chapters have shown that while every organization is different and there are no generically successful schemes, there are nonetheless some common components to successful reward strategies for these groups of staff. These include:

▮ a strong focus on directly rewarding growth in the required competence and contribution of employees, generally through a wide variety of collective and individual, cash and non-cash reward methods, thereby integrating career and reward management approaches so as to encourage and reward short- and longer-term personal development;

▌ a concentration on rewarding customer service measures of performance;

▌ fully engaging staff to perform by providing a genuinely and broadly based rewarding environment at work, with reward and HR policies providing high levels of involvement, job autonomy and an appropriate work-life balance.

The high performing organizations in the Aston study did all utilize some common reward practices, including performance and variable pay, non-financial recognition and harmonized terms and conditions. But in today's society and economy, that is not enough. As Sally Hopson, a director of Asda said at the CIPD's Scottish conference: 'People now want a job with life, not for life... people seek for meaning in their lives.'

So as we detail in other parts of this book, this analysis has shown that as well as pay and benefits, organizations need to use a wider variety of management and HR processes – career development, employee communication and involvement, performance management and so on – to create the supportive and rewarding environment in which employees voluntarily commit to innovating and serving the customer. Reward policies help to provide the context for high staff motivation and performance. The debate has moved on: it's no longer about whether or not money motivates, or should you use performance pay for knowledge and service workers, but instead, how can you best create this rewarding environment that engages staff to commit to high performance.

The lessons for reward professionals are therefore that you have to work with your HR and training colleagues right across the field of HR specialisms to help create this context. But perhaps the key finding from all this research and analysis, as we detail in Chapter 11, is the need to get out there with first line managers. As the Scottish Water manager told us, 'taking account of people's values is vital: it's not just about what you do, but *how* you do it.' The management practice and the employee experience of rewards are what count. The organization has to practise what it preaches on innovation, customer service and reward.

The lesson for company executives in our faster-changing, heavily customer-driven and competitive economy, is that more of you need to follow Asda, Nationwide and the Unite Group's strategy of meeting employee needs, in order to meet customer needs, in order to achieve financial objectives, rather than the reverse.

8

Developments in reward management

Imitating the reward strategies of other organizations gets you nowhere. But an understanding of contemporary external trends in reward management can provide helpful guidance, as long as account is taken of the extent to which they are appropriate for the organization. The fact that a policy such as total rewards has been introduced successfully in a number of prestigious companies in response to external and internal contextual factors may at least suggest that consideration should be given to it.

In this chapter we examine what is happening generally in the UK reward context. We summarize the incidence of different aspects of reward management and consider developments in key areas of total reward, job evaluation, grade and pay structures, and contingent pay. These developments illustrate a key tenet of our concept of contemporary reward strategies in the UK, with a pragmatic tailoring and blending of different HR and reward approaches evident, for example with broad-grading and contribution-related pay, rather than simply copying the strategies and practices of others.

CURRENT INCIDENCE OF REWARD PRACTICES

The CIPD 2005 reward management survey covering 477 organizations (CIPD, 2005a) established that the percentages of respondents adopting different types of reward policies and practices were as follows:

Written reward strategy		45 per cent
Total reward approach		28 per cent
Job evaluation		51 per cent
Pay structures		
	Broad-banded pay structures	36 per cent
	Narrow-graded pay structures	27 per cent
	Pay spines	20 per cent
	Job families	14 per cent
Contingent pay		
	Individual performance-related pay	27 per cent
	Competency-related pay	5 per cent
	Team-based pay	12 per cent
	Contribution-related pay	63 per cent
	Service-related pay	20 per cent
	Cash bonus schemes	52 per cent
Flexible benefits		8 per cent

SPECIFIC DEVELOPMENTS

Total reward

CIPD and e-reward research confirms that total reward is now high on the HR agenda in the UK. There is a general belief that total reward can make a major contribution to enhancing the 'employment value proposition' by being strongly linked to the creation of 'compelling employment opportunities', thus ensuring that the organization is 'a great place to work' and attracting and retaining talent. Several heads of reward emphasized to us that the differentiator in attracting and retaining staff was not so much levels of pay but the total reward package, especially the non-financial rewards, which tend to be unique to each organization. We have commented on this field in earlier chapters.

Job evaluation

In contrast to the USA, where traditional approaches to job evaluation have been largely replaced by market pricing, concern about equal pay has helped to maintain the interest in job evaluation in the UK. The need to be internally equitable is still generally regarded as important. In large sections of the UK economy, especially public services – the National Health Service, local authorities, universities and further education colleges – priority is given to internal equity, and new tailored job evaluation schemes have been introduced in each of these areas in the last five years.

An e-reward survey in 2003 established that 44 per cent of the 246 organizations had a formal job evaluation scheme (e-reward, 2003). Their reasons for using job evaluation are shown in Figure 8.1.

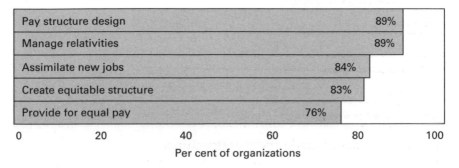

Figure 8.1 Reasons for using job evaluation

Quoted reasons included, 'Provides us with a fair and equitable structure into which we can fit our reward strategy', 'It's objective, transparent and consistent', and 'Transparent and includes staff involvement.' But there were dissenting voices; for example: 'The scheme has decayed to the point of total manipulation', 'Not very robust; time-consuming, inflexible' and, 'Job evaluation bears no relation to salary as we base it on market rates.'

The response has been to reform rather than remove job evaluation. Computerized approaches now speed up administration. More importantly, the trend has been to recognize that job evaluation has a supporting rather than a driving role. It may be used to set up a grading structure and evaluate generic benchmark roles, as in the NHS. But thereafter a faster matching process is used, often with subsequent flexibility to reflect individual and market differences in value.

Although half of organizations covered by the e-reward survey use job evaluation, three-quarters of them also adopt external market-based approaches to pay setting. The delicate process of integrating and balancing these two goals of external and internal worth helps to explain the complex diversity of changes underway in pay structures, and the greater realism and pragmatism evident in contemporary reward strategies.

Pay structures

The incidence of different types of grade and pay structure in the UK as established by e-reward in 2004 is shown in Figure 8.2.

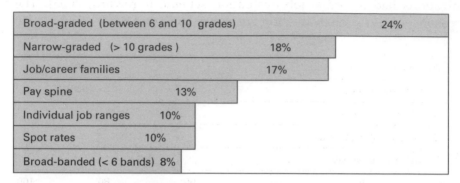

Figure 8.2   Types of grade and pay structures

The major developments as described below have been the replacement of narrow-graded structures with broad-graded structures. Job and career family structures are also more common. However, broad-banding, as originally conceived with fewer than six bands, is comparatively rare.

Broad-graded structures

Broad-graded structures generally have six to 10 grades, rather than the 11 or more grades contained in narrow-graded structures, or the five or less bands contained in the original US versions of broad-banding. In a broad-graded structure the grades and pay ranges are defined and managed in the same way as narrow-graded structures, except that the increased width of the grades means that organizations sometimes intro-duce mechanisms to control progression in the grade, so that staff do not inevitably reach its upper pay limit. Their prevalence is a good illustration of the pragmatic, blended approach evident in reward strategies today in the UK, as employers attempt to combine the benefits of traditional grad-ing structures with the flexibility of broad-banding, while avoiding the potential downsides of both approaches to pay management.

Broad-graded structures have become popular mainly because the use of six to 10 grades is often more in line with the hierarchy of jobs in the organization than a larger or smaller number of grades or bands. They overcome or at least alleviate the grade drift problem endemic in narrow-graded structures – if the broad grades are defined in terms of the various levels of responsibility they represent, it is easier to differentiate them, and matching (comparing role profiles with grade definitions or profiles to find the best fit) becomes more accurate. They cost less to implement than narrow-graded structures. They also alleviate broad-banding problems such as difficulties in controlling progression, perceived lack of opportunities for upgrading and pay inequities. As mentioned below, attempts have often been made to solve this problem by introducing zones in broad bands that in effect converts them to a broad-graded or even narrow-graded structure. Examples are given below.

Broad-grading at Bristol-Myers Squibb

Bristol-Myers Squibb has eight overlapping grades as follows:

D1 Basic clerical, factory semi-skilled

D2 Clerical and factory semi-skilled

D3 Clerical and factory supervisor

D4 Senior supervisor, entry level for professionals (eg scientists), customer-facing sales staff

D5 Customer-facing sales staff

D6 First level manager, head of department

D7 Function heads

D8 Business heads, eg oncology, finance

Broad-grading at COLT Telcom

Nine job levels or grades were introduced at COLT Telecom as a way of:

▌ providing transparency in the organizational structure;

▌ providing an equitable reward framework for base pay, variable pay and long-term incentives;

▌ ensuring consistency and fairness across functions and countries;

▌ allowing cross function and country comparison;

▌ beginning to clarify career development and progression;

▌ supporting the *One COLT* culture and values of open and honest communication;

▌ aiding internal and external benchmarking of remuneration.

Vivian Leinster, Director of Compensation and Benefits, says that:

> COLT levels seek to aid succession planning and promotion; an advantage of having a formal job level structure is that managers will be able to communicate how and when their teams can progress within COLT. As the levels are fairly broad, not all promotions or role changes will result in a level change. However, if your role changes or you move within the organization to a different department, the job level will be reviewed and adjusted as appropriate.

Broad-grading at Friends Provident

At Friends Provident there are eight broad career bands, five for non-management staff, to replace the nine previous grades, and three additional bands to cover everyone below executive director level. Generic skills and competency levels have been established to describe the broad requirements for each band. Each of the career bands is broad and although there is clearly a mid-point, the company tells staff that they should not believe that the rate for the job is the mid-point or control point. As Peter Harris, Reward and Benefits Manager, explains:

> Generally speaking, staff who are developing their role should be in the lower quartile of the range, staff who are fully performing are at the median, while those who are regularly exceeding all requirements should be being paid at the upper quartile. A normal distribution would be 25 per cent developing, 50 per cent fully performing and 25 per cent exceeding requirements.

Broad-grading at Lloyds TSB

Every role in Lloyds TSB has a market reference point, which indicates the normal rate of pay for a fully effective performer. The company has introduced new pay zones within grades 2 to 8 to help indicate normal progression and to give more structure and openness to the way in which pay is managed. An internal briefing paper sent to all staff explains: 'The zones mean that you'll be able to see more clearly how your pay is managed in line with your contribution, and how your salary should increase as you develop in your role.'

There is a published salary range for each grade (in other words, a minimum and maximum salary) based on pay rates within the market, and these are reviewed every year to keep them in line with market movements. Each grade has three zones:

1. *Primary zone*: for people new to the role and still developing in that role. Typically – but not normally in every case – Lloyds TSB expects an employee to be performing to a 'fully effective' level after two or three

years in the role and to move to the next zone. If an employee's salary is currently below the bottom zone and his or her work is judged satisfactory, pay will automatically be adjusted upwards.

2. *Market zone*: if an employee is fully effective in a role, his or her pay should be managed towards or in the 'market' zone (if an employee moves to a new role, pay will start in the market zone as long as he or she has the necessary knowledge, competencies and skills to be fully effective from the outset). Broadly speaking, the market zone reflects the rate that other employers would pay for a particular job. These rates are set with data provided by independent pay consultants.

3. *High performance zone*: if an employee consistently makes a superior contribution to the business, his or her pay is managed towards or in the high performance zone.

Work levels at Unilever

Unilever rejected the notion of broad-banding and introduced its 'work level' structure in the mid-1990s. This is a variation of broad-grading using different nomenclature and a special approach to defining levels. There are six work levels, each subdivided into a number of pay grades. The levels were determined according to the idea of the time-span of discretion developed by Jaques (1961) and also measure the strategic importance of particular jobs. The three principles underlying the levels are:

1. The major tasks of any job fall into a single work level. This is the case despite the fact that a job may include a mixture of tasks, with an executive making strategic decisions also undertaking less demanding administrative tasks.

2. At each successive higher work level, decisions of a broader nature are taken in an increasingly complex environment. Discretion and the authority required to do the job also increase, and more time is required to assess the impact of these decisions. Assigning jobs to work levels involves identifying the decisions that are unique to a job. This helps to highlight differences in management decision making and account-ability, which in turn allows the management structure to be more clearly delineated.

3. Each work level above the first requires one and only one layer of management. A layer of management is necessary only where a manager makes decisions that could not be taken by subordinates, who

may be more than one level below their boss. The company's work levels approach ensures that job holders take decisions that cannot be taken at a lower level.

Broad-banded structures

The 'brave new world' of broad-banding that originated in the USA in the 1980s was greeted with enthusiasm in the UK, at least by consultants and reward commentators like us. It offered freedom from all the rigidity and 'drift' associated with traditional, multi-graded structures. It recognized the significance of market pay and lateral career progression. It was appropriate for de-layered and flexible organizations. It encouraged the devolution of responsibility for pay decisions to line managers (without always considering the extent to which they might be ready to take it on). However, although the concept has been highly influential, 'broader-banding' or broad-grading is a more accurate characterization of the pay structures that have emerged.

One of the problems with broad-banding was that it created expectations for progression that could not be met in an environment of low inflation. The rationale for someone's position in a band was often unclear. Line managers felt adrift without adequate guidance and staff missed the structure they were used to. Questions were asked on the point of having broad-bands when in effect all they consisted of was spot rates determined mainly by market relativities. In one public sector organization it was calculated that it would take even a high flier 50 years to reach the top of their broad-band!

Inevitably, therefore, structure started to creep back in, and a unique mixture of US-driven external market freedom and European internal control has emerged. It started with reference points aligned to market rates around which similar roles could be clustered. These were then extended into market zones for groups of jobs, as illustrated in Figure 8.3. Our research has established that 80 per cent of companies have introduced controls in the form of zones and reference points.

Progressively, therefore, the original concept of broad-banding has been eroded as more structure was introduced in some organizations, for example at GlaxoSmithKline where a broad-banded structure has been divided into zones and grades. There are five bands: A and B for top executives, band C directors and managers, D covers professional and technical staff, and E administrative staff. These bands determine benefit entitlements. Each band is divided into a number of pay zones or grades. For example, band D is divided into six zones, band E has five zones and there are 29 zones in total. The pay range for each zone is approximately 25 per cent either side of the mid-point, and grades are also used for

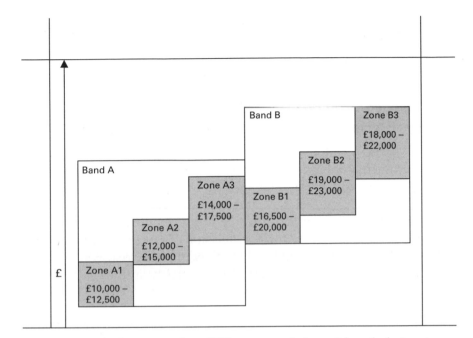

Figure 8.3 Market zones in a UK company's broad-banded structure

determining bonus entitlements. But this zoning approach is not universal, as in the example given below.

Broad-banding at Tesco

At Tesco the structure has six levels and could therefore be classified as a broad-graded structure although its design is closer to the original US broad-banding model. It was introduced because more flexibility in pay management was required. The company was expanding rapidly, especially overseas, and needed a system to support management movement and development. There was also a strong belief that the company was over-managed with a multiplicity of layers.

The new structure converted the previous 22 grades into six 'work levels'. Jobs are placed in levels using a system of internal work measurement and classification based on the thinking of Jaques, as at Unilever. Each level contains what Tesco calls 'pay reference points', developed for around 100 benchmark roles. These are set between the median and upper quartile of pay in around 20 blue-chip service companies, designed to reward staff that perform at the level of the very best individuals in the most successful organizations. Actual pay rates cluster around 10 per cent below pay reference points.

In the new Tesco structure, there are no mid-points or zones, simply very substantial pay bands, which line managers can use (subject to budget constraints) to reward individuals for their contribution. The process is moderated both by senior departmental managers and HR managers. 'It is important to create the right level of expectation,' say the Tesco guidelines. 'The pay band for each work level is broad enough to accommodate the different types of roles and levels of contribution in that level, as well as the different external markets.'

Job and career family structures

An interesting mixture of reward and development approaches is evident in the growing use of job and career family structures in the UK. A job family consists of jobs in a function or occupation such as marketing, operations or finance which are related through the activities carried out and the basic knowledge and skills required, but in which the levels of responsibility exercised differ.

The levels in job or career family structures (usually not more than six to eight) are defined in terms of key responsibilities and competency requirements. Thus they establish career ladders in and between families in terms of what people have to know and be able to do to progress within their own job family or in a different family. The main distinction between job and career family structures is that job family structures typically have separate, market-related pay structures for each family, while career families are applied across a single common pay structure. Job family structures as at Xerox UK are often designed primarily to enable distinct market groups to be set up. In contrast, a career structure is in effect a single graded structure in which each grade has been divided into families and no differentiation is made in the pay ranges to reflect market rates, although market supplements might be paid.

The difference between a conventional graded structure and a career family structure is that in the former the grade definitions are all the same. In a career family structure, although the levels may be defined generally for all families, separate definitions expressed as competency requirements exist for levels in each of the career families. These define career paths and are the distinguishing characteristic of career family structures, which are as much about defining career progression routes as they are about defining a pay structure. Job family structures help organizations to flex rates of pay for different occupations to reflect variations in market rates and therefore provide for competitive pay to attract and retain people with essential skills. The fact that they also define career ladders is an added advantage but not necessarily the main reason for adopting them.

Possible downsides are that they can be divisive and it is more difficult to ensure equity between different families.

Career family structures can be less divisive and operate more equitably than job family structures. They are attractive because they focus attention on career paths between as well as within families and can be seen as an essential part of a total reward approach by focusing attention on opportunities for development and growth. They have been introduced widely in UK universities.

Examples of job and career family structures are given below.

Job family structure in BT

The overall objective of setting up the new grade and pay structure in BT was to be simple and complete, avoiding over-complicated structures. More specifically, the company decided to opt for a system of job families in order to:

▌ achieve internal consistency of reward in alignment with external market rates;

▌ ensure that status, rank and relative position within hierarchies will become less important than what an individual achieves;

▌ help to clarify the roles and potential career paths available to individuals, particularly within a job family and, to a certain extent, between families;

▌ offer visibility of roles and salary ranges across other job families;

▌ achieve more flexibility in managing reward for different occupations to reflect differences in market rates and therefore provide for competitive pay to attract and retain people with essential skills.

The job family structure was developed to replace a traditional graded structure containing eight core grades together with a separate sales structure. Ranges were 'quite broad' with significant overlap. According to the Connect trade union, there were 'deep-rooted problems' with the system. In what was once a typical multi-graded pay structure the emphasis was very much on hierarchy: the only way ahead was upward, through promotion or re-grading. The focus is now on flexible roles and the individual's contribution in the role, and more priority is given to external competitiveness. A salary range provides BT line managers with flexibility in managing reward within their teams. Gone are the days when pay progression and career development at BT were simply a matter of getting promotion to a higher grade.

Job family structure in the Financial Services Authority (FSA)

The FSA has 12 job families, which vary in size from the 38 people in economics and research to 900 in regulatory. Within each job family there are a number of broad levels, ranging from four to six, according to the family. The levels reflect the different contributions that individuals make according to their skills, knowledge and experience, and the roles they perform.

Each level has an associated indicative pay range that has been determined by comparing levels in the markets in which the FSA competes for staff. Pay ranges are used rather than a specific rate for the job, to reflect that there is no single market rate of pay for a given job. Instead, there is a range of pay in the market related to the specific backgrounds, experience and delivery of individuals performing the roles. The broad overlapping ranges are designed to give management the flexibility to reflect the differences in contribution that individuals are making.

Job family structure at Nationwide

Nationwide decided to opt for a system of job families because they:

∎ offer the flexibility to respond to occupational and labour market pressures, in contrast to more rigid systems where market rates may fall outside the grading structure;

∎ encourage flexible working practices and multi-skilling;

∎ encourage people to move jobs and build up a broad base of skills in different areas while still remaining in the same job family, although there must be flexibility in the pay ranges to reward people for this;

∎ clarify routes to career progression; and

∎ flatten the organizational structure, driving accountability down to the lowest possible level so that the person dealing with the customer is empowered to solve their problems.

The job family structure was developed following a detailed analysis of work. Jobs across the whole organization were found to fall into three broad areas – customer service, support services and specialist advice – providing the basis on which to group roles into job families. The project considered whether to construct families on the basis of function or on the basis of similarities in the nature of people's work. They chose the latter because they believed that this would help to keep the number of families to a minimum. It was subsequently decided to base the new structure on 11 job families.

Career family structure at Xansa

There are about 150 generic job titles at Xansa, the IT programming and systems company, covering everyone from receptionists to the board directors. All new recruits must be appointed to one of these jobs, which are positioned on a 'job map' in seven broad bands and 14 career (job) families. The bands reflect the accountability, complexity and influence in the nature of the work undertaken, while career families are groups of jobs with similar skills. For each job there is a generic job description that outlines the main purpose of the job, its key responsibilities and a skills profile that identifies the generic requirements of the job. There is also a competency framework that defines the attributes that contribute to high performance.

The career families fall into four groups:

1. *Delivery* – design; build/integrate; run and support; management; business services; and training.

2. *Consultancy.*

3. *Business development* – general management; sales and strategic development; and client development.

4. *Professional support* – business support; finance; human resources; and marketing/communications.

Career family structure at Norwich Union Insurance

At Norwich Union Insurance a career framework helps staff to understand how their jobs fit within their business unit and the organization as a whole. The career families support movement across the organization, since individuals can identify jobs at a similar level in other families that they might like to join. The skills, knowledge and behaviours profile for each role is published to facilitate this.

This career framework had been used for some time before a pay structure was attached to it. Each family contains between four and seven levels, each with a pay range with an 80 per cent minimum, a market salary guide for competent performance and no maximum.

A career family structure in a university

In this university's career family structure, illustrated in Figure 8.4, the range of pay for all staff in a level is the same. Each of the generic roles has a role profile that is used for job-matching purposes. There are only three families and the structure is presented to demonstrate that while teaching, learning and research are the reason the university exists, managerial and learning support are essential for this purpose to be achieved. This arrangement also facilitates the definition of career paths between families, especially from learning support roles to teaching and research roles.

	Career Families		
Levels	Managerial, professional, administrative and support	Teaching, learning and research	Learning and research support
1	Support Worker		Learning Support Assistant
2	Administrator/ Senior Support Worker		Learning Support Worker
3	Senior Administrator/Section Head/Craft Worker		Senior Learning Support Worker
4	Specialist or Professional/ Activity Leader	Associate Lecturer/ Research Associate	Advanced Learning Support Worker
5	Senior Specialist or Professional Head of small/medium sized department	Lecturer/ Researcher	Learning Support Expert/Team leader
6	Leading Specialist or Professional, Head of Large Operational Department	Senior Lecturer/ Research Fellow/Reader	Leading Learning Support Expert/ Departmental manager
7	Head of Major Department	Professor/Head of Department	Head of Major Department
8	Head of Major Function		

Figure 8.4 Career family structure in a university

Contingent pay (paying for performance, competence or contribution)

Research conducted by e-reward in 2003 looked at 189 contingent pay plans in 100 UK organizations – see Table 8.1. Individual performance-related pay (PRP) was still the most popular approach, although it is regarded by many people in the UK as 'the god that failed'. This is somewhat unfair as not all PRP schemes are failures. But the government championed the use of this apparent North American success story and many organizations, especially in the public sector, introduced it in haste, without adequate thought or consultation, and in the absence of the vital support process of effective performance management.

Academic research studies have since demonstrated that as a result, far from motivating people, PRP often succeeded only in demotivating them. The small proportion of those achieving top performance ratings often received only small differentials in their salary increase. The larger

Table 8.1 Types of contingent pay schemes used in the UK

Type of scheme	% of respondents
Individual performance-related pay (merit pay) – pay related to results (the achievement of objectives, targets or standards)	65
Pay related to organizational performance – pay linked to the performance of the organization as a whole or a major part, eg profit sharing	40
Individual contribution-related pay – pay related to both performance and competence	33
Pay related to service – pay progresses by increments on the basis of service in the job	15
Team-based pay – pay linked to the performance of a team consisting of interdependent workers aiming to achieve a common goal	11
Individual competence-related pay – pay related to the level of competence achieved	8
Individual skill-based pay – pay linked to the achievement of defined levels of skill	8
Other	8

proportion of average performers often felt hard done by, especially when they lacked confidence in their manager's judgements.

Disenchantment with PRP has led to the emergence of a much more varied pattern of contingent pay approaches in line with our observation that a more strategic approach to reward strategy is emerging in the UK. Competence-related pay was for a time promoted as the next US-imported pay 'solution'. But only 5 per cent of UK organizations apply it in its pure form in the latest CIPD study (2005a), with issues raised about its complexity and, ironically, lack of results focus.

We noted in the 1990s the growth of hybrid approaches, which we termed 'contribution-related pay' (Brown and Armstrong, 1999), and the UK has certainly not reacted to its disillusionment with merit pay by returning to the 'bad old days' of inflationary, across-the-board general increases. The 2005 CIPD survey shows that over half of UK organizations now use this contribution-related approach to adjusting pay for at least some of their staff, compared to just 27 per cent who relate base pay increases solely to individual performance.

Contribution-related pay involves pay decisions based on assessments of both the 'outputs', ie results of someone's work, and the 'inputs' in terms of their levels of competence and skill, the 'how' as well as the 'what' of their performance. A model of contribution-related pay is illustrated in Figure 8.5.

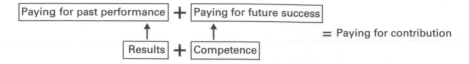

Figure 8.5   A model of contribution-related pay

The term has proved to be immediately appealing to many people because it focuses on what people in organizations are there to do, ie make a contribution. It overcomes the problem with competency-related pay – that it appears to ignore results. It relates to current approaches to performance management that are concerned with behaviour as well as the outcomes of behaviour. It also seems to avoid the mechanistic, limited and target-oriented approach which, somewhat unfairly, people tend to think is characteristic of performance-related pay. It has become particularly popular for the growing numbers of professional staff in UK firms and has been adopted in the higher education sector as an acceptable alternative to performance pay for staff whose work outputs are often intangible and difficult to measure.

As the HR Director of a pharmaceutical company told us:

> Performance in our setting is much more complex than a decision about five 'SMART' objectives. The most measurable is often not the most meaningful... Contribution talks to a broader series of outcomes, is easier to relate to corporate values, encompasses future capability, teamwork and discretionary effort, rather than the sort of tightly-managed, short-term results-focused approach which stifles innovation in many organizations.

It is hard to summarize the many and varied methods of delivering on this goal of contribution-related pay. One interesting example in a not-for-profit organization – The Shaw Trust – is illustrated in Figure 8.6. As well as rewarding competence and results achieved, its system melds together base and variable pay approaches. Growth in competence drives base pay increases up to the market-related reference point, and then a mixture of consolidated and variable pay increases rewards high contribution beyond that.

An approach to contribution-related pay in a UK bank for sales and account management staff based on the balanced scorecard is illustrated in Figure 8.7.

Customer sales and financial performance drive the individual cash bonus, while broader contribution, encompassing work quality and contribution to the team, help to determine base pay adjustments.

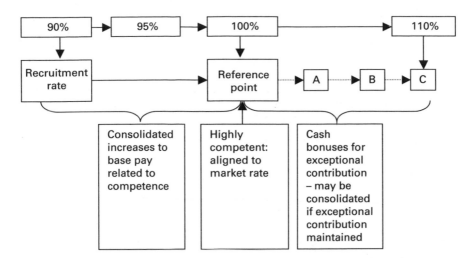

Figure 8.6 Contribution-related pay: The Shaw Trust

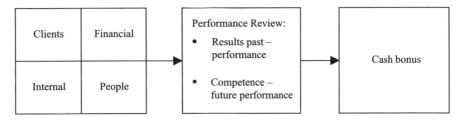

Figure 8.7 An approach to contribution-related pay in a UK bank

The approach to contribution-related pay for sales staff adopted by a car company is shown in Figure 8.8. Base pay reflects the individual's core skills and knowledge, with an annual adjustment to reflect the growth in them; individual sales commission is paid monthly to incentivize personal sales results; and a quarterly bonus is used to reward broader aspects of performance such as customer service and teamwork.

Again, the attention to the different aspects of performance – the core skill requirements and broader behavioural requirements, as well as measurable sales results – and the use of a variety of reward methods (base and variable pay), shows how organizations are abandoning so-called best and market practice in pay and adopting a tailored and genuinely strategic total reward approach.

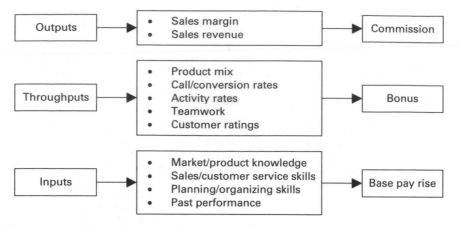

Figure 8.8   Contribution-related pay in a car company

Part 3

Developing and
Implementing Reward
Strategies

9

Developing reward strategy

In this chapter we describe *what* needs to be done to develop and implement reward strategies. We take into account general considerations and requirements, set out what a reward strategy pathway looks like, and describe what needs to be done to assess strategic business needs and achieve vertical and horizontal alignment. The next chapter is concerned with *how* implementation should take place.

BASIC CONSIDERATIONS

As explained in Chapter 2, reward strategy is a business- and people-focused description of what the organization wants to do about reward in the next few years and how it intends to do it. The aim is to provide the organization with a sense of purpose and direction in delivering reward programmes that support the achievement of business goals and meet the needs of stakeholders. It generally starts with a review of the current reward arrangements and situation, then a definition of the desired future state, and the development of reward initiatives and activities to close the gap between the two.

The development of reward strategy may involve a fundamental overhaul of major parts of the organization's reward programmes. This may be necessary following a merger, as at Centrica, GlaxoSmithKline, Halifax BOS, PriceWaterhouse Coopers and the Royal Bank of Scotland. Or it may be an outcome of a fundamental review of business strategy, as at

B&Q, Norwich Union Insurance and Tesco. Or it may simply reflect the belief that only a radical change in present arrangements will suffice, as in BT.

However, the process is often more about continuous improvement than massive change. The five basic considerations that should be taken into account when reviewing and rethinking existing rewards are discussed below.

1. Focus on the context

It's a matter of what works within the context of the organization, rather than the 'next big thing'. Will Astill, Reward Manager at B&Q, explains the thinking behind its reward review:

> An overriding theme running through our review was on the desirability of adopting a strategic approach. It wasn't a case of 'let's follow the best practice', nor were we lured into adopting the latest fads and fashions. Taking what someone has done before will not push you ahead of rivals.

Tim Fevyer, Senior Manager, Compensation and Benefits at Lloyds TSB, has a similar message: 'We need to get away from adopting new initiative after new initiative and move away from a culture of "flavour of the month".'

2. It's about evolution not revolution

Reward professionals rarely start with a clean sheet. They have to take note, and keep taking note, of changes in organizational requirements that are happening all the time. They must track emerging trends and modify their views accordingly, as long as they do not leap too hastily on the latest bandwagon. Even when they are conducting a major review of reward policies, as described in this book at B&Q, BT, Centrica, GlaxoSmithKline, Lloyds TSB, Norwich Union Insurance, the Royal Bank of Scotland and Tesco, they have to ensure that reward strategy can be implemented at a pace the organization can manage and people can deal with. The fundamental change in culture often inherent in such projects takes a lot of time – and trouble – to achieve.

It is helpful to define reward strategy formally for the record and as a basis for planning and communication. But this should be regarded as no more than a piece of paper that can be modified when needs change – as they will – not a tablet of stone. Reward strategy, like business strategy, may be formulated and re-formulated as it is used. As Mintzberg (1987) points out, it may emerge over time in response to evolving situations, to become a 'pattern in a stream of activities'.

3. Manage the balance

A reward strategy can include all sorts of things. But you have to get the balance right, paying attention to the initiatives that are most needed and are most likely to make a difference. You have to establish priorities, reflect realities and make the right strategic choices. If you try to do too much too soon or go too far and too fast in one direction you will run into trouble. For example, it is necessary to balance the often competing claims of pay flexibility against cost control, the devolution of reward responsibilities down the organization against consistency across it, internal equity against external competitiveness, individual incentives against teamwork. It is no use simply setting out these factors as discrete reward strategy objectives without providing guidance on how conflicts between them in the future will be addressed, and where the emphasis really lies.

Managing the strategic reward balance is also about avoiding the problems created by pursuing an initiative without considering what else need to be done to support it: for example, ensuring that performance-related pay is supported by appropriate performance management; equipping line managers with the skills to exercise responsibility for pay decisions before devolving that responsibility to them; and establishing job evaluation to ensure equity across families before setting up a job family structure.

4. Keep it simple

Over-complexity is the bane of reward management. It complicates implementation, puts off the people affected, hampers effective communication and makes the life of line managers difficult. The history of reward management is littered with examples of 'the light that failed' – over-engineered and ambitious plans that did not work.

5. Think implementation

No reward initiative should be planned without thinking about how it is going to be implemented, what problems might arise and how they will be dealt with. It is particularly important to consider the part that will be played by line managers in implementation and whether they are up to the task. It is also necessary to consider the reactions of people generally – the extent to which they might resist change and what can be done about it. Change management has to be planned; it won't work if it takes place on an ad hoc basis after the event.

DEVELOPMENT REQUIREMENTS

As suggested by the CIPD (2004a) there are five key requirements in developing an effective and tailored reward strategy for an organization:

1. Clear reward goals and priorities derived from the business strategy, often referred to as 'vertical alignment'.

2. A strong 'fit' of reward policies with the structure and design of the organization.

3. Alignment of the reward practices with each other in a total rewards approach, and with other HR programmes in the organization, known as 'horizontal alignment'.

4. Addressing employee needs in the strategy and involving staff in its development and delivery (the importance of involving line managers, staff and, if they exist, trade unions in the development programme cannot be overestimated).

5. Treating the strategy development as a process of continuous improvement and interaction between principles and practices.

A further requirement is to communicate regularly and frequently to all concerned the purpose of the exercise, how it is progressing, its outcome and how they will be affected.

THE DEVELOPMENT PATHWAY

The CIPD (2004a) suggests the following key phases in the development of a reward strategy:

1. The *diagnosis* phase, when reward goals are agreed, current policies and practices assessed against them, options for improvement considered and any changes agreed.

2. The *detailed design* phase when improvements and changes are detailed and any changes tested (pilot testing is important).

3. The final *testing and preparation* phase.

4. The *implementation* phase, followed by ongoing review and modification.

We described the practice of strategic reward management in Chapter 1 (illustrated in Figure 1.1, on page 15). In this chapter we expand on that model by examining in more detail the reward strategy development pathway, as shown in Figure 9.1.

Example of environmental analysis

B&Q provides an example of a thorough investigation into the context of the organization – its internal and external environment – and the characteristics of the existing reward system, while taking account of the views of all the relevant stakeholders. Its aim was to get, via an in-depth research exercise, a full understanding of the present arrangements, changing employment situation and future requirements. The company gathered and marshalled data from two perspectives.

External perspective

The analysis of the external environment included:

▍ an examination of the changing labour market;

▍ a literature review of employers' responses to emerging employment trends and how their competitors reward staff;

▍ gaining a more in-depth understanding of how specific reward elements are used and integrated in the market; B&Q drew on research and surveys including Watson Wyatt's work on the HR and reward strategies typically adopted by high performing organizations;

▍ a survey by Watson Wyatt of 50 high-performing people in a sample of 20 high performing organizations, examining what these staff need in their reward package;

▍ two commissioned surveys of 200 people each to examine 'external' perceptions of B&Q as an employer;

▍ a benchmarking exercise using retail industry salary surveys undertaken by Alan Jones, Hay Group, Mercer, Tesco's bespoke survey and Watson Wyatt.

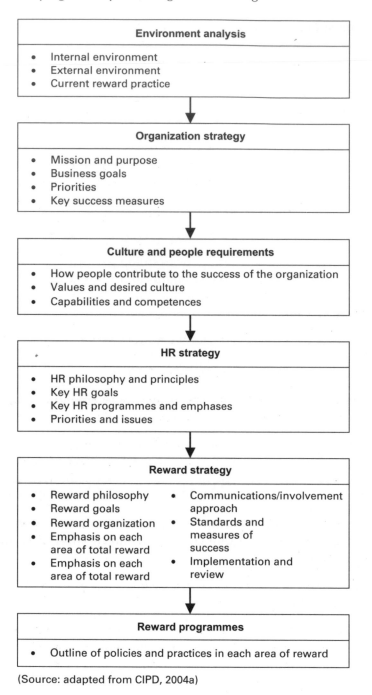

(Source: adapted from CIPD, 2004a)

Figure 9.1 The reward strategy development pathway

Internal perspective

The analysis of the current internal reward environment included:

▌ a full audit of the current reward investment and its focus;

▌ consideration of the existing use of bonus schemes;

▌ an examination of pay for performance arrangements;

▌ the current provision of financial and non-financial rewards;

▌ findings of 20 focus groups comprising people from different levels and different divisions in B&Q.

The external and internal benchmarking exercises provided a picture of reward strategies, practices and policies in top performing organizations and helped B&Q to identify the strengths and weaknesses of its current arrangements relative to the competition. From there it could examine the reward issues facing the organization and diagnose any changes or improvements required.

An example of a summary analysis of all the work carried out in their reward strategy development pathway in the new start up division of a European financial sector organization is shown in Figure 9.2. Summarizing a strategy as simply and clearly as this is very tough but also highly desirable, and this company used the diagram to explain the reward arrangements to their staff.

ASSESSING REWARD STRATEGY REQUIREMENTS

The key activity in the development programme is the assessment of reward requirements. This should be carried out with the full participation of senior managers, line managers, employees and their representatives. The following are examples of tools and exercises we have used successfully in top management discussions, workshops and focus groups to help analyse the components of the reward strategy. They have generated the involvement and interest of those involved, thus producing valuable guidance and, importantly, helping to create a sense of ownership in the outcomes. The example provided of an opinion survey can also be used to inform discussions, as well as providing a picture of staff attitudes to existing and possible future reward practices.

Business strategy	HR and cultural requirements	Future reward strategy	Future reward components
• Incredible customer experience • Increased sales volume and efficiency • Launch new operation successfully • Information management	• Skilled staff committed and able to form strong relationships with customers • Strong(er) performance/ results focus • Flexibility/ adaptability • Commitment • Support values of service, teamwork, quality and fun	• Support business goals • Reinforce performance, contribution and values • Flexibility within a 'one company' framework • Openness and understanding • Total rewards	• Base pay related to key displayed competencies: customer service, teamwork, etc • Sales bonus focused on core targets with quality/ service thresholds • Corporate/team bonus focused on corporate/ business targets • Flexible working hours and benefits • Extensive recognition awards

(Source: CIPD, 2004a)

Figure 9.2   Example of reward strategy development pathway

Rating reward strategy goals

The rating framework shown in Figure 9.3 can be used to obtain overall views and generate discussion on reward strategy.

These common goals (and any other relevant ones) can be rated by managers, staff and reward specialists in accordance with their views on how relatively important they are and the effectiveness (or otherwise) of their current delivery. The aim is to start the process of defining and drafting specific objectives and priorities for reward. Quite often there will be low effectiveness scores given on some of the most important objectives, while different individuals may differ on what they see as important goals. This exercise can be also used as the basis for a group discussion on what the key reward goals and priorities for the organization should be, for unless senior managers, for example, agree on the priority of objectives, then no set of reward practices will ever satisfy them all.

Objectives	Importance*	Effectiveness*
• Reinforce the achievement of organizational goals		
• Recruit and retain staff of the required calibre		
• Facilitate staff mobility		
• Strong relationships between pay and performance		
• Reinforce organizational values		
• Motivating for employees		
• Cost effective		
• Well communicated and understood by employees		
• Managed effectively in practice by line managers		
• Efficient to operate/maintain		
• Flexible, to react to change		
• Others (list)		

* Scale: 10 = high; 1 = low

Figure 9.3 Rating framework for reward strategy goals

Gap analysis

When examining reward arrangements and needs it is useful to carry out a gap analysis to compare the current and desired reward characteristics in the organization using the framework set out in Figure 9.4. It involves comparing and contrasting what are thought to be the critical goals and choices in the organization, such as adopting a high or low stance in the external market place, or operating consistent policies in the organization versus varying practices in different parts of it. Respondents are asked to indicate the current emphasis in reward arrangements on the variables shown, and any others that may be relevant. They are then asked to indicate the desirable position. Comparing the largest gaps with the current situation helps to indicate the priority issues to be addressed.

Senior managers can be asked to complete the grid individually, indicating where in their view the emphasis should be on reward policies. Their average scores are plotted and a group meeting held to review the findings and discuss the priorities they highlight. The same approach can be adopted in staff workshops or focus groups.

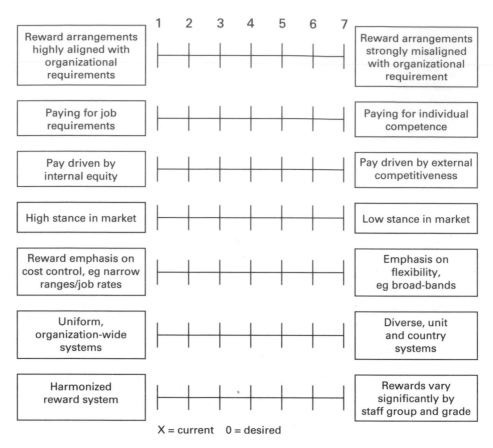

	1	2	3	4	5	6	7	
Reward arrangements highly aligned with organizational requirements								Reward arrangements strongly misaligned with organizational requirement
Paying for job requirements								Paying for individual competence
Pay driven by internal equity								Pay driven by external competitiveness
High stance in market								Low stance in market
Reward emphasis on cost control, eg narrow ranges/job rates								Emphasis on flexibility, eg broad-bands
Uniform, organization-wide systems								Diverse, unit and country systems
Harmonized reward system								Rewards vary significantly by staff group and grade

X = current   0 = desired

Figure 9.4   Example of a reward gap analysis grid

An example of a gap analysis conducted in a pharmaceutical company is shown in Figure 9.5. The plot shown averages the scores given by all senior managers. Here it can be seen that there is general support amongst the senior management population for rewards in future to reflect better the skills and competencies of staff and their performance, greater consistency of approach across the organization and improved reward communication and understanding.

Total reward analysis

A method of analysing the total rewards strategy in an organization, derived from the Towers Perrin model described in Chapter 1, is shown in Figure 9.6.

Groups of managers and/or staff can be asked to describe the current total rewards provision using this grid. They can then be asked to describe the improvements and changes in content and emphases they would like

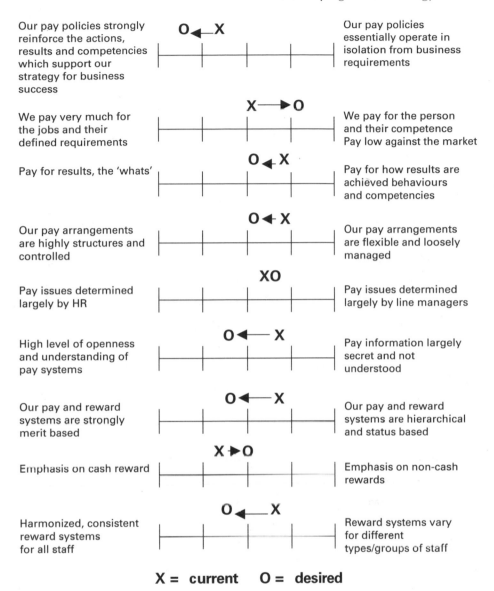

| Our pay policies strongly reinforce the actions, results and competencies which support our strategy for business success | O◄─X | Our pay policies essentially operate in isolation from business requirements |

X──►O

We pay very much for the jobs and their defined requirements — We pay for the person and their competence Pay low against the market

O◄─X

Pay for results, the 'whats' — Pay for how results are achieved behaviours and competencies

O◄ X

Our pay arrangements are highly structures and controlled — Our pay arrangements are flexible and loosely managed

XO

Pay issues determined largely by HR — Pay issues determined largely by line managers

O◄── X

High level of openness and understanding of pay systems — Pay information largely secret and not understood

O◄── X

Our pay and reward systems are strongly merit based — Our pay and reward systems are hierarchical and status based

X►O

Emphasis on cash reward — Emphasis on non-cash rewards

O◄─X

Harmonized, consistent reward systems for all staff — Reward systems vary for different types/groups of staff

X = current   O = desired

Figure 9.5 Example of a reward gap analysis in a pharmaceutical company

to see to better support the business of the organization, and make it a more rewarding and motivating place to work.

The current and required total reward strategy in a public sector organization, developed by this process with their top 50 managers working in groups, is shown in Figure 9.7.

PAY	BENEFITS
• Now	• Now
• Future	• Future
LEARNING	ENVIRONMENT
• Now	• Now
• Future	• Future

Figure 9.6 Total reward analysis grid

PAY	BENEFITS
Now	**Now**
• Secure	• Family-friendly
• Below average	• Paternalistic
• 'One size fits all'	• Secure
Future	**Future**
• Aligned to business goals	• Individually tailored
• Market rates	• Flexibility
• Flexible	• Valued by employees
LEARNING	ENVIRONMENT
Now	**Now**
• Good learning opportunities	• Comfortable
• Spoon fed	• Family
• Structures	• Formal
Future	**Future**
• More targeted training	• Challenging
• Focused on business goals	• Responsive
• Good opportunities as before	• Enjoyable

Figure 9.7 Current and required reward strategy

Opinion survey

As the example in Figure 9.8 illustrates, an opinion survey can be used to obtain views from a wider audience on current and desirable reward arrangements. They are now very commonly used as part of the initial review to determine the future shape of the reward strategy.

REWARD OPINION SURVEY					
I believe that:	**Strongly agree**	**Inclined to agree**	**Neither agree nor disagree**	**Inclined to disagree**	**Strongly disagree**
1 My pay adequately rewards me for my contribution	1	2	3	4	5
2 The pay system is clear and easy to understand	1	2	3	4	5
3 It is right for staff to be rewarded according to their contribution	1	2	3	4	5
4 The basis upon which my pay is determined is fair	1	2	3	4	5
5 I am paid fairly compared to other jobs in the organization	1	2	3	4	5
6 Rates of pay in the company are not consistent with levels of responsibility	1	2	3	4	5
7 My rate of pay compares favourably with rates paid outside the company	1	2	3	4	5
8 My pay does not reflect my performance	1	2	3	4	5
9 The current pay system encourages better performance	1	2	3	4	5
10 The pay system badly needs to be reviewed	1	2	3	4	5
11 I am clear about the standards of performance I am expected to achieve	1	2	3	4	5
12 I do not understand the competence levels I am expected to reach	1	2	3	4	5
13 The performance management scheme is helpful	1	2	3	4	5
14 I receive good feedback from my manager on my performance	1	2	3	4	5
15 My manager is not really interested in carrying out my performance review	1	2	3	4	5
16 I am motivated by my performance review meeting	1	2	3	4	5
17 The process of setting objectives and reviewing achievements is fair	1	2	3	4	5
18 The assessment of my performance by my manager is objective and fair	1	2	3	4	5
19 Performance management does not help me to improve my performance	1	2	3	4	5
20 Performance management clearly indicates areas where I can learn more about how to do my job	1	2	3	4	5

Figure 9.8 A reward and performance management opinion survey

ACHIEVING ALIGNMENT

As we have noted several times in this book, reward strategy development involves ensuring so far as possible that there is vertical alignment or fit between the reward strategy and the business strategy, and horizontal alignment between the reward strategy and other HR strategies and policies.

Vertical alignment

Vertical alignment means that business and reward strategies are in harmony. Reward goals are linked to business goals and reward strategies are defined in a way that spells out how they will contribute to the achievement of the business plan. As Will Astill, Reward Manager at B&Q, commented on its reward strategy review:

> Remember that strategy formulation is an evolutionary process. Our business is changing rapidly and there are significant differences in our business needs compared with, say, the early 1990s, so we need policies, procedures and people to follow them. We work on the basis of an emerging strategy and there is always a three-year rolling plan. New challenges emerge through the business changing. There are whole new profit areas of B&Q that simply didn't exist a few years ago, for example the financial services and installation part of the business. Clearly, this has an impact on the type of people we recruit and the way we reward them. Customer advisers now need to be educated to sell financial services.

The business strategy issues that may impact on reward strategy are:

∎ intentions concerning growth or retrenchment, acquisitions, mergers, divestments, diversification, product/market development;

∎ proposals on increasing competitive advantage through innovation leading to product/service differentiation, productivity gains, improved quality/customer service, cost reduction (downsizing);

∎ the felt need to develop a more positive, performance-oriented culture.

Respondents to the CIPD reward survey (CIPD, 2005a) were asked to assess the extent to which their reward strategy was aligned to their business strategy on a scale of 1 to 5, where 1 is not aligned while 5 is fully aligned. On the whole, they felt that they were doing a good job – 39 per cent reported scores of 4 or 5, and almost two-thirds felt that the level of alignment had improved. Those from private sector firms felt that they did better than those from public sector organizations.

However, there are three common problems in achieving vertical alignment. First, while it may be possible to establish the strategic goals of the organization it may be more difficult to identify reward strategies that are specifically aligned to them. There is a risk of producing bland proposals that would fit any situation. There can be few circumstances where the management would not recognize that they need to attract, retain and motivate high quality staff and that reward processes can contribute to doing this. Similarly, few if any organizations are uninterested in improving performance, so that anything the reward function proposes which claims that it will achieve this is likely to be welcomed as something that will support the business's strategic aims.

Secondly, fit may exist at a point in time but circumstances will change and fit no longer exist. An excessive pursuit of 'fit' with the status quo will inhibit the flexibility of approach, which is essential in turbulent conditions. A third factor that will make the achievement of vertical alignment difficult is that the business strategy may not be clearly defined – it could be in an emergent or evolutionary state. This would mean that there could be little or nothing with which to fit the HR strategy, but the attempt must be made nonetheless.

Dealing with the first problem of achieving specific alignment is possible if the business strategy is carefully analysed into its component parts and a reward approach that demonstrably addresses the business issues is developed. For example, in a car company one of the strategic aims might be to improve customer retention rates. An investigation might reveal that there should be more emphasis on customer service and better teamwork in getting repeat orders from customers. The aligned reward strategy in this case might be: 1) to develop a set of competencies that focused on different aspects of customer service and relate individual payments to competency assessments under these headings; 2) to institute team bonuses related to the volume of repeat orders.

One approach to linking business and reward strategies is to relate the latter to the firm's competitive strategies, for example, the generic strategies listed by Porter (1980). An illustration of how this might be expressed is given in Table 9.1.

To deal with the second problem of maintaining fit over a period of time, it is necessary to bear in mind the fundamental point made in Chapter 1 as expressed by Tyson (1997) about reward strategy, indeed any strategy. This is that strategy is emergent and flexible – it is always 'about to be', it never exists at the present time. It is essential therefore to track developments in business strategy and be prepared to modify the reward strategy accordingly.

Dealing with the third problem of the lack of a clearly defined business strategy is more difficult. It could be argued that in these circumstances

Table 9.1 Linking HR and competitive strategies

Business strategy	Reward strategy
Achieve competitive advantage through innovation	Provide financial incentives and rewards and recognition for successful innovations
Achieve competitive advantage through quality	Link rewards to quality performance and the achievement of high standards of customer service
Achieve competitive advantage through cost-leadership	Review all reward practices to ensure that they provide value for money

the whole concept of vertical alignment becomes meaningless. But it is possible to take note of the notion put forward by Mintzberg *et al* (1988) that strategy can have a number of meanings other than that of being 'a plan, or something equivalent – a direction, a guide, a course of action'. Strategy can also be a pattern, ie consistency in behaviour over time, or a perspective, an organization's fundamental way of doing things. If this is accepted, then at least an attempt can be made to analyse the overall strategic intent of the organization and its 'pattern' of doing things, and consider how reward strategy can support these broad approaches.

Achieving horizontal alignment

Horizontal fit is achieved when the various HR strategies including reward cohere and are mutually supporting. This can be attained by the process of 'bundling' or 'configuration'. Bundling involves analysing the scope for linking the various HR and reward practices together so that they reinforce one another. This may mean identifying integrating practices such as the use of competency-based processes that impact on recruitment, training, performance management and reward. In particular it is necessary to explore how reward practices can support the recruitment and retention of high quality staff, talent management and learning and development.

The aim is to achieve coherence and this means adopting a holistic approach – no innovation should be considered in isolation. It is necessary to seek opportunities to create synergy by looking for ways in which one practice can support another practice, and to identify common requirements that can be met by initiatives in different areas of HR practice, as long as they are deliberately linked. The holistic concept of total reward provides an important basis for achieving horizontal alignment accompanied by more specific strategies in the areas of grade and pay structures, performance management and contingent pay. Examples of how reward

Table 9.2 Examples of the horizontal alignment of HR and reward strategies

HR strategy area	Reward strategy contribution
Resourcing	• Total reward approaches that help to make the organization a great place in which to work
	• Competitive pay structures that help to attract and retain high quality people
Performance management	• Contingent pay schemes that contribute to the motivation and engagement of people
	• Performance management processes that promote continuous improvement and encourage people to uphold core values
Talent management	• Non-financial rewards such as recognition and opportunities for growth and development
	• Policies that recognize talented people for their contribution
	• Career-linked grade and pay structure, for example a career family structure
Learning and development	• Performance management processes that identify learning needs and how they can be satisfied
	• Career family structures that define career ladders in terms of knowledge and skill requirements
Work environment	• Total reward approaches that emphasize the importance of enhancing the work environment
	• Work-life balance policies

strategies can be linked to and therefore support HR strategies are given in Table 9.2.

Examples of aligned reward strategy

B&Q

B&Q summarizes the alignment between its business and HR and reward strategies as shown in Figure 9.9.

GlaxoSmithKline

Here the business strategy is very different from that adopted by B&Q but, similarly, it is reinforced by the HR and reward strategies; see Figure 9.10.

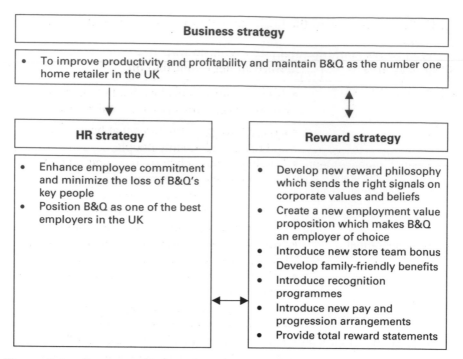

Figure 9.9 Integrated reward strategies at B&Q

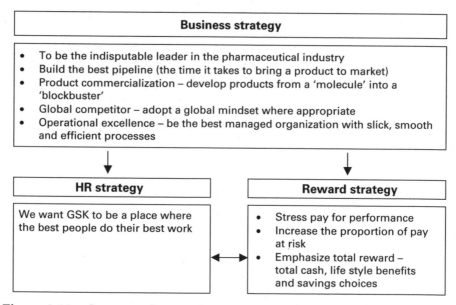

Figure 9.10 Integrated reward strategies at GlaxoSmithKline

Lands' End

This mail-order clothing business regularly tops the best places to work listings, and its HR and reward strategies are integral to its business strategy; see Figure 9.11.

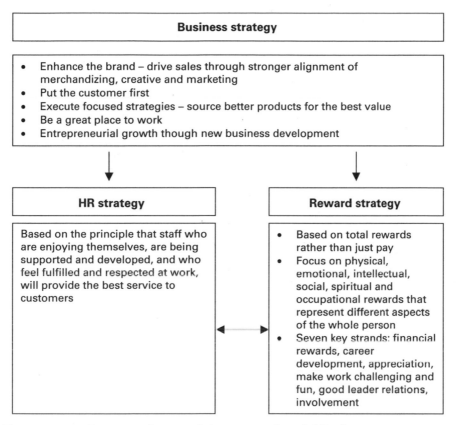

Business strategy

- Enhance the brand – drive sales through stronger alignment of merchandizing, creative and marketing
- Put the customer first
- Execute focused strategies – source better products for the best value
- Be a great place to work
- Entrepreneurial growth though new business development

HR strategy

Based on the principle that staff who are enjoying themselves, are being supported and developed, and who feel fulfilled and respected at work, will provide the best service to customers

Reward strategy

- Based on total rewards rather than just pay
- Focus on physical, emotional, intellectual, social, spiritual and occupational rewards that represent different aspects of the whole person
- Seven key strands: financial rewards, career development, appreciation, make work challenging and fun, good leader relations, involvement

Figure 9.11 Integrated reward strategy at Lands' End

These simple diagrams of course summarize an enormous amount of work in developing the reward strategy and then, as we consider in the next chapter, trying to make it an operating reality in the organization. There are many textbooks that can give you a step-by-step outline of what a reward strategy should in theory contain. But we have seen that it needs to be much more than just an isolated statement of desirable reward goals. What we have tried to do in this chapter is give you a more realistic view of how the development process in UK organizations has evolved into a near continuous process of review, action and reflection, as well as illustrating examples of the key tools used and the main learning points drawn from some leading organizations' experiences.

10

Implementing reward strategy

The aim of implementation is to make the reward strategy an operating reality by building the capacity of the organization to put into practice the proposals worked out in the development stage. It is always essential to design with implementation in mind.

Purcell (1999) believes that the focus of strategy should be on implementation. As explained by Thompson and Strickland (1990): 'Implementation entails converting the strategic plan into action and then into results.' An effective reward strategy is a living process and, in the words of Kanter (1984), an 'action vehicle'. The way in which it is implemented and operated is critical to that process. As Quinn (1980) points out, many strategies fail because 'they did not lend themselves to coordinated implementation'. Many so-called reward strategies amount to no more than a list of policy goals and schemes without any proper consideration having been given to how to make them work. This chapter aims to indicate how to overcome this problem and covers:

▍ an overall assessment of the problems arising from the 'say/do gap' in reward, that is the distinction being saying you are going to do something and actually getting it done;

▍ approaches to implementing worthwhile, achievable and realistic strategies;

▍ dealing with common problems that arise;

▌ project management;

▌ change management;

▌ an analysis of typical problems and issues relating to specific strategies for implementing job evaluation, grade and pay structures, performance management and contingent pay;

▌ an examination of the success criteria that should be used when carrying out the essential task of evaluating the impact of the reward strategy;

▌ a concluding description of how BT tackled the implementation of a massive reward strategy project involving action in all of these areas, and how it measured its success.

Each organization is unique and so rather than attempt to provide simple universal step-by-step guidance, we instead give many examples of how leading organizations are addressing the continuing challenges of reward strategy implementation.

THE SAY/DO GAP

All too frequently there is a say/do gap between the reward strategy as designed and the strategy as implemented. The CIPD reward survey (2005a) compared the assessment by heads of reward of what they believed to be the three most important reward management activities with those activities they found were most time-consuming. A sample of their assessments, shown in Table 10.1, reveals that strategy considerations were important but not very time-consuming, while administration was much less important but much more time-consuming (we discuss these findings in more detail in Chapter13).

This is the 'rhetoric/reality gap' identified by Gratton and Hailey (1999) on the basis of their research. They commented that there is 'a disjunction between rhetoric and reality in the area of human resource management, between what the HR function says it is doing and that practice as perceived by employees', or, as Troilus said when rejecting Cressida's

Table 10.1 The most important and time-consuming reward activities

Activity	Most important	Most time-consuming
Supporting the business strategy	65%	13%
Developing reward strategy	62%	33%
Reward administration	18%	63%

explanation of her treachery, 'Words, words, words, no matter from the heart.'

The following reasons for this gap between the rhetoric and reality of HR polices have been suggested by Gratton and Hailey:

▮ the sheer complexity of the organization and its strategies, which might make it hard to achieve any coherence across a diverse range of activities and plans;

▮ senior managers who want quick fixes which lead to individual initiatives that are isolated from complementary HR activities – the most common example of this is the introduction of performance-related pay without the existence of embedded performance management processes;

▮ incremental and reactive approaches to the development of HR practices, possibly arising from management pressures or the existence of financial constraints;

▮ difficulty in deciding which 'bundles' of HR practices are likely to be most appropriate in the circumstances, and in deciding the order in which they should be implemented;

▮ lack of understanding amongst HR practitioners of the need actively to achieve integration and lack of the skill and knowledge required to implement integrated practices;

▮ implementation difficulties where, even when there is a 'grand design' and much rhetoric, the reality is different – the links are difficult to maintain, line managers are indifferent or incapable of playing their part, and employees are suspicious of or hostile to the newly linked initiatives.

These issues apply particularly to reward practices.

Issues and problems of reward strategy implementation

The say/do gap in reward strategy often occurs when the reward strategy as conceived at the development stage is unrealistic and unduly complex, and implementation has been hurried without adequate pilot testing or analysis of the likely consequences. Problems can be caused by poor project management, inadequate attention to managing change, and neglecting to ensure that the supporting processes such as performance management are in place. Failure to achieve acceptance, understanding of and commitment to the strategy by involving line managers, staff and their representatives in the design and testing of processes and by communicating properly are common reasons for implementation problems. Underestimating the importance of providing guidance and training to line managers to ensure they are capable of playing their part in implementing and operating the strategy can also create difficulties.

THE PROCESS OF IMPLEMENTATION

Strategy must be 'implementation orientated' (Galbraith and Kazanjian, 1987). As we have said many times, but it bears repetition, effective implementation is dependent on good design, and good design is always concerned with producing something worthwhile that will work. Will Astill, B&Q's Reward Manager, emphasizes that no initiative should be implemented without examining the return on investment: 'Make a business case for everything. The return on investment analysis also justifies what priority you assign to implementation.'

The following reward strategy questions need to be answered at the design stage:

▌ How will it add value?

▌ How is it going to be put into effect?

▌ What supporting processes will be needed and can they be made available?

▌ Who is going to be involved in implementation?

▌ How are we going to make sure that those involved know what they have to, know why they are expected to do it, believe that it is worthwhile and have the skills to do it?

▌ Are people likely to react negatively to the proposed strategy and if so, how do we deal with their concerns?

▌ How much time will be needed; how much time have we got?

▌ Will any additional resources be required and can they be made available?

▌ Are there any likely implementation problems and how will they be dealt with?

Particular attention should be paid to issues arising from process factors (*how* the strategy will work), involving people and communicating with them, and the part played by line managers.

Process factors

Implementing reward strategy is much more about process than design – *how* it will be done rather than *what* will be done. Change management, as discussed later, is mainly concerned with process rather than technical details. The principles of procedural and distributive justice apply. People must feel that the procedures used to determine their grades, pay level and pay progression are fair, equitable, applied consistently and transparent. They must also feel that the awards distributed to them are just in terms of their contribution and value to the organization.

The infrastructure required to do this consists of the methods used to evaluate and grade jobs, the operation of an effective performance management scheme, a fair and consistent process for determining pay increases, and open procedures for reviewing and appealing against grading and pay decisions. For example, performance-related pay schemes will demotivate rather than motivate people if the process for assessing performance is perceived to be biased or unfair. It is very risky to introduce any contingent pay scheme until, following pilot tests, it is reasonably certain that performance management provides a proper basis for decision making.

Involvement and communication

A constantly recurring theme in this book is the importance of involvement and communication. The approaches used in a number of leading organizations to involving people are given below.

Involvement at B&Q

As Will Astill Reward Manager, B&Q explains:

> A key challenge is getting the people in all of the different departments involved in the project – recruitment, employment policy, internal communications, human resources and reward – to work together. If change strategies do not carry everyone in the organization willingly forward, the process can be painful and even damaging. So it's vital that the reward manager builds relationships with the right people. You need to get key individuals to work together without them feeling that they are losing control of their initiatives. Never underestimate the value of in-depth employee consultation. It is necessary to spend money on professional research – market research, HR consultants to design and facilitate focus groups – as though you are conducting a market research exercise. Employees are consumers. You need to sell the initiative to them and help them understand why it is taking place.

Involvement at Centrica

At Centrica, employee involvement in designing the new reward package was considered vital. Focus groups were held, attended by some 200 staff. These took the form of structured workshops that looked at pay, progression, bonuses, holidays, pensions and attitudes to flexibility both in benefit provision and in working time. The focus groups explained current provision for British Gas Trading and ex-Enron staff and flagged up options for the future. But their most important role was to get an idea of what employees wanted. A union representative attended all the focus groups, and played an important part in reassuring staff that the changes were voluntary, and that the function of the workshops was to gain input as to how the pay and benefits spend could be redistributed in a way that suited staff better than the current arrangements.

The outcome of the workshops was that staff believed, correctly, that they were driving the redesign of the reward package, and this helped to dispel any suspicions as to what the company might be planning. What employees wanted was:

▌ pay in line with the market;

▌ transparency in pay progression;

▌ reviews based on performance;

▌ meaningful bonus potential;

▌ more frequent bonus payments;

▌ to be able to retain the final salary pension;

▌ to keep existing holiday entitlement;

▌ to be able to trade holidays for other benefits;

▌ flexibility and choice over benefits.

The next step was to validate these findings. This was done through a series of additional workshops and presentations to the workshop participants, who were asked to confirm that they agreed with them. Once this had happened, work began on designing a reward package that would meet employees' requirements.

Implementation at Diageo

Nicki Demby, Performance and Reward Director at Diageo, believes that an essential feature of any implementation programme is the very clear, effective and regular communication of aims, methods of operation and the impact. Transparency is essential. But for Nicki Demby it is imperative not only to explain the planned changes, the rationale behind them, and how it affects the workforce, but also you need to communicate details of who was involved in the development process so that unnecessary fears are allayed. 'Cross-functional teams develop better solutions,' says Nicki Demby.

Involvement and communications at Lloyds TSB

Tim Fevyer, Senior Manager, Compensation and Benefits, Lloyds TSB, recommends that:

> The success of new reward systems depends heavily on talking to people, and asking what they would like to see. There is much to be said for involving line managers and listening to what employees and their representatives regard as important.

Indeed involvement is seen as a cornerstone of the bank's total reward programme. A range of approaches are used to involve employees, to capture meaningful data and to gain an understanding of employee needs and the rewards that motivate them to deliver results. But Lloyds TSB finds that the best ways are through carefully crafted attitude surveys, focus groups and the like:

> When creating our compelling employment offer, we talked to people and found out what the key trends were. We undertook research about what is really compelling for employees. It is an essential preliminary to any reward strategy.

Lloyds TSB feels it is imperative to communicate to staff in advance of launch and at every stage of the process, explaining the planned changes, the rationale behind them, and how it affects the workforce. It is necessary to continue to give progress reports to employees and obtain their input on an ongoing basis thereafter. It requires consistent communication to employees, who must have a clear understanding of why total reward is being introduced and how it will affect them.

However, as Tim Fevyer admits, communicating a wide-ranging change programme is onerous: 'Getting a consistent message across and getting people to understand what the business is trying to achieve is very difficult when rolling out a reward strategy over six, seven and eight years.'

We comment in more detail on communication issues in Chapter 13.

The importance of line managers

As Purcell *et al* (2003) emphasize, it is line managers who bring HR policies to life. This probably applies to reward policies more than to any other aspect of HR. Reward specialists will be involved in the design of the strategy and planning and executing its application. They will be there to provide guidance and help. But ultimately, it is the line managers who make the recommendations on pay increases and upgradings, who, often, fix salaries on appointment, or at least exert influence over them, and who conduct performance management reviews. All these activities are fundamental to the success of a reward strategy. The role of line managers and how their capability and commitment can be enhanced is discussed in Chapter 11.

DEALING WITH IMPLEMENTATION PROBLEMS

Common implementation problems can arise because of over-engineered reward systems, misalignment, and acting precipitately, as discussed below.

Over-engineering

Implementation problems are often caused by over-engineering the reward strategy and its components. The temptation presented to reward specialists (both practitioners and consultants) is to design highly detailed processes that are hard to explain and justify and even harder to operate. It is a temptation people often find difficult to resist. Nicki Demby, Performance and Reward Director at Diageo, explained to the e-reward researcher:

> It is essential to assess the extent to which changes will add value rather than create work. Reward processes and schemes will not be introduced or updated without assessing whether there is a good reason for doing so. Does it give energy or take it away? For example, is the reward plan so complicated that by the time you have waded through it you wish you hadn't? If so, you are taking away an effective management tool.

So how does Diageo take complexity out of the reward system? 'Our mantra is "keep it simple, but simple isn't easy!" It's just as hard as making something complicated, but in terms of effectiveness, well thought through simplicity can pay huge dividends,' says Nicki Demby.

Misalignment

Implementation problems can be created if alignment with the business and HR strategies is disregarded when formulating reward strategy. Lack of vertical alignment means that there is a risk of reward policies becoming isolated or irrelevant. Line managers will be less willing to implement them and their impact will be reduced. Failure to achieve a measure of horizontal alignment will diminish the impact of reward practices by reducing the amount of mutual enhancement and support that can be achieved through 'bundling' HR policies.

Approaches to achieving vertical and horizontal alignment were examined in Chapter 9.

Precipitant implementation

Those involved in developing reward strategy naturally want to get results, and this particularly applies to top managers who often tend to put project managers and their teams under pressure to deliver the strategy quickly. The risk of taking precipitant action is that new policies and practices will not have been tested properly to identify any problems that might be met in their implementation, through inappropriate or poor design, or the absence of adequate supporting processes such as performance management. This has been a major reason for the failure of many new reward schemes to live up to expectations.

It is essential to allow time in the project plan to reflect on the implications of proposals and identify potential problems and areas where particular care has to be taken in avoiding them. These problems may include the capacity of line managers and employees to understand what they have to do and acquire the skills to do it, the snags that inevitably occur and are difficult to deal with over a short time scale, and the failure of existing processes such as performance management to provide adequate support.

There are essentially two ways of dealing with these problems. First, wherever possible, the new or significantly altered reward process should be pilot tested in a division or department or with a selected sample of employees. This applies particularly to performance management and contingent pay schemes (performance, competency or contribution-related pay).

The tests should be designed to establish the extent to which line managers can and will carry out their responsibility; the support that HR will need to provide; any inadequacies in existing processes; the approach that should be adopted to informing employees generally and individuals in particular on how they will be affected by the strategy; and the need to involve people in further discussions on the proposals. The outcome of the tests could be the amendment of the proposed practice or existing processes and the improvement of involvement, communication and training processes, as well as a better understanding of what problems may arise and how they can be solved.

The second approach, which can be used where there is more than one component of the reward strategy, is to phase the introduction of the different parts. An incremental approach means that people are given the time to absorb and adjust to the new practice, and the resources such as HR support required to deliver the strategy are not over-stretched. For example, a large local authority phased the implementation of a comprehensive reward strategy initiative that included a major cultural shift from service-related increments to contribution-related pay. First they developed and introduced a new job evaluation scheme. Then they amended the grade and pay structure by reference to job evaluation scores and a market rate survey, retaining the existing incremental system. Next they introduced a measure of contribution pay by making increments dependent on achieving satisfactory levels of competence. Finally they implemented a full contribution-related pay scheme, rewarding people both for their outputs (results) and their inputs (competence).

PROJECT MANAGEMENT

The development and implementation of a reward strategy often constitutes a complex project that has to be managed effectively. Failure to do this adequately may result in serious implementation difficulties, especially when there are a number of dependencies in the project. For example, the design of a grade structure depends on having job evaluation data, which in turn may be dependent on the development and testing of a new scheme; the pay structure to be attached to the grade structure is dependent on the provision of market rate data; the introduction of contribution-related pay depends on the existence of effective performance management and a pay structure that is designed to accommodate it. The project plan has to determine priorities, resource requirements and interdependencies over a period of time to achieve planned results.

A project management procedure has to be instituted which:

▎ specifies objectives and deliverables;

▎ defines who is to be responsible for directing and managing the project and the degree of authority they have;

▎ sets out what should be done (activities), who does what, and when it will be done;

▮ involves senior managers/heads of department as sponsors, who provide comment, guidance, support and encouragement;

▮ breaks down the project into stages with defined starting and completion dates to produce the programme;

▮ clarifies interdependencies;

▮ defines resource requirements – people, outside advisers, finance;

▮ defines methods of control, eg progress reports, meetings;

▮ ensures that everyone knows what is expected of them and has the briefing, guidance and resources required;

▮ sees that progress is monitored continuously against the plan as well as at formal meetings;

▮ ensures that corrective action is taken as required; for example, amending timings, and reallocating resources;

▮ evaluates progress and the end result against objectives and deliverables.

A bar chart as shown in Figure 10.1 (based on an actual example) on page 170 is a useful way of planning, illustrating and controlling the project. The illustrated chart does not cover the initial analysis, diagnosis and planning stage.

In addition, a clearer picture of the interdependencies can be presented in the form of a network, as shown in Figure 10.2 (page 171).

A project manager should be appointed to plan and control the whole project. It is common practice for the project manager to work with a project team or task force comprising management and employee representatives. The team would be involved in the development of the reward system but may not deal with pay issues, especially if there is a trade union with negotiating rights (unions usually prefer to negotiate pay levels and assimilation and protection policies). A steering committee of senior managers and trade union officers may also be established to oversee the project.

A description of the typical phases and activities in a reward strategy project is given in Figure 10.3 (page 172).

CHANGE MANAGEMENT

The implementation of reward strategy may result in major changes to the ways in which people are rewarded. Those initiating the changes may truly

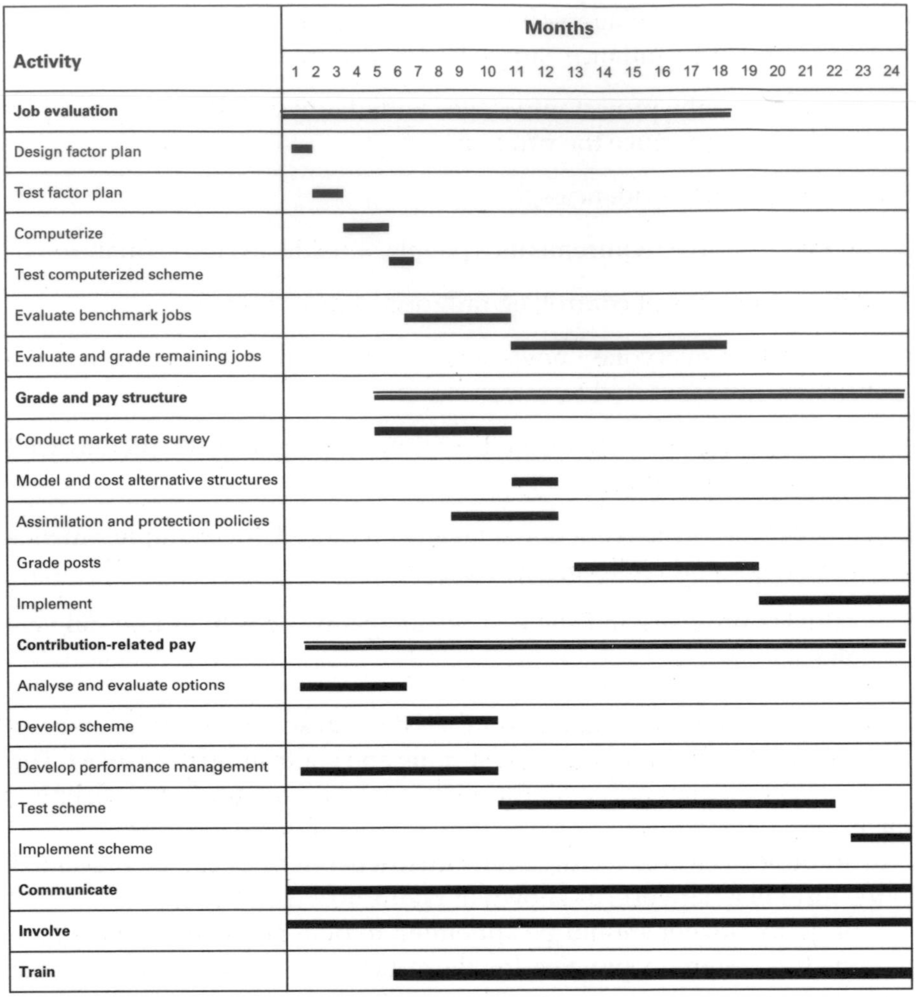

Activity	Months 1–24 (bar span)
Job evaluation	1–17
Design factor plan	1
Test factor plan	2
Computerize	3–4
Test computerized scheme	5
Evaluate benchmark jobs	6–8
Evaluate and grade remaining jobs	11–17
Grade and pay structure	4–24
Conduct market rate survey	5–8
Model and cost alternative structures	10–11
Assimilation and protection policies	9–11
Grade posts	14–18
Implement	19–24
Contribution-related pay	1–24
Analyse and evaluate options	1–3
Develop scheme	5–6
Develop performance management	1–3
Test scheme	11–19
Implement scheme	23–24
Communicate	1–24
Involve	1–24
Train	4–24

Figure 10.1   Reward strategy design and implementation control chart

believe that it is for the good of employees, as well as the organization. The employees may think otherwise. In a large local authority great care was taken to communicate the reasons for and the impact of the new job evaluation scheme, emphasizing that it would result in fairer gradings through a more transparent process. The trade union representatives on the working party accepted this, but the bulk of employees did not, at least at first. They felt that it was just a device to reduce their pay. The opposite can happen – people can expect too much from change. In a housing association the staff were convinced that job evaluation meant more money all round and had to be persuaded that this was not the case. In either situation, great efforts had to be made to get people to understand and accept what was really going to happen to them.

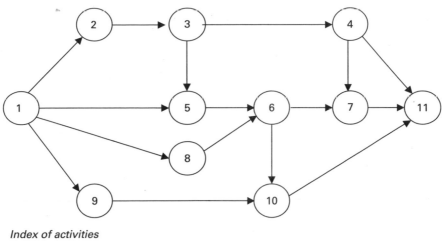

Index of activities

1 Develop strategy
2 Design and test job evaluation
   scheme
3 Evaluate benchmark jobs
4 Evaluate remaining jobs
5 Design grade structure

6 Grade jobs
7 Conduct market rate survey
8 Attach pay ranges to grade structure
9 Consider and assess contribution pay options
10 Develop and test contribution pay scheme
11 Implement

The timing and responsibility for each activity would also be indicated.

Figure 10.2   A reward strategy development and implementation network

Approaches to managing change

The management of change is a key process in introducing new or considerably altered reward policies and practices. Thurley (1979) produced one of the most practical descriptions of approaches to managing change:

1. *Directive* – the imposition of change in crisis situations or when other methods have failed. This is done by the exercise of managerial power without consultation.

2. *Bargained* – this approach recognizes that power is shared between the employer and the employed and change requires negotiation, compromise and agreement before being implemented.

3. *'Hearts and minds'* – an all-embracing thrust to change the attitudes, values and beliefs of the whole workforce. This 'normative' approach (ie one which starts from a definition of what management thinks is right or 'normal') seeks 'commitment' and 'shared vision' and should include extensive involvement and communication. It is likely to fail if it does not.

	Phase 1	Phase 2	Phase 3	Phase 4
Purpose	Diagnosis of current situation, setting the future direction and principles, development of the future reward architecture	Detailed design of the components of the future reward strategy	Preparation and testing, building the capacity to deliver	Implementation and ongoing review and adjustment
Outputs	• Full understanding of present reward situation • Identification of key reward issues • Future reward strategy, definition and components • Defined employment 'deal' • Prioritization of schemes and changes • Detailing and communication plan • Buy-in and support of relevant interest groups	• Detailed scheme design, eg pay structures and levels, base pay reviews, incentive and bonus plans, benefits • Schemes initially modelled and tested • Preparation plan • Senior management agreement	• Agree finalized changes/schemes • Fully tested and costed reward schemes • Trained managers and staff with clear understanding of reward strategy and changes • Defined implementation and operating responsibilities and policies • Appropriate phased implementation plan • Branded reward	• Detailed implementation communication • Effectively implemented and operating reward schemes • Operation of review mechanisms and modification as required • Further development of management skills and staff training
Typical stages	• Planning • Formation of project team • Management interviews and staff/representative group discussions • External market analysis: reward levels, practices, trends • Internal data review • Project team workshops: review findings, develop and critique opinions, agree changes • Senior management	• Design team meetings • Drafting of scheme designs • Testing of new schemes on sample of jobs • Further consultation • Initial costings and modelling • Staff updates and briefings	• Further testing of designs, eg pilots • Analysis of transition from present situation • Detailed modelling and costing • Development and delivery of communications and training support • Trade union negotiations • Design of operating, administration and control procedures	• Full and properly tested installation • Regular audits of effectiveness • Design of any required modification to schemes

(Source: CIPD, 2004a)

Figure 10.3 A phased project pathway to developing and implementing a reward strategy

4. *Analytical* – a theoretical approach to the change process, which proceeds sequentially from the analysis and diagnosis of the situation, through the setting of objectives, the design of the change process, the evaluation of the results and, finally, the determination of the objectives for the next stage. This is the rational and logical approach much favoured by consultants – external and internal. But change seldom proceeds as smoothly as this model would suggest. Emotions, power politics and external pressures mean that the rational approach, although it might be the right way to start, is difficult to sustain.

5. *Action-based* – this recognizes that the way managers behave in practice bears little resemblance to the analytical, theoretical model. The distinction between managerial thought and managerial action blurs in practice to the point of invisibility. What managers think is what they do. Real life therefore often results in a 'fire, aim, ready' approach to change management. This typical approach to change starts with a broad belief that some sort of problem exists, although it may not be well defined. The identification of possible solutions, often on a trial or error basis, leads to a clarification of the nature of the problem and a shared understanding of a possible optimal solution, or at least a framework within which solutions can be discovered. The extent to which change is really managed in these circumstances is limited.

It is interesting to note that the 'hearts and minds' approach is becoming increasingly popular, but whichever approach is used, change management programmes have to take account of the fact that many people resist change, and these include top management and line managers, as well as staff. There are those who are stimulated by change and see it as a challenge and an opportunity, but they are usually in the minority. It is always easy for managers to select any of the following 10 reasons for doing nothing:

1. It won't work.

2. We're already doing it.

3. It's been tried before without success.

4. It's not practical.

5. It won't solve the problem.

6. It's too risky.

7. It's based on pure theory.

8. It will cost too much.

9. It will antagonize the union/the workers.

10. It will create more problems than it solves.

Employees and their representatives are likely to take a pragmatic view expressed by the phrases, 'What's in it for us?' or, 'What's the catch?' or, 'What's the hidden agenda?' or, 'What's the downside for us?'

Change management guidelines

A change management programme must anticipate and deal with both the objections that may be raised by managers and the questions posed by staff.

Change management at General Electric

The following comprehensive guidelines for managing change, produced by the HR department at General Electric, require those involved to ensure that:

∎ employees see the reason for change;

∎ employees understand why change is important and see how it will help them and the business in the long and short term;

∎ the people who need to be committed to the change to make it happen are recognized;

∎ a coalition of support is built for the change;

∎ the support of key individuals in the organization is enlisted;

∎ the link between the change and other HR systems such as staffing, training, appraisal, and communication is understood;

∎ the systems implications of the change are recognized;

∎ a means of measuring the success of the change is identified;

∎ plans are made to monitor progress in the implementation of change;

∎ the first steps in getting change started are recognized;

∎ plans are made to keep attention focused on the change;

∎ the likely need to adapt the change over time is recognized and plans can readily be made and implemented for such adaptations.

Change management at Friends Provident

As Peter Harris, Reward and Benefits Manager at Friends Provident, explained to the e-reward researcher:

> We often read that 'the only constant thing is change itself and during periods of change: communicate, communicate, communicate'. How right they are. Over the past four years we have continuously reviewed and evolved our reward and benefits package to ensure we can differentiate reward by

performance, have a set and range of benefits that are valued and which are effectively communicated. The changes we have made have certainly helped to move the company forwards, given us the opportunity to reinforce the link between individual performance, company performance and reward, and personally given me the opportunity to make a positive difference. I'm confident that the latter is true for all reward specialists.

Change management at GlaxoSmithKline

Paul Craven, Compensation Director, R&D, summed up the approach to change management in a major reward strategy development project at GlaxoSmithKline when he commented: 'Don't expect people to change overnight and don't try to force change. It is better to reinforce desirable behaviour than to attempt to enforce a particular way of doing things.'

Change management at Lloyds TSB

According to Tim Fevyer, Senior Manager, Compensation and Benefits, Lloyds TSB the success of any total reward programme will hinge on the degree to which employees feel a sense of ownership. 'The aim is to get "ownership" – a feeling amongst people that the change is something that they are happy to live with because they have been involved in its planning and introduction – it has become *their* change.'

Change management at Xansa

Following the introduction of its new approach to reward and HR generally, the following important lessons were noted at Xansa:

▍ establish a clear vision and senior management sponsorship;

▍ free up the best resources to work on the project and ensure sufficient resources continue to be made available;

▍ establish baseline metrics and desired future metrics;

▍ a phased approach meant that some 'quick wins' could be achieved;

▍ manage resistance by focusing on the positive aspects of the change programme;

▍ communication plans need to vary for different audiences, for example, managers, employees and the HR team;

▍ don't give up!

SPECIFIC REWARD IMPLEMENTATION ISSUES

The problems and issues arising in four of the most common areas of reward management that feature in reward strategies, and the advice on dealing with them provided by practitioners, are discussed below.

Job evaluation

The development and introduction of a new or substantially changed job evaluation system can create a number of problems with employees. First and foremost, employees often fail to appreciate the purpose of the scheme and are not convinced that it operates fairly. They may expect too much from it (all-round pay increases) or worry because they suspect that it is part of a cost-cutting exercise.

The scheme itself may, in the words of Peter Wickens (in Armstrong and Baron, 1995) 'create work but fail to add value'. Job evaluation schemes are in danger of being or becoming bureaucratic and paper-intensive, as well as inflexible, time-wasting and costly. Also, they are not always consistent with the ways in which work is often carried out nowadays, involving greater flexibility and more scope for individuals to engage in discretionary activities. It is necessary to recognize this by paying for the person rather than for what is assumed to be a tightly defined job. Finally, the job evaluation scheme may fail to convince people that it is fairly and consistently measuring the relative value of jobs. These issues all arise at the design and development stage, but they also have to be taken into account when implementation takes place.

To deal with the main issue of reactions to job evaluation, regular and pertinent communication with staff is important throughout the implementation programme. It is necessary to manage expectations by restating the intention behind bringing in the new job evaluation scheme, making it clear that no specific pay decisions will be made until the evaluation programme is complete; and (if that is the case) emphasizing that no one's pay will be reduced as a result of introducing the scheme and stressing that the pay of individuals will not necessarily increase. It is also important to explain the evaluation process, who is involved and what their different roles are, to present the principles of the new grade structure and, if appropriate, the new pay arrangements before any individual grades are made known.

To deal with implementation issues arising from the scheme design it is essential to test the scheme thoroughly before launching it. The following design tips were provided by the respondents to the e-reward (2003) job evaluation survey:

▌ Simplify.

▌ Make schemes less wordy and subjective.

▌ Make sure the scheme covers the whole organization.

▌ Consider factor definitions more carefully.

▌ Use a computer-based system.

▌ Allow for flexibility and creating new job families.

▌ Use more meaningful and less generic job descriptions.

▌ Define clearer boundaries between bands.

▌ Move towards job families and wider bands.

▌ Clarify promotion routes and career paths.

The tips given by survey respondents on introducing job evaluation were:

▌ Prepare the technical work within HR. Present to senior managers with a good description of the advantages to them (some real-life examples they can relate to). Then communicate the project to the whole organization (a specific project team needs to be working on the plan). Use different media to give information to employees.

▌ Overkill communication.

▌ Explain more thoroughly.

▌ Involve all stakeholders early on.

▌ Try to ensure a greater understanding of the scheme at an earlier stage.

▌ Gain greater business buy-in and support so that it is seen as a business tool rather than an HR process.

▌ Widen the pool of trained evaluators.

▌ Introduce through a rigorous process of pilot testing.

▌ Run like a project with specific success criteria and regular reviews. No one should be afraid to amend it as appropriate, rather than letting the job evaluation system run the organization.

▌ Set more reasonable time scales to manage employee expectations.

Grade and pay structures

Again, the issues arising when implementing new grade and pay structures often occur at the design stage if insufficient attention has been paid to developing a structure that fits the culture and operational requirements of the organization; is acceptable to employees; is based on robust job evaluation and market rate data; and can be implemented without undue cost. A particular problem with all schemes developed on the basis of point-factor job evaluation is that of defining the boundaries in a graded structure. 'Boundary problems' can easily arise where the evaluation scores for jobs are very close to the boundary with the next higher grade, and these can lead to many time-consuming and potentially demotivating appeals.

At the implementation stage problems may arise concerning assimilation into the new structure and pay protection for those whose pay is above the maximum for their redefined grade. The cost of implementation may be higher than expected. There can be dissatisfaction not only amongst the 'losers', who are now overpaid and red-circled, but even amongst the green-circled 'winners', who are underpaid and will receive pay increases – they may be discontented because they feel they have been previously underpaid, and ask, 'Why has it taken so long to sort that out?'

The 'dos and don'ts' of developing and implementing new or amended grade and pay structures, as expressed by respondents to the 2004 e-reward survey (2004a), are set out in Table 10.2.

Converting to a broad-banded structure from a traditional narrow graded structure can present special problems. The operation and effect of broad-banding – the positioning of people in bands and how far they can progress – are often difficult to explain and manage. While broad-banding tends to make the job evaluation process simpler and less demanding, it requires much higher-quality and active base pay management. Broad-banding processes have to be strong enough to cope with the increased demands that will be placed on HR and line managers, and they have to be developed and described in ways that clarify for employees how broad-banding will work, how it is different, and how they will be affected by it.

A building society decided to add one band to its initially agreed new banding structure as it prepared to implement it. While it had been thought desirable in a flatter organization structure to put front desk employees and supervisors in the same band, consultation with staff showed that it would have caused widespread opposition from existing employees and represented a cultural 'step too far'.

Table 10.2 Grade and pay structures dos and don'ts

Do	Don't
• Make the structure congruent to the values and methods of work in your business	• Be rushed into launching before you are ready – all employees will want to know what it means for their pay and progression on day one, so have the answers before you launch
• Ensure it fits with how the organization wants to operate	
• Ensure that the company is ready and supports broad approach and that flexibility over structure is valued	• Lose sight of the detail when discussing the strategy!
	• Expect people to understand first time round
• Work out why you are doing it and if anyone else will understand it	• Try to put in a structure that other companies have and then adapt it as yours
• Keep the structure as simple as possible – if people don't understand the structure, it is too complicated	• Try to do it without a process for job evaluation
	• Spend a fortune implementing an unwieldy system
• Resource your project full time, not in someone's spare time	• Rely on one survey – make sure you have other sources to verify data you are gathering
• Ensure you have accurate data relating to each job and person within it	• Be secretive about the process
• Get good market data but be honest about their limitations	• Underestimate levels of internal resistance to change
• Monitor internal consistency	• Assume that launch communication will be sufficient to enable structure to be fully understood – reinforcement of message is required over a longer period of time
• Ensure you have the buy-in of senior managers	
• Talk to the line managers (at least 20 times!)	
• Get line managers involved at an early stage	• Underestimate the resources such a project will use up
• Allow managers flexibility	• Underestimate the level of perseverance required
• Allow time for managers to adapt to new approach and support appropriately	• Be pressurized into a system that does not fit your organisation culture, eg by a US parent
• Ensure you have a structure that can be managed without becoming cumbersome	• Think of a structure and force fit the jobs into it
	• Neglect the 'status symbol' that grades have for certain people (they can be a very emotive subject!)
• Ensure you have the correct processes in place to deal with movements and changes of job	• Expect to please everyone

- Ensure that performance management disciplines are embedded
- Make sure that the structure is available to all staff with no hidden agenda. People like to know there is something to work towards and that the system is fair
- Communicate very widely and very often what is being done and why
- Involve key operational sponsors throughout
- Be determined to achieve!
- Keep the faith!

- Assume anything or try to hide the unpalatable – be honest about any aspects that aren't ideal
- Misunderstand the amount of work involved in changing, either partially or totally, elements of current pay framework/system
- Try for perfection – fit for purpose will do
- Regrade people in response to market pressures on pay
- Introduce it without training managers (ensuring they understand the system) and the rest of the employees

Phased implementation, as at the BBC, with a progressive reduction in the number of grades over a number of years, moving at a pace consistent with the development of line management capability and employee understanding and acceptance, is a common strategy in implementing pay restructuring.

Richard Sullivan, Group Reward Manager at Tesco, recommends that the following guiding principles should be borne in mind when introducing broad-bands, many of which apply to any reward innovation:

1. Don't underestimate the old culture – it will take time to change it.

2. Deal with the move to broad-banding as a conversion rather than a new initiative, to minimize change issues.

3. Be prepared to challenge any return to the old ways.

4. Management capability is key to communicating issues.

5. Deal with cost issues before changing to broad-bands.

6. If broad-bands are not used for all staff, explain why carefully.

7. Consider equal pay issues.

8. Use market data, but ensure that it is credible before making it public.

9. Allow at least nine months to move to broad-banding.

10. Employee communication is key to having the new system understood.

11. Don't have less than five layers across the business in a broad-band system.

12. Obtain managers' input when designing the new process; this will help them explain it to others and will increase their commitment to it.

Performance management

Performance management is perhaps the most prominent example of an HR process that is fairly easy to design but incredibly difficult to introduce and operate effectively. The main problem is getting line managers to do it conscientiously and well, as was confirmed by the outcome of the e-reward survey of performance management in 2005. The survey established that more training or coaching for managers was the most popular method of dealing with the issues. A number of respondents were reviewing the process and some were seeking greater support from top management. Here are some typical comments:

▌ There is a shift in culture from long-term employees feeling that performance management is just something they have to go through, but that they will be in the job for ever anyway, to a more business-like approach to performance management, with accountability, and competency.

▌ Structured programme of line management training is being established with great success. Ongoing coaching of those managers.

▌ Line managers tend to give the average 3c rating, and back away from dealing with poor performance. We conduct regular coaching sessions with line managers to encourage them actively to performance manage.

▌ After introducing a new scheme three years ago, last year we carried out a refresher training workshop specifically tackling how to carry out performance reviews, feedback and dealing with poor performance. The majority of managers found this useful, but there remains a significant number who believe that the training was unnecessary.

▌ Generating leadership from the top of the hierarchy to support/ encourage the need for managers to tackle poor performance head on in a fair and positive manner.

▌ We are seeking ways of getting the executive team to take ownership of our performance management system and to get the buy-in of their management teams to work with it for the benefit of the organization. Alongside this, we are asking them to encourage their management teams to participate in relevant development to improve their skills so that they may be more effective.

▍ Nagging, nagging, nagging, motivating, threatening, nagging, etc.

Contingent pay

Even the most committed supporters of contingent pay (pay for performance, competence or contribution) acknowledge that it is difficult to introduce and manage well. This particularly applies when shifting from a service-related progression scheme – a massive culture change that is almost always resisted by trade unions because they believe the process will be fundamentally unfair. So, one of the key issues addressed in the e-reward (2004b) survey was that of conditions for success when implementing and operating contingent pay schemes.

Survey participants were asked to spell out their key tips for successful implementation. The five most important actions they recommended were:

1. Keep the scheme as simple and as easy to understand, communicate and operate as possible (stated by 44 per cent of respondents).

2. People must feel that the decision-making process and performance measures are fair and consistent (37 per cent).

3. Align to business objectives and reward behaviour the organization wants to reinforce (36 per cent).

4. Transparency is essential (27 per cent).

5. Communicate fully on what is going to happen, why it is going to happen and how people will be affected (26 per cent).

Other tips included:

▍ Good, well-operated performance management process on which to base reward decisions.

▍ Simple – not too many factors influencing (or confusing) decisions.

▍ Ability to clearly differentiate on the grounds of performance.

▍ Based on measurable performance that adds to the bottom line of the business.

▍ Clear guidelines as to what constitutes levels of competence and performance.

▌ As objective as possible in measuring the relevant factors affecting the payout level.

▌ Based on factors over which the employee can exert a reasonable degree of influence.

▌ Meaningful reward to the employee, such that all levels of employee can see what they need to do to increase their pay.

▌ Applied consistently and fairly.

▌ Clearly defined and above all transparent.

▌ Buy in from all staff.

▌ Designed to reinforce the culture of the organization.

SUCCESS CRITERIA

Effective implementation ultimately depends upon having clear objectives and success criteria, and then monitoring and evaluating the process closely against those criteria throughout the project. A good example of a clear definition of success criteria is provided by Centrica, where the nine keys to success for its reward strategy have been:

1. Partnership
    - between reward, pensions, HR services and the business.

2. Preparation
    - consultation with all affected parties and trade unions at the outset;
    - expectations set and timelines agreed;
    - regular communication took place throughout the planning stages;
    - clear exploration of current terms and conditions in operation and early identification of issues;
    - financial modelling commenced at the beginning of the process;
    - communication strategy devised.

3. Business engagement
    - consultation with each key stakeholder on a one-to-one basis;
    - identified drivers for the business: high performance culture, team working, flexibility, one consistent Centrica contract and attractive new joiner proposition;
    - illustrated how each element could be achieved via total reward;
    - building robust business case in conjunction with finance gained credibility;

- illustrated to employees the importance of total reward to the business via communication process.

4. Financial modelling
   - costing and financial modelling the transition from existing to new arrangements in conjunction with finance department.

5. Union engagement
   - consulted with the union at the outset of the project;
   - maintained communication with union representatives throughout the planning and implementation process;
   - offered employees choice: it was not a 'forced move';
   - involved union representatives in the focus groups and communication processes;
   - utilized the union as a point of support for the employees;
   - built a partnership with the union.

6. Employee engagement
   - series of employee focus groups: in excess of 200 employees attended;
   - collated feedback and fed into reward proposition;
   - served to confirm a number of assumptions and to drive some amendments;
   - revalidated findings with initial focus group attendees;
   - employees felt that they owned the package as they could see the link between their input and the options available: it ceased to be just an HR initiative;
   - attendees publicized the initiative in the business and stirred interest;
   - allowed the business to position the introduction of new terms and conditions;
   - provided a forum to address any negative perceptions prior to full roll-out;
   - consultation process served to build trust with employees, stopped them looking for the 'hidden catch'.

7. Communication
   - began communicating at early stages of the project and continued throughout;
   - ongoing communication maintained employees' interest in the new proposition;
   - utilized variety of communication formats, including e-mails, in-house magazines, road shows and one-to-one meetings.

8. Project administration
   - dedicated HR contact key to effective coordination of the project;
   - do not underestimate the administrative burden!
   - over 1,000 comprehensive information packs were produced;
   - individual packs were created for each employee;
   - 'variances' dictated by different terms and conditions in operation;
   - data integrity of packs is dependent on good employee data;
   - undertook a large validation process, requiring line management ownership of data to ensure accuracy;
   - utilized a single project office to create packs;
   - scheduled a week to create packs: this was achieved but timescales were tight.

9. Business-as-usual administration
   - engaged HR services at outset of the project;
   - identified dedicated contacts in both payroll and the Employee Service Centre (ESC).

THE BT APPROACH TO IMPLEMENTATION

Kevin Brady, HR Director, Reward and Employee Relations at BT, commented to Paul Thompson of e-reward in 2005 that: 'Introducing the new reward framework represented a formidable challenge. It was a major exercise in change management. It certainly involved a lot of learning along the way.' He believes the following seven key learning points for change need to be remembered when planning the implementation of reward strategy.

1. Business sponsorship and ownership is key

From the outset, BT's aim was to secure 'sponsorship and ownership' amongst senior people – a feeling that the change is something that they are happy to live with because they have been involved in its planning and introduction – it has become *their* change. But Kevin Brady admits that problems may arise in achieving sponsorship and the unwavering commitment by all concerned – these difficulties should never be underestimated. The harsh reality for BT was that the degree of sponsorship that it thought it had achieved was not really there. 'If I'm brutally honest, it's easy to put across a very positive message about sponsorship – that people are doing all the right things and they're signed up to it – and the CEO wants it,' says Brady. 'But if people haven't got an active interest in the project and it's not their top priority, they don't realize what the impact is until way down the road. That's when they suddenly come back to you.'

Brady describes the process of organizational change management as a 'continual circle whereby you constantly need to go back to sponsors and reconfirm their responses and re-engage' with them:

> People will tell you they are happy with the project and they'll nod it through, but you actually need more than that. You have to keep going back and reinforcing the sponsorship and then you can stand up and be counted. It's only human nature. People were only too happy to delegate and say, 'I'll let so-and-so design the structure for me and whatever they say goes.' But then when we published the structure we'd get dozens of e-mails, saying, 'This is nuts. I can't believe you've done this.'

Above all, Brady thinks it is crucial to avoid the programme being tagged as just another HR or reward initiative, rather than as something that is owned by the organization as a whole:

> It's essential to get continued operational ownership of the programme. It's not about an HR project – it's about a fundamental shift in terms of the business. And it's a business-driven change initiative. We're trying to shift the culture of the businesses.

2. Don't underestimate resistance

Kevin Brady believes that the level of resistance that may arise when reorganizing reward systems should never be underestimated, hence the importance he places on sponsorship, communication and training. 'I've had resistance from my own team, resistance from senior operations directors and resistance from the businesses,' says Brady. Almost inevitably, changes in reward systems can be perceived by people as not only potentially hitting them where it hurts – in their pockets – but also undermining their status. They can be unsettled, unduly apprehensive and resist anything that alters an existing arrangement. This is an area of great interest to people and their expectations must be managed:

> It's about being aware that as you go into the change, not everyone is going to be happy with the change. Reward is such a sensitive area. Even little things that you believe to be beneficial, which you would think would convey a positive message, are not seen that way. In fact, we almost managed to snatch a defeat from the jaws of victory. People still perceived that they were losing status – because they previously had been entitled to a car and although they were still going to get that car, someone doing the same job working alongside them wouldn't now receive a car. Therefore that was a slight on them.

3. Understand the internal dependencies in your current structure

BT discovered that when it scrapped its grading structure, which had been in place for 15 years, many of its systems and authority levels were grade-driven. As Brady explains:

> What tends to happen is that people build all the systems around grades, so in terms of sign-off levels we had something like 360 systems that still referred to the old grading structure. All of our operating systems that are embedded in the system are built around grade. All of our internal customer service systems have got grade in there. Finance systems are all driven off grade.

For the duration of the transitional period, BT decided that each individual employee would maintain his or her current grade. This was necessary to allow 'business as usual decisions' to be made and processes to operate, whilst appropriate systems work was carried out as part of a change to role-driven systems.

4. Project management skills are critical

BT reckons that the introduction of the new reward framework was one of the largest change management programmes of its kind in the UK. It was certainly the most ambitious and complex project that BT has ever undertaken. 'To be successful, your new reward programme should be implemented by means of a carefully planned and managed project to organize and shape work more effectively,' says Brady:

> The normal rules of project management should apply. So, you need to establish a steering committee, appoint sponsors from each line of the business, ensure that you have clear and agreed objectives, prepare a project plan with project milestones and clear change control processes. But, above all, with something on this scale and complexity with a huge number of internal dependencies, you need a full-time, dedicated individual, trained in project-management, who can manage all aspects of the project. In hindsight, our project management could have been better and we could have done things differently.

5. Cost can restrict speed of change

All too often, huge amounts of money are spent devising and implementing new reward systems, but BT has developed its new reward structure without making a substantial financial investment. Clearly, if there is limited additional investment, in terms of increased pay and benefits, then the 'process of change can be impacted,' says Brady:

In our case, launching a new structure at the same time as a very tight annual review, meant people blamed the structure rather than the commercial pressures. The project was broadly cost-neutral, whereas often a big reward change like this would be driven by a merger or something like that, and there's some money to smooth the way. We had very limited amount of additional funding to do that.

6. Engage, engage, engage!

Kevin Brady believes that ownership and acceptance is much more likely if the maximum degree of engagement of all concerned is built into the entire change programme:

Stop and talk to people, involve them in the implementation process, let them know their views are important. Involvement in the programme of introducing new reward systems is a key component of the change management process. It gives people the chance to raise and resolve their concerns and make suggestions about the form of the change and how it should be introduced. Employees should be given every opportunity to participate and contribute to the decision-making processes concerning the development of the new reward programme.

For BT, this was a matter of undertaking attitude surveys, involvement in focus groups – made up of representatives of all of the lines of business – along with briefings and roadshows. 'We did everything you can think of to make sure that people understood the message we were trying to get across,' says Brady.

7. Clear, consistent communication

In Kevin Brady's view, an essential feature of any reward change programme is the very clear, effective and regular communication of aims, methods of operation and impact. Transparency is essential. His recommendations are these:

▮ It is vital to reinforce your key principles through all communication. The importance of ensuring that communication is consistent cannot be overemphasized, says Brady. 'We have tried to be more consistent about putting across what are the key reward principles for this part of the workforce. The core message has not really changed, but it has evolved, as we have taken on board comments and developed it as we have gone along.'

▮ It is essential to communicate consistently and wherever possible use one signatory or one voice. 'Lines of business CEOs fronted many of our reward communications. It's about them embedding that in their organization,' says Brady.

▌ It is imperative to communicate to staff at every stage of the process – even in advance of launch – using one bank of collateral copy and images, without any 'reinvention'.

▌ Early engagement with trade unions and works councils, where appropriate, is important.

▌ 'Line HR is a priority for advance briefing and up-skilling,' says Brady. They must have a clear understanding of what the change is, why it is taking place and, importantly, how it affects employees. As part of this process, BT developed training programmes – for example, in role mapping – to ensure that everyone acquired the skills needed to manage the new processes and play a part in them. Brady is confident that BT's reward communications have become 'much crisper' as the implementation programme has progressed. 'Communication has improved immensely in terms of clarity. But the harsh reality is that all too often the feedback you get is along the lines of, "You don't tell us enough." However, more recently, one of the positives is that people have told us that they were unsure why they had received the latest call, as there was nothing new in it. This means that the message is getting through. But you've got to reinforce continuously.' Without doubt, the introduction of job families at BT has constituted a major culture change. 'I think employees were saying that intellectually they get it, but emotionally they didn't. They were telling us that their grade had been taken away. People can find it difficult to accept that they have lost their old grade, which defined their status, and are now placed in a role that they may share with others who were previously in lower grades. That is why the process of communicating to staff generally and as individuals the rationale for job families is so important.'

Measuring success at BT

It is always vital to specify the objectives and success criteria for reward strategies and changes, and to put some processes in place to assess how well your new systems and schemes are working. No thorough-going shift in reward is complete until you find out if it has worked. So far as possible, you should be able to demonstrate that it has made a difference. So, how has BT measured the effectiveness of its new reward programme? Kevin Brady outlines five key measures of success.

1. Language of total reward

Are people talking differently? Brady is confident that a 'total reward' mindset is gradually being established within BT, and people now recognize that there is more to their reward than just base pay. He reckons employees are increasingly focusing on the external market:

> People are talking more about the external market, whereas two years ago they might have been comparing their salaries with what someone in Retail received, or what someone in Wholesale gets. I think we have shifted the whole debate around reward forward. Are we fully there yet? No, but I don't think on a journey like this you change things overnight. This is a five- or 10-year programme to change the culture, you are trying to change the perception of employees.

2. Clear impact on salary, bonus and make-up of package

Is the mix of the reward package any different? In BT's case it has shifted, with increased levels of variable pay, which was a key requirement at the start of the project.

3. Confidence in market data

Acceptance by employees of the validity of the market data used to set salary ranges remains a source of concern, admits Brady. 'The view tends to be, "If it's not the right message for me personally, I don't believe the data".' But he points out that employee 'churn' is still well below external benchmark comparisons.

4. Employee relations

'If you are in open warfare with your union, you'll have problems,' warns Brady. BT says it worked closely with Connect, the main union, throughout the entire change project. 'We engaged them on almost a weekly basis. They were fully involved,' says Brady.

5. Cost neutrality

Kevin Brady emphasized that, 'The new reward framework is emphatically *not* about saving money – the factors which determine the annual budget will remain the same.' Nor is it designed to inject new funding, but it is about using that budget more effectively to ensure that BT can recruit and retain the people it needs by aligning reward more closely to performance and the external market.

The verdict

Results from employee surveys are encouraging, says Brady. 'They show that the rationale for the new framework is generally understood and supported. I'm very pleased with how well communication of the new reward framework worked,' he says. As many as 94 per cent of respondents reported that they received some form of briefing, while over three-quarters said they had read the *Your Guide to Reward* booklet and visited the intranet site devoted to the reward changes. The vast majority of BT managers and professionals surveyed also 'understand and support' the changes.

Kevin Brady's openness and honesty as to the successes and the challenges of BT's reward strategy journey is a fitting conclusion to this chapter, and an appropriate antidote to traditional checklists of reward strategy implementation steps. Reward strategy in reality is a marathon, not a sprint, the 'continuous cycle' that Brady refers to. Recognition of this and a realistic, long-term approach to the implementation and near-continuous review of reward strategies is vital to managing expectations about what rewards can and cannot do, and to realizing in practice the huge potential benefits of a strategic approach to reward.

11

Role of the front line manager in managing reward

In a reward symposium held by the CIPD and e-reward in July 2005, the importance of line management capability was stressed by participants throughout the day. It was generally agreed that employees experience HR policies through the way their managers interpret them, and through the management skills they apply. Problems with understanding, conviction, capability and consistency were raised, and it was a more or less universal opinion that line managers needed more training and support if they were to carry out their reward duties such as performance management or recognition effectively. Line managers have to both commit to the reward strategy and be capable of implementing it.

Research conducted by Purcell and his colleagues (2003) at Bath University established that high levels of organization performance are not achieved simply by having a range of good HR policies. What makes the difference is how 'line managers implement and enact policies, show leadership in dealing with employees and in exercising control'. Line managers are described as the 'Achilles' heel' in the delivery of contemporary HR and reward strategies. A department manager in Clerical Medical commented to the team: 'It is the quality of team leaders that is important. If they take a close interest in people and processes, it makes a big difference. You can see this by comparing my two teams.'

The trend in the UK is to devolve more responsibility for managing reward to line managers, but managers may not always do what HR professionals expect them to do and if compelled, they can be half-hearted in their response. Reward professionals can initiate new policies but it is the line that has the main responsibility for implementing them. In other words, 'HR proposes but the line disposes.'

This puts a tremendous onus on reward specialists to develop line management capability; initiate processes that can readily be implemented by line managers; promote understanding by communicating what is happening, why it is happening and how it will affect everyone; and to provide guidance, help and training where required.

Yet in the CIPD's reward survey (2005a), HR functions consulted line managers in developing their reward strategies in fewer than half of the organizations, and some did not even share the strategy with them. Hardly a recipe for effective understanding and implementation!

This is essentially an implementation issue. To a very large extent line managers have the ultimate responsibility for making things happen in all aspects of people management, especially with regard to reward. Consideration is given in this chapter first to the overall role of front line managers in putting HR policies to work, and then to their particular reward responsibilities. The chapter concludes with a discussion of what steps an organization can take to ensure that line managers have the commitment and skills they need.

OVERALL ROLE OF FRONT LINE MANAGERS

Front line managers as defined by Hutchinson and Purcell (2003) are managers who are responsible for a work group to a higher level of management, and are placed in the lower layers of management, normally at the first level. They are concerned with the day-to-day running of work rather than strategic matters and tend to have employees reporting to them who themselves do not have any management or supervisory responsibility.

However, the CIPD survey on employee well-being and the psychological contract (Guest and Conway, 2005) established that too many line managers are failing to motivate and improve the performance of people whom they manage. Under half of the respondents to the CIPD survey reported that they were regularly motivated by their line manager, only 45 per cent were happy with the level of feedback they received, and just 37 per cent said that their manager helped them to improve their performance. This supports the familiar saying that people leave managers, not organizations, and suggests that the organizations concerned were failing to get managers to understand their role in motivating people and were also failing to manage performance as effectively as they might. As the report emphasizes: 'One of the biggest challenges for HR is to support line managers in managing and developing their people.'

THE LINE MANAGER'S ROLE IN IMPLEMENTING HR POLICIES

As pointed out by Purcell *et al* (2003), high levels of organizational performance are not achieved simply by having a range of well-conceived reward policies and practices in place. What makes the difference is how these policies and practices are implemented. That is where the role of line managers in people management is crucial: 'The way line managers implement and enact policies, show leadership in dealing with employees and in exercising control comes through as a major issue.' Purcell *et al* noted that dealing with people is perhaps the aspect of their work in which line managers can exercise the greatest amount of discretion. If they use their discretion not to put HR's ideas into practice then the reward strategy rhetoric is unlikely to be converted into reality. Performance management schemes often fail because of the reluctance of managers to carry out reviews or conduct them effectively.

Another factor affecting the role of line management is their ability to do the HR tasks assigned to them. People-centred activities such as defining roles, interviewing, reviewing performance, providing feedback, coaching, identifying learning and development needs and making and communicating pay awards all require special skills. Some managers have them: many don't. Performance management and performance-related pay schemes often fail because of untrained line managers.

Further research and analysis at Bath University (Hutchinson and Purcell, 2003) confirmed that: 'The role of line managers in bringing policy to life and in leading was one of the most important of all factors in explaining the difference between success and mediocrity in people management.'

DEVOLUTION OF REWARD RESPONSIBILITIES TO LINE MANAGERS

It can be argued that the whole implementation programme for any reward initiative should be the responsibility of the line management concerned, on the grounds that it is their system and they should own it. But HR and reward specialists can play a vital part in giving guidance and help in monitoring progress. The devolution of reward responsibilities to line managers is often mainly concerned with pay decisions, as in the following examples.

Aegon UK

In Aegon, the insurance group, pay decisions have increasingly been devolved to line managers, who have been given the freedom to manage the pay of their staff in accordance with policy guidelines and within their budgets (by reference to information on market rates and relativities within their departments).

Friends Provident

The rationale behind the new approach to salary management at Friends Provident was the need to match salaries directly to the market and to give line managers greater accountability for staff salaries and career progression. Providing line managers with the means to reward the best performers was a top priority at a time when the organization was trying to change the culture from paternalism to high performance.

Lloyds TSB

Lloyds TSB has increasingly devolved pay decisions to line managers, who are given more freedom to manage the pay of their staff using relevant policy and budgetary guidelines. The HR function at Lloyds TSB had traditionally controlled the implementation of pay policies and practices. Line managers had tended to do what they were told. During the 1990s, the company gradually replaced these centralized, command and control arrangements with a system of devolved pay management. It was felt that managers who were on the spot were best equipped with the information to manage pay and rewards.

As Tim Fevyer, Senior Manager, Compensation and Benefits, explained:

> Lloyds TSB considered that the best place for making decisions about people's basic pay is where the majority of information is. Most of the information, skills and knowledge are held at the local level with the line manager. Rather than dictate pay adjustments from the centre or set pay matrices, which to a slightly lesser degree dictated adjustments from the centre, pay management decisions were devolved. Line managers were given a pot of money and were free to allocate it where the need was greatest and where circumstances dictate.

As part of this process, Lloyds TSB pursued a 'progressive phasing' policy, moving from a fixed merit matrix, via a variable matrix the following year with more flexibility for managers in the level of award they could allocate, and finally to a position where salary decisions were made and budgets held locally. The final stage in the devolution of pay decisions to line managers was the scrapping of the variable pay matrix. Line managers were given freedom to manage the pay of their staff within pay budgets held locally, following policy guidelines and referring to information on market rates and relativities within their departments supplied by HR. The system was designed to provide greater scope for progressing individual pay according to a line manager's judgement about an employee's performance, competence and contribution in relation to market trends.

Tesco

Richard Sullivan, Group Reward Manager, explained to the e-reward researcher that:

> Now our line managers have the freedom to reward performance, contribution and potential, we are going to see that they use this to produce the top class staff we need to enable Tesco to continue to succeed. With just six work levels, the new Tesco structure provides line managers with much greater flexibility to manage the career development and pay of their teams. Detailed guidelines have been issued to all line and human resource managers to help them manage pay within the new work levels.

THE VARIED REWARD RESPONSIBILITIES OF LINE MANAGERS

Pay determination is often regarded as the major area for devolving reward decisions, and ways in which this takes place are described below. But there are other important aspects of reward management that can and often should be devolved to line managers, namely: implementing a total reward policy, using performance management as a reward process in its broadest sense, and explaining reward policies and decisions.

Pay determination

Line managers are often involved in deciding on individual pay increases or awards. Examples are given below.

Aegon UK

At Aegon UK department managers make pay recommendations for all their staff within the budgets agreed for each individual business unit, which is further devolved down to line managers in some areas of the organization. The recommendations are based upon the individual's actual performance over the previous year, as evidenced by the performance management review system. In cases where the target rate has moved, the affected individual's existing salary in relation to the target rate and performance zone is also taken into consideration.

Guidance is provided to line managers on the pay review process, taking into consideration the individual's performance against his or her job description and required competences. Managers are able to make larger or smaller awards, providing there is sound basis for their decision, so that the reward system is responsive to the individual performance of each member of staff.

As each department has different reward needs – dependent upon the profile of staff within the area – there is scope for flexibility in the guideline budget at departmental level. So, a department with a high number of staff developing into their roles but under their relevant performance zone threshold, may require a higher level of pay funding than a similar department where the majority of staff are already competent and continue to perform at a competent level.

Lloyds TSB

Broad guidelines are provided by Lloyds TSB to line managers, which suggest that in making pay decisions they should consider:

▌ what the individual's current role and pay position in the salary range are;

▌ what people in the same or similar roles are being paid;

▌ how they value the individual's skills, competencies and performance in this role, relative to the nearest pay reference point;

▌ the function and geographical market rate for this role;

▌ what recent pay awards they have received;

▌ entering into a 'dialogue' about expectations – managers should talk to their people about where they are and where they could be;

▌ any other relevant factors such as the degree of challenge of the job, the amount of learning required, and their recent performance history.

Line managers are now provided with a pay pot, which could be worth, say, 3.5 per cent of the pay budget, and are free to distribute it to reflect each individual's contribution. They are supplied with details of the salaries they would be expected to pay a typical employee who is fully experienced and consistently delivers a fully effective level of performance over a sustained period of time in a given role. This illustrates where

Lloyds TSB expects them to be paid according to their skills, competencies and performance.

Additionally, managers are supplied with details of actual salaries in their department or area to enable them to make comparisons against the relevant internal market. They are also given the pay reference points for the appropriate benchmark roles. An individual may be paid at, below or above this pay reference point, depending on the contribution of his or her role relative to the nearest benchmark role, and on the individual's experience, skills and contribution in his or her particular role.

Pay decisions are made on the basis of the manager's overall budget pay pot, the market and internal equity, and they are scrutinized by the manager's manager and the HR manager for fairness and consistency. There is a perceived need to exercise control to achieve what is regarded as a proper degree of equity and consistency. Besides adherence to the pay budget, additional control is provided by careful monitoring of the distribution of pay in bands to ensure anomalies and unusual pay distributions do not occur. The structure provides line managers with much greater flexibility to manage the career development and pay of their staff: 'HR now has more of a support or consultative role rather than a decision-making role,' says Tim Fevyer.

Implementing total reward

Line managers also have a key role in implementing total reward policies, as described in detail in Chapter 1. They are the people on the spot who can recognize achievement, provide scope for individuals to develop, increase autonomy, enhance skills through coaching, create a rewarding work environment, influence the design of jobs and deal with work-life balance issues. HR and reward specialists may define what total reward means, but line managers put it into effect. Involving line managers in the development of total reward strategies (as illustrated in Chapter 9), training managers in the operation of total reward schemes and giving them appropriate online support; using them to communicate schemes to their staff – these are all ways in which reward professionals can partner line managers to deliver total reward strategies in practice.

Performance management

The only people who can make performance management work are line managers. It stands or falls on their commitment, efforts and skills. It is line managers who discuss role requirements with their staff in terms of objectives, skills and competencies, agree performance improvement programmes and take part in dialogues with individuals about their performance and learning and development needs. However, they don't always do it very well or even want to do it. In the e-reward survey of performance management in 2005 the issues most frequently mentioned by respondents were:

▌ line managers do not have the skills required – 88 per cent;

▌ line managers do not discriminate sufficiently when assessing performance – 84 per cent;

▌ line managers are not committed to performance management – 75 per cent;

▌ line managers are reluctant to conduct performance management reviews – 74 per cent.

Gaining the commitment of line managers to performance management takes a lot of time, effort and persistence but it has to be done. Here are some of the approaches that can be used.

The role of top management

Top management has a crucial role to play in implementing performance management. They have to communicate and act on the belief that performance management is an integral part of the fabric of the managerial practices of the organization. They should demonstrate their conviction that this is what good management is about and this is how managers are expected to play their part.

Communicate

The message to line managers is that managing performance is what managers are expected to do. It should come from the top and be cascaded down through the organization. It should not come from HR except, incidentally, as part of a training or induction programme. The message should be built into management development programmes, especially for potential managers. It should be understood by them from the outset that performance management is an important part of their responsibilities and that these are the skills they must acquire and use. The significance of performance management can also be conveyed by including the effectiveness with which managers carry out their performance management responsibilities as one of the criteria used when assessing their performance. Three hundred and sixty-degree appraisal systems can also help to indicate how well line managers, in reality and the eyes of their staff, are carrying out their performance management and reward responsibilities.

Keep it simple

Willing participation in performance management activities is more likely to be achieved if managers do not see it as a bureaucratic chore. Forms should be as simple as possible, no more than two sides of one piece of paper. It should be emphasized that performance management is not a form-filling exercise and that the important thing is the dialogue between managers and individuals that continues throughout the year; it is not just an annual event.

Reduce the pressure

Line managers can feel pressurized and exposed if they perceive that performance management is just about carrying out an annual appraisal meeting in which they have to tell employees where they have gone wrong, rate their performance and decide on the pay increase they should be given. This pressure can be reduced if the emphasis is on performance management throughout the year, as a continuous process. It should be regarded as part of normal good management practice that involves recognizing good work as it happens, dealing with performance problems as they arise and revising roles and objectives as required. The annual review meeting takes the form of a stocktaking exercise – no surprises – but more important, becomes a forward-looking exercise – where do we go from here?

Pressure can also be reduced if managers do not have to make and defend ratings, although they still have to reach agreement on areas for development and improvement and what needs to be done about them. A further reduction of pressure can be achieved if the emphasis in performance management is primarily forward-looking and developmental, rather than purely about performance rating and the resulting pay award.

Involve

Involve line managers in the design and development of performance management processes. They can also be involved in reviewing the effectiveness of performance management. Commitment can be enhanced by getting line managers to act as sponsors and as coaches in developing performance management skills and as mentors to managers unfamiliar with the process. The more performance management is owned by line managers the better.

Encourage

Line managers can be encouraged to believe in performance management through communities of practice – gatherings of managers during which information on good practice is exchanged. They are more likely to take notice of their peers than someone from HR. But HR can still play a useful role in encouraging managers.

An example of dealing with the line management issue

One of the respondents to the e-reward 2005 survey of performance management explained that they were dealing with this problem by:

▮ generating leadership from the top of the hierarchy to support/ encourage the need for managers to tackle poor performance head on in a fair and positive manner;

▮ getting senior management to lead by example;

▮ tackling the negative connotations associated with performance management through cultural mindset change;

▮ providing education and training on how to do this effectively;

▮ ensuring that people see the link between individual performance and overall organizational performance.

Explaining reward policies and decisions

As has been mentioned frequently in this book and will be discussed thoroughly in Chapter 13, it is vital to ensure that employees understand reward management policies in general and the reward decisions that affect them in particular. This can be done centrally by senior management and HR but it is the face-to-face contact that matters most. Line managers must be capable of providing clear explanations of policies and giving people information on their pay and benefits. Following a major revision of the reward system, BT's line managers received letters from their HR business partner for each member of their team, containing their role mapping, on-target bonus level and benefits package. Each line manager was asked to ensure that the role and job family details for each individual were correct. They then printed and presented the letter to the employee in a one-to-one session, to ensure that there was an opportunity to answer any questions that the individual may have had. The responsibility was clearly with the line manager, with background HR function support.

ENSURING THE COMMITMENT AND CAPABILITY OF LINE MANAGERS

The following suggestions were made by Hutchinson and Purcell (2003) on how generally to improve the quality of front line managers in people management:

▌ ensure they have the time to carry out their people management duties that are often superseded by other management duties;

▌ pay more attention to the behavioural competencies required when selecting them;

▌ provide them with the support of strong organizational values concerning leadership and people management;

▌ encourage the development of a good working relationship between them and their own managers;

▌ give them sufficient skills training to enable them to perform their people management activities.

In particular, the following approaches can be used to secure the commitment and improve the capability of line managers with regard to their reward management responsibilities.

Provide leadership from the top

Top management must deliver the message that managing reward and implementing a total reward policy is an integral part of the fabric of the managerial practices of the organization. They should demonstrate their conviction that this is what good management is about and this is how managers are expected to play their part.

Communicate

Simply telling line managers that reward management is a good thing will not be very productive, but the message has to reach them that they are expected to adopt a total reward approach and manage performance. The message should be built into management development programmes, especially for potential managers. It should be understood by them from the outset that this is an important part of their responsibilities and that these are the skills they must acquire and use. For example, the significance of performance management can also be conveyed by including the effectiveness with which managers carry out their performance management responsibilities as one of the criteria used when assessing their performance.

Don't over-engineer

Reward management processes should not be over-engineered, neither should they be designed to require knowledge and skills that line managers are unlikely to possess or be able to develop. The design of the reward system should always take into account what line managers will have to do to implement it.

Provide clear guidelines

Managers should know exactly what is expected of them. In the case of pay reviews they should know how to interpret the review guidelines and the pay data they will be given and understand the principles they should follow in making recommendations on pay increases. By developing clear principles, Diageo ensures that when line managers are faced with choices, the right decisions will be more obvious. As a result, 'less demand will be placed on reward experts in the business, who can spend more of their time on value creating enhancements to our processes, plans and communications,' says Nicki Demby, Performance and Reward Director.

Involve

Develop ownership and commitment by involving line managers in the design and development of reward management processes as members of project teams or by taking part in pilot studies. This could be extended by the use of focus groups and general surveys of opinions and reactions.

A major Scottish financial services group extensively involved a team of 30 line managers from all parts of the company in developing a new reward strategy and more market- and performance-focused approach. The new system was pilot tested in the marketing department and then progressively rolled out across the organization, drawing out and spreading key learning points and improvements as they went along. In a pharmaceutical company, a team of line managers were trained as coaches to assist their colleagues in managing the new pay system, generating enormous credibility and ensuring successful implementation.

Brief and train

Line managers need to be briefed thoroughly on the procedures they should follow and trained in their use. Formal training is necessary in the performance management skills managers need to use such as preparing role profiles, defining objectives, giving and receiving feedback, taking part in review meetings, identifying learning needs, and preparing and implementing personal development plans and coaching.

Formal training should take place when launching new reward processes but, importantly, also during management development programmes for potential managers and induction programmes for new managers. Coaching and guidance for individual managers should be provided to supplement formal training. This can be given by HR specialists although, better still, experienced, committed and competent line managers can be used as coaches and mentors.

Provide personal support

Do not expect that reward management will come naturally to line managers. They need support. As one head of reward told us: 'I had to do a lot of hand holding when we introduced our new pay structure.' This should be provided by HR supplemented by mentors. Paradoxically, devolving reward responsibilities to line managers increases rather than decreases the onus on HR to help make it work. Individual coaching and guidance needs to be provided, especially on the introduction of new reward practices and for newly appointed managers.

Provide systems support

Systems support for line managers in conducting pay reviews can be provided by information technology. In a financial sector company, technology is used to move the reward function away from a salary administration role – preparing for mid-year and year-end performance management reviews – to a function with a much more dynamic approach to reward management. The company has purchased a software application from Link Consultants, which helps it to develop an in-depth compensation reward modelling capability and put more decisions in the hands of line managers. The pay review modelling software enables the company to develop performance matrices for deployment to line managers and generate reports analysing the distribution of pay by almost any variable, to assist in managing and auditing the reward system. These reports are standardized across the business and provided to the managers responsible for pay decisions.

Spreadsheets can be developed, as at Bass Brewers, which provide managers with the data they need on the distribution of pay amongst their staff and on market rates, and enable them to model alternative distributions of awards and, after a series of 'what ifs', achieve the optimum distribution of their pay review budget to individuals. However, technology should be used to support, rather than replace the crucial role of line managers in putting reward strategies into practice.

The common difficulties we have seen in this chapter with line managers exercising these responsibilities should be enough to make reward professionals think more deeply before putting the simple statement of 'line management ownership' as an objective in their reward strategies. The steps to overcoming these implementation issues are themselves surprisingly simple and obvious to state – training, involvement and so on – but much, much more difficult to deliver on.

Yet the evolving approach to reward strategy we are profiling in this book at least goes beyond the confines of the HR function to acknowledge and address the critical role of line managers in effective reward management. As Nicki Demby described it and as we detail in the next chapter, effective partnering with the line is critical to reward professionals effectively carrying out all aspects of their multiple and shifting roles.

12

The strategic and multiple roles of the reward professional

Go to any reward conference or read any book or magazine on compensation and benefits issues and the content is overwhelmingly concerned with the technical design of schemes. The historic focus of the training and development of reward professionals has displayed a similar emphasis. When we started to specialize in the area many years ago, the training courses we attended focused on numbers and financials, painting a picture of a complex and impenetrable science or 'black art', with detailed rules, procedures and formulas. For many of those starting out in the profession today the picture may not be dissimilar, and the reward option in the CIPD's professional development scheme was never one of the most popular.

In our discussions with reward executives as part of our research for this book a similar bias was often evident. They would wax lyrical about what the latest legislative changes mean for executive share plans or maternity pay, how they are responding to pension plan deficits, what the outlook is for pay budgets and inflation, and so on. But when we raised the issue of the role they personally play, the competencies they need and the requirements for success, an element of reticence, even shyness seemed to be evident. Was this indicative of natural British modesty at their increasing impact, or reflective of a deeper-seated worry about their changing role and contribution?

Ironically, the one theme universally mentioned when we forced them to talk about their work and roles, aside from the increasing volume and challenge, was that of the shift from purely administrative and design work to a more strategic role for them and the whole HR function in their organization, which this book has primarily been concerned with. According to Paul Bissell, Senior Manager Rewards at Nationwide, 'organizations are realizing what a powerful lever reward is and how it needs to complement their business strategies, whereas historically people have tended to view it in glorious isolation.' A number mentioned the change in their title, from compensation and benefits to reward heads and managers as illustrative of the shift to a more strategic, integrated and holistic perspective.

The concept of this strategically contributing role for reward and HR professionals is not new, of course. In the mid 1990s Dave Ulrich, Professor of Business at Michigan University, defined his highly influential framework of four roles that HR functions needed to play in the future to deliver high added value, most famously that of strategic partner to the business (Ulrich, 1997). Look through any list of HR job vacancies today and 'HR business partners' are clearly in demand.

Do these developments represent a huge opportunity or a threat? The CIPD's latest study of career experiences and aspirations amongst HR and reward professionals reveals a degree of concern about 'over-specialization' in areas such as reward, with one individual lamenting the 'long hours, little reward and recognition' in his own reward job (CIPD, 2005e). Other studies highlight the continuing focus, in reality, of reward staff on the traditional technical and administrative tasks.

So just how has the concept of strategic HRM and the business partnering role impacted on the work of compensation and benefits specialists? Are they being elevated to greater boardroom impact or being outsourced into oblivion? How are they adding most value, where are they focusing their efforts and what do they need to do more and less of? What are the main changes in the roles they play in contemporary organizations? What are the key requirements and competencies required in these roles to be successful?

In this chapter we describe the responses to such questions that have resulted from our research. The picture that emerges today is of a future for reward practitioners that certainly looks ever busier, more complex and challenging. Yet it also highlights the tremendous growth, impact and opportunities for the profession and the vast range of ways in which we can and are using reward expertise to positively influence the strategic direction and success of organizations. As one of the CIPD's survey respondents expressed it, their work on compensation issues represents for them 'the most rewarding career'.

MORE DEMAND, MORE PEOPLE, MORE STRATEGIES

Given some of the reward challenges and activities that we have described in the rest of this book, it is perhaps not surprising that there has been a significant growth in the demand for and numbers of reward specialists in UK organizations in recent years. In the private sector, recruitment and skill shortages have pushed the resourcing, reward and retention of talented employees up to the top of the concerns of chief executives, according to a recent global survey by Accenture (Berry, 2005).

With a raft of new bonus and reward schemes to operate, BOC Gases now has a team of five compensation and benefits specialists servicing its UK workforce of 6,000 from their HR service centre (Arkin, 2005). There was none when it was set up five years ago. Bissell's team at Nationwide has grown from three to 11 in the past five years, as the range and complexity of rewards offered by the winner of *The Sunday Times* Best Large Employer to Work For survey has spread.

In the public sector, the modernization and reform agenda in central government, the implementation of the local government single status agreement, the new pay framework in higher education and Agenda for Change pay reforms in the NHS all present an enormous reward agenda, as well as giving individual organizations more responsibility for determining the pay arrangements of staff than in the past. Geoff White from the University of Greenwich explains, 'National agreements are more flexible and can be interpreted more at the level of the institution – providing it has the necessary expertise.'

In the voluntary sector Peter Geoffrey, HR director at St Mungo's charity for the homeless, sees a more demanding and competitive environment forcing 'more focus on performance' and moves away from often public-sector-derived arrangements (Arkin, 2005). St Mungo's is introducing job evaluation and a new pay structure, along with contribution-related pay progression.

Across all parts of the economy therefore, it is perhaps not surprising that 41 per cent of the 500 organizations in the CIPD's reward management survey (2005a) have increased the numbers of rewards specialists they employ in the past three years, to an average of six full-time staff (see Figures 12.1 and 12.2). A third of these organizations have a distinct reward function or department, with HR generalists managing reward issues in the remainder. That proportion is higher in the private sector (42 per cent) and in the largest organizations, with seven out of 10 employing over 5,000 staff having a specialist function.

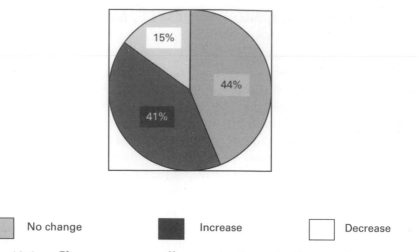

| | No change | | Increase | | Decrease |

Figure 12.1 Changes across all organizations in the employment of reward specialists in the UK, 2002–2005

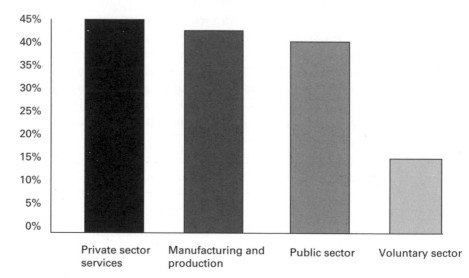

Figure 12.2 Changes in the employment of reward specialists in the UK, 2002–2005, analysed by sector

This demand is also evident in the pay levels for reward specialists, both inside and outside of major employers. Far from being a restricted backwater and career dead-end, the CIPD's data shows that it is increasingly financially rewarding to be in reward. The average base pay for a rewards manager in their annual survey is £50,000, representing a premium of 30 per cent over the pay of equivalently experienced and qualified HR generalists. Movement into often higher paying external consultancy roles is also on the increase, with a tenth of those in the CIPD's HR careers study now working for consultancies, and 15 per cent of employers in the reward management survey using external consultants to work on aspects of their reward strategies.

The agenda for this expansion is unashamedly strategic, with a focus on total rewards, major pay systems overhaul, employee engagement, and the other strategic issues highlighted in this book. Most reward functions deal with the complete range of pay, benefits and recognition activities and, as Malcolm Douglas, BAT's remuneration and benefits manager explains, the core purpose is achieving business alignment, addressing questions such as, 'If these things are important to the business, why aren't we rewarding them?' Reward strategy and business alignment are at the top of the agendas of reward professionals in the CIPD survey, and well over half of them have such strategies in place. A survey of Watson Wyatt's Reward Network participants demonstrated an increasing focus on rewarding performance and total rewards, with less emphasis on administration, tax and National Insurance type issues.

In terms of the roles HR and reward professionals are playing in delivering this agenda, the priority is therefore on being a strategic business partner, which is the current focus for over half of functional heads in the CIPD's most recent study of the HR function (CIPD, 2003b). Regarding the other roles defined by Ulrich, being an agent of change is the priority for almost a third, while only a quarter and 12 per cent respectively see their priority role as being administrative experts and employee champions (see Figure 12.3).

Strategic partner	Change agent
Management of strategic human resources to execute business strategy	Building the capacity for change to create a renewed organization
• Current priority role 56%	• Current priority role 28%
• Future priority role 73%	• Future priority role 30%
Administrative expert	**Employee champion**
Building an efficient infrastructure of HR processes	Increasing employee commitment and capability
• Current priority role 24%	• Current priority role 12%
• Future priority role 4%	• Future priority role 6%

Figure 12.3 The focus of HR roles in UK organizations (source CIPD, 2003b, based on Ulrich, 1997)

Some proponents of the strategic role for HR and reward professionals see it in black-and-white terms. Thomas Stewart, editor of the *Harvard Business Review*, described it a decade ago as a simple choice: 'HR has come to the proverbial fork-in-the-road. One leads to a highly automated service operation, the other leads straight to the CEO's office' (Stewart, 1996).

Using this type of 'either/or' interpretation, there are some worrying indications as to just how effectively reward professionals are actually playing a strategic, business-impacting role, as opposed to their more traditional technical design, administrative and reactive one. The clearest evidence of this is in the apparent mismatch between what they see as being their most important and value enhancing activities, and how they actually spend their time, as shown in the CIPD reward survey responses (see Figure 12.4).

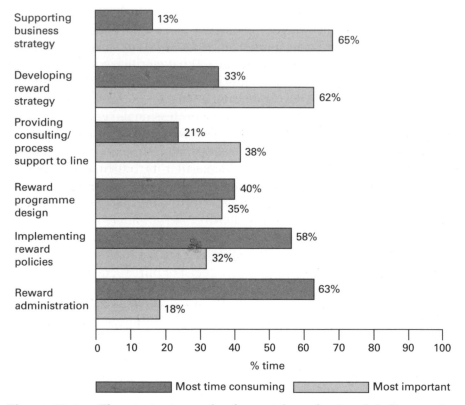

Figure 12.4 The strategic work of reward professionals? Contrasting their most important and time-consuming activities

The most valuable activities are clearly in developing reward arrangements that support the business strategy and working with line managers as consultants to support this: 'Shifting our culture to a more performance-oriented business and aligning reward policies accordingly', as one head of compensation in the survey put it. Yet significant portions of the function's time are still being absorbed in routine administrative activities and responding to immediate queries and crises.

The evidence we have considered in other chapters regarding the difficulties in actually implementing and realizing their reward strategies, which a majority of organizations own up to in the CIPD's research, also might suggest that many rewards professionals have taken the 'wrong' fork of Stewart's road. The implementation problems rarely seem to be to do with an inappropriate strategy or scheme selection, but more often are about the processes of making changes actually happen: of improving line managers' skills and commitment to making pay decisions; of helping employees to understand and trust decisions and changes to their rewards.

Some commentators are highly critical. Purcell (1999) characterizes many reward strategies as well-presented plans that don't relate to the reality of what goes on in the organization and what reward professionals actually do. Zingheim and Schuster (2002) have criticized total rewards strategies in North America for simply creating a vast array of benefits and increasing costs, with no corresponding impact on performance.

As we have seen, many HR and reward professionals report difficulties in actually performing their strategic roles. One study found that only 40 per cent of HR department reorganizations were successful, and another revealed commonly experienced problems after introducing HR business partners, such as releasing enough time to focus on the genuinely strategic, and actually having enough staff with the formidable list of required competencies to play such roles (CIPD, 2004b).

Yet these issues are hardly surprising. The reality of organizational life today is far too fast-changing and complex to make the simplistic option of strategic or non-strategic activity, strategist or bureaucrat, presented by Stewart a decade ago a realistic or possible way forward for reward functions. Reward professionals can't suddenly drop all of their traditional work to focus exclusively on the boardroom and business strategy. Of course, bonus decisions need to be made and coordinated, market data gathered and reviewed, pay reviews conducted and administered, remuneration committees serviced, legislation and immediate disputes responded to, payrolls run and so on.

Indeed the leading business thinkers today paint a picture of business strategy not as a fixed long-term plan developed in the boardroom, but an emergent, dynamic and adaptive process occurring throughout the organization. Professor Charles O'Reilly at Stanford refers to the ambidextrous organization, while Linda Holbeche similarly characterizes strategic management as dealing with complexity and contradictions, combining multiple goals and tasks to try to achieve the 'dynamic stability' underpinning high performance (Holbeche, 2005). The same is true of effective reward and HR strategies and the professionals responsible for them.

Ulrich in fact always emphasized that his four defined roles all represent ways in which HR functions can potentially add value to the organization and partner with the business, and that they must 'learn to be both strategic and operational, focusing on the long and the short term' in order to be successful (Ulrich, 1997). His updated version of the model (Ulrich and Brockbank, 2005a) emphasizes that HR functions in reality have a 'cacophony of roles' that they need to perform. Building the personal credibility needed to play a genuinely strategic role in partnership with line managers depends on carrying out activities such as pay and benefits administration effectively and efficiently, for example.

This is very much the message that reward managers have given us during the research for this book. When Peter Christie asked Watson Wyatt's network of heads of reward to draw a picture of their current roles on a flipchart, they drew an octopus, illustrating the diverse and multifunctional roles and activities performed by their functions, with 'tentacles' engaged in an increasingly wide range of activities through all parts of the organization. They had no fears of lack of strategic business impact because of this, and were well aware of the research described in this book, demonstrating the links between good people and reward management and business performance.

Rather than justifying the existence of their in-demand and growing functions, or removing the administrative component, the key challenge for these senior rewards practitioners appears to be that of becoming slightly more focused and 'shark-like', providing a clearer and more consistent, better coordinated, comprehended and supported direction to their necessarily varied diet of activities, and building the multiple skill sets in their departments required to deliver them.

Quite a number of HR and reward functions in large multinationals we know are now moving on a global or regional basis to a structure that represents a simplified 'three-legged' version of Ulrich's model, to help to try to achieve this sharpening. It comprises:

▮ an administrative outsourced or in-house shared service operation, to administer transactional processes such as bonuses and payroll and related queries as efficiently as possible;

▮ technical centres of expertise, setting out reward policies and acting as internal reward experts and consultants in assessing and designing reward 'solutions' to meet business needs;

▮ business partners and change agents, working with directors and line managers to develop the strategic vision and then effectively deliver these reward strategies into practice, so as to deliver business results through improved people and reward management.

Reward professionals are playing a vital role in each of these three areas and all of them have a strategic dimension. We move on to consider the common components of each one in turn, and finally the competencies and skills that are required to perform them and how they can be developed.

REWARD PROFESSIONALS AS ADMINISTRATIVE AND IT EXPERTS

We learnt early in our careers the importance of cost-efficient and error-free reward administration processes and the costs that can be incurred, for example by the inclusion of a few rogue noughts in notifications of redundancy payments. This role is just as important in today's faster-moving and more complex organizations, although thankfully we typically have a lot more computing and IT power at our disposal to help deliver these goals.

Standard Chartered Bank runs its own HR service centre in Chennai in southern India. From here the payrolls of over half of the bank's 33,000 employees across 56 countries are administered, as well as 27 pension plans, all of their employee share schemes and the administration for internationally mobile staff. The emphasis is on using single, standardized processes wherever possible, delivered via web-enabled technology. The centre has been highly successful in achieving the objectives of cost reduction, but also improved quality of HR service (there is an associated enquiry contact centre) and liberating the HR and reward functions to engage in higher value-adding activities (Scott-Jackson, 2005).

Reward applications such as payroll were of course some of the earliest applications for IT systems in large organizations, as well as more recently of the phenomenon of HR service outsourcing. Seventy-seven per cent of UK organizations across all sectors have an HR information system (HRIS) according to the CIPD's survey (CIPD, 2005f), and reward applications are some of the most common functions. The technology is moving rapidly, and 40 per cent anticipate that they will change or modify their HRIS in the next two years.

When considering the role of reward professionals in this field, the emphasis tends to be placed on the objective of cost saving and the need for technology skills and understanding to achieve this. The HR competency toolkit developed by SHRM and the University of Michigan, for example, has HR technology as one of its five components (Cohen, 2005). Such knowledge is essential for a wide range of reward tasks, from selecting the most appropriate external systems to purchase, through to gathering and manipulating external pay survey data and administering computerized job evaluations.

A key obstacle to the achievement of the cost-saving objective at present appears to be the preponderance in almost two-thirds of organizations of stand-alone systems covering different applications, for example pay review administration, performance management and so on, which are not integrated with each other or the wider IT systems across the organization. They were presumably often bought reactively to meet a specific need without considering the wider organizational picture. In the proposed changes they want to make, participants in the CIPD survey see improved integration as a key requirement, as well as in some cases moving to fewer administration centres to realize economies of scale, as Standard Chartered has done.

Customizing and tailoring systems to better suit the specific needs of the organization is also an important objective of future upgrades and system changes, illustrating the mix of strategic and operational roles in this area. The lack of fit of off-the-shelf systems was a common complaint in the survey.

Reward professionals are also increasingly using technology to help improve communication and partnering with line managers and their employees in the business, as well as to save costs and free up their valuable time. Seventy per cent of organizations now have an intranet, typically used to provide a whole range of information on reward and HR policies to staff. There may also be specific and restricted information for line managers, for example to help them model and cost pay review awards for their staff, or work out the potential value of their share options. BG Group, working with external partners, recently introduced a new system to calculate the value and taxation of expatriates' share awards, reducing administration costs by 60 per cent (Lovewell, 2005a).

Also rapidly growing are HR self-service applications for tasks such as personal records updating and flexible benefits selection, illustrating this dual agenda of greater efficiency but also improving communication and relationships.

Rather than simply systems knowledge and IT skills therefore, even in this apparently administrative role, as Paul Bissell at Nationwide told us: 'The ability to communicate is at the core of reward work these days, the maker or breaker of everything.' For example, the potential advantages of a flexible benefits system can be lost, however excellent the components and the IT system, if staff fail to understand and appreciate it and the take up is low. Outsourcing provider Vertex created an internal HR service centre and implemented HRPlus, a dedicated area on the intranet to carry reward and HR policies and guidelines and incorporating various elements of employee self-service (*Personnel Today*, 2005). HR staff worked with the communication team to launch an education campaign briefing nearly 6,000 staff, enabling the system to achieve its target savings and supporting the desired shift in HR staff work from transactional to more strategic.

Following Aon Insurance's successful implementation of a flex scheme for its own staff, reward director Michael Rose also emphasizes the importance of relationship and project management skills (Stibbe, 2005). As well as some of its own consultancy's reward and benefits experts, the cross-divisional project development team included IT staff, lawyers and the firm's tax director to deal with the Inland Revenue.

The same appears to be true of outsourced reward administration services. Scott-Jackson's (2005) research demonstrates that the extent of HR service outsourcing has actually been exaggerated, and again, it is nothing new for reward professionals, who for many years have dealt with external suppliers and consultants, both to add expertise and save costs.

A key conclusion of his research is that the assumption that you can save costs and improve service levels by simply handing over your poor reward administration processes to someone else is a false and dangerous one. As Randal Tajer at UBS warns, 'don't outsource what you don't understand' (Scott-Jackson, 2005). Following a well-planned and managed process, from building a strong understanding and case for change, through developing and comparing in-house and outsourced options for improvement, to selecting the most appropriate and working with relevant partners to deliver it, is essential. As Jeremy Arwas of BT sees it, reflecting on its massive outsourcing deal with Accenture, 'everything is sortable if the relationship is good.' BT claims administrative cost savings of more than 30 per cent.

TECHNICAL EXPERTISE: THE ROLE OF STRATEGIC CRAFTSPERSON

According to Gautam Ghosh, 'HR people can no longer make choices about whether they will be business generalists or technical specialists in the organization; they have to be both' (Kearns, 2003). The heads of reward functions we have interviewed very much supported this view.

Ulrich's highly influential original framework of HR roles was criticized by some commentators for downplaying the importance of technical knowledge and expertise in areas such as compensation and benefits, describing them more as 'needed to play' than 'needed to win' competencies. Yet in his more recent updating, Ulrich specifies a new value-adding role of functional expert. He explains: 'By mastering the concepts and research for foundation HR practices and ensuring their alignment with key business priorities, HR professionals will optimize their impact on business performance (Ulrich and Brockbank, 2005a).

Our senior reward interviewees regard their technical expertise as a continuing and vital component of their role, both in terms of time spent and business added value. It explains much of the recent growth in the size of HR functions in the UK, with 37 per cent of organizations having recruited more technical specialists in the last three years. Keeping up to date with technical knowledge and trends in areas such as reward was also regarded as important for HR generalists and business partners in the CIPD's study of what makes for effectiveness in the latter role.

Rolling out a flexible benefits plan for thousands of managers across multiple countries and tax jurisdictions in a multinational consumer goods firm, or implementing a new common grading structure and skills-related progression system for over 1 million employees under Agenda for Change within the National Health Service; these and many other current examples represent major technical design challenges for the reward professionals leading them, who are increasing their worth, power and influence as a result.

Such initiatives are also the key to progressing the strategic agenda and business goals in these organizations – of increased growth, improved profits, better service levels, culture change and so on. Our discussions with reward professionals about the technical design aspects of their work have highlighted a major evolution in the way they are being carried out and the skills and knowledge required to succeed. They are becoming more strategic in a number of senses.

First, as we have seen in earlier chapters, whereas in the past many compensation and benefits specialists could concentrate just on one aspect of reward, such as pay or pensions, today the emphasis is on 'lateral integration' and total rewards, in order to create a totally rewarding environment in which staff commit to delivering high performance and are rewarded as a result. Knowledge and integration, not just across the entire reward field but also people management as a whole, is essential. HR functions are having to break down the traditional functional 'silos' between, for example, pay and training roles to achieve this.

At retailer Harvey Nichols (Sloman, 2005), Training Manager Karen McKibben rejected a generic training course to improve the skills of sales assistants, recognizing the dangers of being over-prescriptive and failing to address the crucial issue of the motivation of staff to learn and improve. Instead it introduced the Brand Champion approach, involving the immediate allocation of recognition awards to staff who demonstrate that they are living the company's values, and providing specialist advisers and high performing 'buddies' to help those not doing so well. Is it a training or a reward initiative? Who cares, as long as staff satisfaction and customer service improve.

Similarly, many compensation and reward professionals essentially left pensions as a distinct field for the actuaries and specialists to determine and administer. No longer. As Otto Thoresen, the chief executive of Aegon UK explains, current trends in pension scheme design reflect a much wider set of issues, such as the shift in resourcing approaches and diversity policies required to address the aging workforce, as well as the financial risks, that are crucial to the survival and success of employers over the next 30 years. Reward professionals and advisers have to help their organization 'think through how they are going to adapt their whole philosophy for the development of people', rather than just deal with 'the narrower issue of what their employee benefits package should look like' (Bolger, 2005). To give another example in terms of the theoretical underpinnings of their work, while economists and psychologists may never communicate with each other, reward professionals need a good understanding of both disciplines to inform their work.

Second, as with any effective business strategy, reward strategies and the schemes within them have to reflect a good understanding of the external context and environment, as well as of internal conditions and resources. Traditionally reward professionals may have had good information on the pay rates in other organizations, but in some cases they were much less aware of the different approaches evident in areas such as variable and bonus pay, or international reward approaches. Now, Ulrich defines 'knowing external realities' as the first of his HR value propositions (Ulrich and Brockbank, 2005), and a full knowledge of the range of possibilities for technical reward 'solutions' to business and motivational issues is a critical requirement of the technical reward role.

This technical design role today, however, is definitely not one of copying supposed 'best practice' from outside, and carrying out isolated design work on paper and computer screen. As Guest (2000) puts it, reward and HR practices developed in 'laboratory-like isolation' are never going to work effectively.

Competitive and organizational success is delivered not by copying but by differentiating, by tailoring design arrangements to suit the goals and character of each employer and its workforce, of delivering 'best fit' not 'best practice', which is the third aspect of a more strategic design role. It is why business understanding and awareness are every bit as important today for the reward professional as their technical knowledge of pay and benefits schemes.

At a recent e-reward/CIPD conference, Helen Murlis characterized this critical role as that of the technical design craftsman, expert in all the techniques of pay and reward, knowing all the possibilities and the potential of their craft, and then designing something unique to meet the exact needs of the user, rather than 'banging' out standard products on the performance pay or broad-banding production line.

Hence, as described earlier in this book, we are increasingly seeing tailored and hybrid reward schemes operating in organizations in place of unthinking and over-generalized design formats, with, for example in pay structure design, job families overlaid on to broad pay bands, as at IBM; fixed pay rates with variable performance and retention-related top ups, as at Pret A Manger; and over 3,000 hybrid pension plans in the UK with more than 300,000 members (an example might be a defined contribution scheme with a defined benefit underpin on pay rates up to a certain level).

Fourthly, design work is becoming more strategic in that it does not stop with the implementation of schemes. Reward professionals today are placing a much stronger emphasis on defining clear objectives and goals for reward schemes, and then measuring and reviewing their effectiveness in achieving these. Historically, too many executive incentive plans, for example, have had no clear goal beyond a vague rationale to 'match the market' and no demonstrable return evident on the costs of payments. As Ulrich writes, 'to create value, HR professionals must begin not by focusing on activities but by defining the deliverables' (Ulrich and Brockbank, 2005b).

The current range of measures being used to assess the effectiveness of reward schemes is illustrated in Figure 12.5. There has been much progress in the field in recent years, encouraged by the increasing use internally of broad scorecards of performance, and externally by the demands to report a broader range of non-financial performance information to external stakeholders. The CIPD's latest reward survey shows that two-thirds of organizations do now try to assess how effective their reward arrangements are, with surveys of staff attitudes and satisfaction being the primary method for doing so.

Around a third of them attempt to relate the success of reward schemes and changes to common measures of HR performance such as labour turnover, recruitment acceptance rates and absenteeism. The Royal Mail, for example, reduced absence by 11 per cent after the introduction of its attendance bonus scheme in 2004, and GAP tripled employee participation rates in its pension plan after a redesign and communication exercise. Fewer organizations currently conduct cost-benefit analyses and can relate their reward initiatives to overall productivity and performance, but the progress at firms such as Nationwide in modelling customer, financial and reward variables illustrates the potential.

The evolution in the technical reward role illustrates that reward design now is based on a fundamentally different premise from the past. Technical reward knowledge is essential for reward professionals: the job simply cannot be done without it. But rather than reward design work being

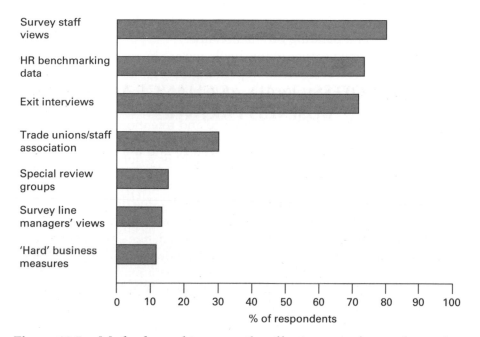

Figure 12.5 Methods used to assess the effectiveness of reward practices and changes

regarded as an engineering science based on the assumption of design perfection, of developing a clock-type mechanism that you can implement and let run for ever more, the approach now is a biological and organic one, of introducing schemes that interact with the environment in which they operate and need to evolve in conjunction with them. Change is assumed and essential rather than being regarded as failure. As Will Astill, Reward Manager at B&Q, told us: 'Always evaluate the effectiveness of programmes, generally making improvements over a number of years.'

Dennis (2005) describes how at building society Britannia, Philippa Harrison led an exercise in 2002 which introduced broad pay bands to address the inflexibility and unhealthy emphasis on hierarchy that existed in job design and pay arrangements. The initiative has been successful in supporting more flexible working and roles and greater pay transparency internally. Reviews in 2004/5 have led to further changes and improvements, changing the job evaluation approach and introducing a more accurate market fix for roles within the bands, to help staff and managers work with the structure.

In fact, initiatives such as Agenda for Change in the NHS are much more than just technical design exercises, representing major organizational changes in their own right, and needing to be managed as such. The reward roles and competencies regarded by senior reward professionals today as their highest adding-value work are those of change leadership and management.

REWARD PROFESSIONALS AS CHANGE AGENTS AND BUSINESS PARTNERS

The core thesis of this book is that we need to and are seeing a shift in contemporary reward strategies and activities from planning to process, from intent to implementation, which is essential if reward professionals are to realize in practice the full potential added-value of their work.

Successfully implementing, say, a flexible benefits plan, of course represents a technical design and administrative challenge – what benefits to include, how much choice to give employees, how to manage enrolment and updating, and so on. But key challenges and a really crucial role of reward professionals appear to lie in managing and influencing the process of implementation and operation – how to communicate the plan and educate employees, how to secure senior management approval and support, how to develop and retain line manager understanding and support, negotiating the detail with trade unions.

Such reward schemes cannot be technical ends in themselves but the means to an end, which ultimately is the creation of, as Pfeffer (1998) puts it: 'A fun challenging environment in which individuals are able to use their abilities, are shown appreciation... (and) enhance motivation, building their discretionary commitment that will drive the success of the organization.' Creating such an environment takes far longer, and puts a much more challenging set of demands on the reward professional than just designing a few schemes, but it is where their true added-value lies.

The CIPD's research on the competencies underpinning successful HR departments in multinational companies brought out the technical knowledge required in disciplines such as compensation, and the importance of business and contextual knowledge and understanding (Sparrow *et al*, 2004). But the key differentiating competencies were the high-level process and political skills, of cultural sensitivity and diversity management, managing uncertainty and conflict, playing the diplomat and consultant. One HR director described his role as 'getting people together from across the business and making things happen, getting big ideas to come alive'. The Michigan HR competency studies have similarly highlighted the significance of the ability to manage change and culture.

Thus any reward redesign exercise needs to be managed, as Kevin Brady, Reward and ER Director at BT puts it, 'as a change management exercise, not a reward change'. In implementing a wide range of reward changes, including a new pay structure and progression system at BT, the key points he highlighted at a recent conference were about managing the process of change, such as the importance of business and line sponsorship and ownership; not underestimating staff resistance; good project management; setting an appropriate speed of change related to the resources devoted to it; and communicating and engaging extensively with line managers and staff.

John Campbell, HR Vice President for Citigroup, emphasizes the multiple, octopus-like requirements of the European regional compensation roles that he manages. They need to provide line managers with reliable external market data, set guidelines for and help to administer and police the merit review and annual bonus processes, design new bonus schemes and so on. Technical design skills are essential. But he sees their key contribution being as internal consultants and business partners:

▌ bringing parties together to facilitate and make sustainable and effective decisions;

▌ sharing experiences and transferring successes, while tailoring and adapting to local needs;

▌ encouraging a focus on long-term sustainability and future development;

▌ managing and coordinating communications;

▌ having the cultural sensitivity to successfully build relationships and teamwork based on trust and respect.

Above all, as he describes it, he needs in these jobs 'confident, bright people who can inform thinking, gain credibility, understand change, and move the business agenda along in a collaborative but influential role'. It is no use reward professionals just being 'strategic' in their thinking, any more than that they can only design schemes on paper. They are equally concerned with service delivery – in the words of Professor Guest, they must 'deliver the deal' and make things happen in practice.

The link with line and business managers is of course key from a number of standpoints, so key in fact that Ulrich's latest version of his value-adding HR roles framework merges the two formerly distinct roles of change agent and strategic partner, so intertwined have they proved to be. Some organizations pursuing the model of distinct technical reward experts and HR business partners, who are solely responsible for the relationship with the line, have found that it can create implementation issues. For example, there can be problems if the technical experts develop their flex benefits plan in isolation with external consultants, and then simply pass it on to the internal business partners and their teams to worry about implementation.

Seamus Elliot, HR Director at the East Anglian Ambulance Trust, trained all his HR managers and staff representatives in reward management to assist with the implementation of a new set of employment terms and conditions (Arkin, 2005). More widely, Sandy Wilson, head of policy and reward at Norwich Union Life, told the CIPD Reward Conference how the company had put all 600 staff managers through a two-day training exercise in the new pay review process, to support its effective operation. As he explained: 'Line managers need to live and breathe it, they need to own it and realize how important it is to the business strategy to make it work. If they don't make it work we're scuppered' (see Chapter 11).

The knowledge transfer required for effective partnering is therefore a two-way process. Reward managers have to understand the business context and dynamics, and forge strong personal relationships with line managers if they are to play the business partner and change agent role effectively. As Purcell and his colleagues (2003) put it, 'line managers implement and enact policies'. In fact, a quarter of UK HR departments have recruited from other functions, particularly general management, in the last three years, to help forge a stronger partnership of HR and business management expertise. The line managers correspondingly need to understand and fulfil their responsibilities in reward management, not only to make reward strategies operate in practice, but also to deliver their broader resource and change management roles and function.

Professor Richard Whittington's recent research into major organizational restructuring found that lack of attention to HR processes such as reward and lack of involvement of HR professionals were primary contributors to failure (CIPD, 2004c). Almost two-thirds of the participants said that in future they would pay more attention to the potential effects on rewards systems before undertaking major organization redesigns. In fact, a quarter of HR functions in the UK now have the lead role for organization design and change management in their employers.

REWARD PROFESSIONALS' ROLES, SKILLS AND LEARNING

In summary, therefore, working with line managers in navigating and negotiating their way through the cultural complexities of their employers is clearly a critical, demanding but highly valuable role and set of skills for reward professionals, and helps to explain the pay premium they demand in the UK. Technical design knowledge is essential but no longer sufficient. Copying a reward scheme design from a textbook is relatively straightforward, but working with managers and employees in real life to accept it, implement it and operate it so as to demonstrably deliver the intended motivational and business benefits – that appears to be where the real value-added of the function lies in the future.

Our evidence from senior reward professionals in the UK paints a positive future for the function. There are more of us with more diverse, challenging, changing but also more impacting roles. The multi-legged roles and skill sets required of reward functions are a necessary reality of organizational complexity and life today.

Administrative and technical design skills and knowledge remain critical to effective performance, and we have described the ways in which these roles have evolved. We can no more claim an exclusive boardroom positioning in the strategic partner role than we should retreat back into a historic, tactical and bureaucratic control function. But these skills have to be married with a wider understanding of the strategic business and cultural context. Ultimately the HR and reward function's highest potential contribution to their employers appears to be in making strategy happen.

This dual agenda of technical knowledge and wider business and strategic understanding and perspective is at the heart of the CIPD's new Advanced Certificate in Reward Management. Reward training today has to focus on technical design in the context of business and cultural diagnosis and fit, rather than isolated pay formulas and procedures. The SHRM/University of Michigan HR competency toolkit similarly highlights HR technical and business knowledge, as well as strategic thinking and HR technology skills, for HR to perform its value-adding roles effectively (Cohen, 2005).

The third crucial component, underpinning the personal credibility competency in the five-fold SHRM model, is the area of personal relationship, process and change management skills. The CIPD's (2003b) study of staff in HR and reward functions reveals these high level change management, consulting and influencing/process management skills as being the most important for future success as illustrated in Figure 12.6. Such skills certainly can't just be developed in the classroom.

Angela O'Connor, director of HR for the Crown Prosecution Service, has led a major and successful restructuring of her own function. All staff have a personal development plan, and the development framework for the reward and HR staff encompasses:

▌ technical and specialist knowledge and professional competence;

▌ business knowledge;

▌ team building across the function;

▌ personal and management and leadership skills.

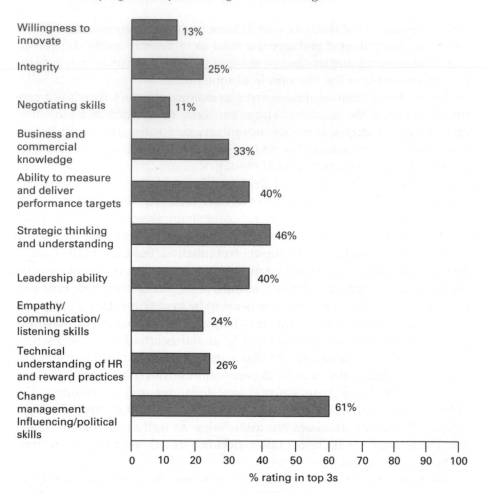

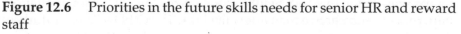

Figure 12.6 Priorities in the future skills needs for senior HR and reward staff

These skills, behaviours and knowledge are developed through a wide variety of learning methods including work shadowing, visits to courts and other departments, action learning sets, conference attendance and internal expert briefing sessions, secondments, as well as the CIPD qualification.

Perhaps the blackest cloud on the horizon for the reward profession is that not enough organizations are following the lead of the CPS in developing the more skilled and competent reward professionals that are required to play the diverse, multi-faceted and increasingly valuable roles we have described. Incomes Data Services' review of the jobs market for reward specialists concluded: 'Organizations across all industrial sectors and regions are finding it difficult to recruit compensation and benefits professionals at all levels' (IDS, 2005c). Recruiters Badenoch and Clark believe that 'reward specialists are the most sought after function'.

A company value that the recognition scheme at Harvey Nichols we described earlier in this chapter is designed to reinforce is that of being 'exclusive but available'. The current upside for rewards staff of having the first without the second is a pay premium, but the longer-term implications are less attractive for UK organizations. Jon Sutcliffe, pay adviser to the Employers Organization for Local Government, blames the slow rate of progress in the implementation locally of single status agreements on a shortage of reward management know-how. Geoff White is similarly worried by a 'real capacity problem' across the public sector in reward expertise, which threatens the achievement of many of the current reward and wider modernization reforms in government (Arkin, 2005).

This lack of attention to developing enough of the required professionals and professionalism may also have a personal dimension. Given the fast-changing and expanding nature of reward roles, in a function also typically having a lead role in learning and development in organizations, you might anticipate that we would be investing considerably in our own personal development, to keep up and ahead of these demands. Yet Watson Wyatt's unpublished survey of participants in its Reward Network found that on average, heads of reward were only devoting 5 per cent of their time, less than three hours a week, to their own personal development. They thought that this was less than half the amount that they should be spending. The opportunities are there – of reading, getting out with colleagues, attending networks, conferences and workshops and so on – but the issue appears to be prioritizing the time to take advantage of them.

Personally and nationally, therefore, employers and individuals have to devote more resources to developing the demanding set of competencies that we have seen are required to play the diverse roles that will make reward and business strategy happen on a more widespread basis. As we have seen from examples throughout this book, the potential is huge, but we need to invest more to achieve it.

13

Communicating reward strategy: from telling and selling to involving and engaging

'It's all in the communication'; 'You simply can't over-communicate'; 'Total reward is all about communication'; 'Communication is key'; 'A communication strategy is essential'. Throughout all our research for this book, the HR and reward professionals we have spoken to and the books and studies we have read overwhelmingly emphasize that employee communication is the 'make or break' of successful reward strategies, policies and plans.

In this chapter, we look at why communication is so important and illustrate the wide range of ways and media now being used to get messages on rewards over to staff. Rewards arrangements are an integral part of the increasingly popular approach of employer branding, which is being used by organizations attempting to increase their attractiveness in the recruitment market and to encourage staff loyalty.

We go on to question how much substance and real employee involvement and engagement there is under much of the hype about creating these 'great places to work'. Only a more open and two-way, dialogue-based approach to reward communication, we argue, will realize the full potential of strategic reward management, and we illustrate the benefits of this approach, particularly at times of reward changes and challenges.

THE IMPORTANCE OF COMMUNICATION

When the CIPD asked its reward survey respondents to list the barriers to effectively operating their reward strategies, they did not generally refer to issues of wrong scheme selection or bad design. Predominantly they listed the 'softer' process issues of changing staff attitudes (26 per cent) and poor communication (25 per cent). As one manager told us, 'employees aren't getting the information, don't understand or trust decisions on pay'.

There are perhaps three fundamental reasons why communication is so important to the delivery of reward strategies and why good communication is so difficult to achieve. First, reward can be a technically complex field, and the contemporary developments we have described, such as the moves towards total rewards and the greater tailoring and personalization of reward packages, make full employee understanding both more important and more difficult to achieve. As American satirist Dave Barry wryly observed, 'I can't understand my pension, no matter how many beers I drink.'

Secondly, unless staff do understand their rewards arrangements then the employer is not investing what is generally their largest cost item in an effective way. A recent consultancy study found that the majority of UK employees substantially underestimate the real costs of their benefits package, and despite the rapidly escalating costs, a third of staff were not even aware that their employer contributed to their occupational pension plan. Attitude surveys in a major technology company suggested that up to $10 million of pay and employment costs were in fact having no effect on employee attraction, retention or motivation.

Moreover, the desired goal of using rewards to reinforce those behaviours driving the business strategy will not be achieved if staff don't understand their rewards and what they are designed to do. The directors of a car manufacturer were delighted with the level of strategic alignment that consultants apparently delivered to them in a new plant incentive. Each of the firm's six strategic priorities was reflected in a measure in the incentive plan. Yet an attitude survey in the plant 18 months later found that the majority of employees didn't understand the measures in the plan or felt unable to influence them, and so most favoured a return to the previous pay arrangements. In fact, given the complexity of many contemporary long-term incentive plans, it must be questionable as to how many executive participants really understand what they have to do in order to drive up the performance measures and payments.

Thirdly, rewards are an unavoidably emotive issue. So many personal needs are tied up in them – for security, recognition, status and so on – that discussion of and particularly changes to them almost inevitably generate emotional and sometimes hostile responses from at least some employees.

Hence, as we saw in previous chapters, the importance of treating any alteration to reward packages as a significant change management exercise in which effective communication has a critical role to play. BT made a major series of pay and benefits changes in implementing its new reward strategy. Director Kevin Brady emphasizes the importance of employee communication and advises others not to underestimate the scale of employee and trade union resistance based on this experience.

COMMUNICATING THE REWARD STRATEGY

Figure 13.1, drawn from the CIPD's annual reward management survey (CIPD, 2005a) illustrates the wide range of vehicles organizations now use to communicate about reward strategies and issues to their staff. IT and company intranets have clearly been embraced by reward professionals as they try to get the rewards message across, alongside the more traditional employee handbooks and policy manuals.

		Percentage of respondents by sector			
	All	Manufacturing and production	Private sector services	Voluntary sector	Public services
Intranet	62	51	64	74	64
Through line managers	60	51	61	59	67
HR presentations/ meetings	46	37	51	29	51
Staff handbook	45	44	40	65	44
Part of recruitment/ selection/induction process	40	40	44	48	29
Through staff groups	37	28	28	53	60
Reward/benefit statements	32	30	44	24	11
Newsletters	26	21	23	17	40

Figure 13.1 Getting the message across? Popular ways of communicating the reward strategy

The fifth Workplace Employee Relations Survey (Kersley *et al*, 2005) confirms an increasing variety of direct communication methods are in evidence across this large sample of UK organizations, with:

▌ 91 per cent operating staff or team briefing meetings (up from 85 per cent in 1998);

▌ 74 per cent using notice boards, 38 per cent e-mails and 34 per cent intranets;

▌ 45 per cent staff newsletters;

▌ 42 cent carrying out employee surveys.

Through such channels, more than two-thirds of organizations claim that their staff now receive information on the salary grade they are in, their pay range and their positioning in it, the evaluation system and how jobs are placed in grades, the pay increase policy, the appraisal system and the benefits package.

In fact, go to any rewards or benefits exhibition and you might be forgiven for thinking from the enormous range of communication advice and aids on offer that the problem in this area for UK employees in our media-obsessed age has become one of information overload rather than ignorance.

Total rewards concepts have given a big stimulus to this activity, for as Darren Smith, a communications consultant at Hewitt Bacon and Woodrow explains, they give the opportunity for 'staff to see everything together in one place and recognize its overall value' (Hadaway, 2005). Organizations are using increasingly sophisticated techniques derived from customer market research to analyse the needs of their workforce and deliver tailored and flexible packages to meet them.

A good example is Royal Bank of Scotland, which offers a comprehensive package of benefits and wide range of employee choices. The bank operates a sophisticated human capital measurement system, but with 125,000 employees worldwide, rewards communication is still a key challenge. Messages on rewards are kept as simple as possible and, through the use of technology, the aim is to enable employees to answer as many of their own questions as possible. Total rewards statements have been redesigned and this has improved staff appreciation of the value of their package. These statements are being moved online and an interactive pension's modeller is being introduced (CIPD, 2004d).

Reviewing examples in this area, Robertson's (2005) advice on communicating total and flexible rewards programmes is that organizations should:

▌ develop a communication plan;

▌ talk to staff to assess their motivations;

▮ use a wide range of communication methods, including information technology, road-shows and face-to-face briefings; 15 per cent of organizations now provide some form of online modelling tools to help managers and staff to plan, for example, the distribution of their pay budget or their future retirement savings;

▮ make the programme and its communication clear and simple, only offering choices that staff actually want, keeping a minimum core of benefits, and with clear communication themes;

▮ keep it fresh by regular fine-tuning of schemes and communication updates.

COMMUNICATION SUCCESSES

There is an increasing body of research evidence and case examples to show that where considerable attention is paid to communication then the objectives of reward strategies and programmes are more likely to be achieved. Three examples are given below.

AstraZeneca

Pharmaceutical giant AstraZeneca was created from a merger in 1999 and as HR VP Malcolm Hurrell explains, 'Employees told us what they valued and from that we created a total rewards philosophy' (Thompson, 2002). The work 'took us into the area of branding and marketing that are not traditional strengths of our function'. The company set out clear goals for the reward strategy including common terms and conditions, increasing the firm's attractiveness to talented people, focusing on performance, and introducing personal choice and flexibility.

A total rewards package focused on excellent development, an energized environment and competitive and flexible rewards was developed to deliver this, providing employees with an attractive package and wide range of lifestyle, health, financial and security options. The programme was rolled out across the organization in a series of carefully planned communication phases: six months of awareness raising, three months engagement-building, three months enrolment, followed by continuous embedding thereafter. The success can be seen in over 90 per cent of employees choosing to flex their package, and the enhanced image and appeal of the company in the recruitment market.

GAP

Clothing retailer GAP surveyed its 6,500 mostly part-time and female employees as part of a wide-ranging review of its reward policies in 2003. One of the findings was that staff were generally unaware of and did not understand the company's two existing pension schemes, so in common with the sector as a whole, participation rates were very low. As a result, UK Compensation and Benefits Manager Sue Hayes developed a new stakeholder pension plan (CIPD, 2004d). GAP also devoted considerable attention to developing an innovative approach to communication that would appeal to their generally young and image-conscious workforce, utilizing the firm's expertise in customer marketing.

The programme was rolled out in several stages starting in September 2003 and involved:

▮ a short leaflet and personalized example sent to employees' home addresses;

▮ group presentations, followed by personal meetings with individual financial advisers;

▮ a new website with a financial modeller;

▮ a 24-hour helpline run by the scheme's advisers;

▮ posters at all sites, strongly branded with the GAP image, with few words and frequent changes to maintain interest.

It is this strong, simple design focused on the company brand which Sue Hayes believes has contributed most to the success of the scheme. Feedback has been gathered from staff via questionnaires and focus groups, with very positive results. Since the scheme's relaunch, overall take-up rates have trebled, with a ten-fold increase in the number of shop staff who have joined.

Nationwide

Nationwide employed similar techniques and with similar success when making changes to its pay structure and to its pension arrangements (CIPD, 2004d). A variety of communication methods were used when the new pay bands were introduced, including:

▮ cascading the information from executive management to all levels of staff;

▮ consulting with the Nationwide Group Staff Union;

∎ publishing articles in the staff newspaper;

∎ setting up a dedicated intranet site;

∎ producing a briefing on audiocassette and CD;

∎ personalized letters for each employee.

As a result, only 85 appeals against the new pay positioning were made out of a total workforce of over 15,000.

Good communication had also helped to achieve a 93 per cent employee participation rate in Nationwide's pension plan. As well as short, simple booklets with much 'jargon busting' in evidence, the firm provides an annual pensions review to all staff in the form of an in-house magazine. It also issues all staff with combined benefits statements showing them the value of their state pension as well as their Nationwide benefits, to help their financial understanding and emphasize the need to save. All new staff are shown a short, witty video about the benefits available. The pension's team also provide pension clinics and one-to-one information sessions, though with a dispersed branch structure, the internet is assuming increasing importance, and in 2005 staff received their annual statement online.

A funding deficit in 2003 forced Nationwide to review its scheme and to move from a final salary to a career average pension plan, accompanied by an increase in staff contributions. This potentially difficult message was got across in a variety of ways, and the staff union even had an article in its magazine to emphasize that the change was necessary and had been a joint decision. Participation rates have remained unchanged and Nationwide retains the very positive staff attitudes which in 2005 saw it voted as the *Sunday Times* Best Large Employer to Work For.

COMMUNICATING THE EMPLOYER BRAND

All three of these examples illustrate how the concept of reward communication in recent years has expanded beyond the simple objectives of building employee awareness and appreciation to embrace wider goals of employee attraction and engagement. Beaumont and Martin (2003) document how the increasing evidence of the association between employee and customer attitudes that we described in Chapter 7 has encouraged the importing of the branding concept from external marketing to the workforce of the organization and potential recruits. As they explain, rewards are a key component of this branding, which they define as 'what it is like to work at a company, including tangibles such as salary and intangibles such as culture'.

Winning out in the talent war and in an environment of severe skill shortages, the argument goes, requires an attractive and distinctive branding and rewards package to attract and then retain good people. Forty-seven per cent of those in the CIPD's annual recruitment and retention survey (CIPD, 2005b) are responding to recruitment difficulties by promoting a more positive employer image in the external marketplace. For fast-growing information search company Google, 'the rewards and culture, the great brand, are always going to be attractive to people', according to markets head Russ Kohn (Lovewell, 2005b). Its rewards package emphasizes concern for the security and welfare of staff, with free meals and medical benefits for example, as well as an annual company skiing trip.

Job advertisements are a good place to spot the emphasis on different aspects of reward in a company's employer brand. For example, amongst retailers, Timberland asks potential store staff: 'Do you reflect our core values, humanity, humility, integrity and excellence? Do you mirror our product, durable and hardworking?'

Pret's offer is 'Good jobs, good people... making great food. We pay our wonderful, hardworking staff as much as we can afford rather than as little as we can get away with.' Staff in each location have the final say on whether job applicants get taken on after their day's trial, to help ensure their cultural fit.

Aldi advertises its position in *The Times* top 100 graduate employers, but makes a more traditional offer to potential area managers of '£37k plus Audi A4'.

The external 'Extra' Hollywood-style advertising campaign at the Halifax is mirrored in the recruitment advert contained on its current bank statements to customers:

> If you'd like to join the friendliest and best motivated workforce around there's no better time. We want extraordinary people to join our star cast and deliver extra special service. If you give extra – to our customers and colleagues – we'll give extra to you.

Illustrating the concept for existing staff, at recruitment agency Ajilon, created after a merger in 2002, group HR director Julie Bowen explains that the new total rewards package 'was the first group-wide initiative under the Ajilon banner'. The communication material reflected the company's red and white corporate logo (Lovewell, 2005c).

At the other extreme, an Audit Commission report (2002) noted that the common failure of public sector bodies to promote a positive image of the breadth and value of their reward package was hampering recruitment and retention, rather than it being purely an issue of low pay levels.

Becoming an employer of choice with this clear and distinct employment and reward brand has become an increasingly common strategy for UK organizations and objective for UK HR and reward directors, with a mushrooming number of contests and awards on offer. Reviewing the learning from one of the most popular of these, the *Sunday Times* Best 100 Companies to Work For survey, Leary-Joyce (2004) draws out the importance of reward and recognition, but particularly employee communication, amongst the highest placed companies.

Asda is one of the top companies profiled in her analysis. Despite the bulk of staff in the stores being on comparatively low pay levels, over 90 per cent enjoy their jobs and are proud to work there, and staff retention rates are high for the sector. Making work meaningful, creating a sense of belonging and listening to people are key components of Asda's people strategy. 'We're Listening', the staff survey, is run annually, supplemented by monthly temperature checks. Colleague circles are run in each business and used to drive the morale and business agenda. Asda also makes extensive use of employee recognition with local initiatives and an annual awards ceremony, as well as offering staff a wide range of flexible working options.

Catering company Compass's strategy is similarly to employ great people who deliver great service that produces great results. It collects and compares customer and staff attitudes on the extent to which it delivers on its corporate values such as teamwork and quality. As a result of its various initiatives, it claims a 2 per cent reduction in labour turnover, 10 per cent improvement in productivity and a large increase in job applications.

All staff at Flight Centre, another highly placed company in the *Sunday Times* listing, are required to attend a monthly 'buzz night', when all staff get together to learn, celebrate success with numerous awards and have a generally good time. While some of these specific branding and reward techniques might appear to be an acquired taste, and Schuster and Zingheim (2000) criticize such initiatives for simply creating benefits cost escalation, the facts are that the best companies in the *Sunday Times* listing achieved an average annual shareholder return of 12.1 per cent between 1998 and 2003, when the FTSE All Share index as a whole fell by 5.8 per cent.

All of these examples would suggest that:

▌ your employment brand is a measurable thing that you should define, review and assess;

▌ integrated, total rewards approaches help to cement a clear employment brand;

∎ you should compare your investment in the various aspects of your rewards package with your employees' perceptions of them, ensuring that they are aligned;

∎ you should communicate this brand identity, but keep it simple and possibly not oversell it;

∎ a key issue is whether your managers can actually deliver the promised rewarding experience in the workplace.

INVOLVEMENT AND ENGAGEMENT?

A more valid criticism of all of this reward communication and employer branding activity is that it is heavily focused on 'telling and selling' the rewards and benefits of employment, rather than on genuinely involving and engaging with staff. This is a critical point, because some of the research on high performance workplaces that we reviewed in Chapter 3 does show relationships between high performance and specific communication and reward practices. Pfeffer (1998) for example, found associations with the provision of business information and operation of performance pay schemes, most of them highlighting the necessity of wider employee involvement and engagement.

As the work of Purcell *et al* (2003) demonstrates, the key factor in high performance organizations is how they use reward and other HR practices to support a positive workplace climate in which employees voluntarily commit to deliver those levels of performance. It's no use having a well-designed incentive plan in a workplace if employees don't feel involved and are never consulted on how the performance the plan measures might be improved. They, not the incentive plan, nor even dare one say their managers, produce those improvements. The general picture on UK employee attitudes, rewards and engagement from a 'bottom-up' rather than a 'top-down' perspective is a much less positive one.

Guest's (2004) work has done much to develop and illustrate the idea of the psychological contract, the web of mutual obligations and commitments between employers and employees that underpin the high performance workplace, as modelled in Figure 13.2.

As in the West (2005) research reviewed in Chapter 7, he demonstrates, as shown in Figure 13.2, how employee attitudes in three crucial areas are at the centre of this positive contract: how trusting I am of my employers and its management, how fairly I think I am treated and rewarded, and the extent to which the promised reward brand is actually delivered in practice. These in turn are influenced by factors such as appropriate and fair reward practices, communication and involvement

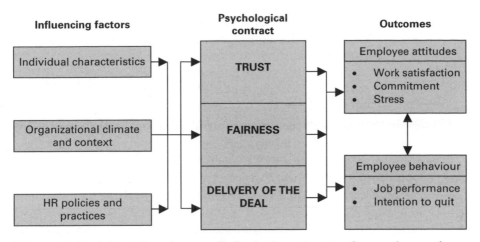

| Influencing factors | Psychological contract | Outcomes |

Figure 13.2 Managing the psychological contract: a figure drawn from Guest's 2004 research

mechanisms, well-designed and autonomous jobs, the provision of training, as well as the general workplace climate and support of managers. These attitudes are also strongly related to employee outcomes including levels of stress, intention to leave, commitment to the employer and performance.

So just how healthy is the general state of the UK psychological contract between employer and employees revealed by Guest's regular studies of thousands of employees over the last decade? In essence, although most employees are broadly satisfied with their employer, the picture is much less rosy than the branded recruitment adverts would lead us to believe:

▮ on trust, only 25 per cent of employees trust senior management to look after their interests, and the trend is downwards;

▮ similarly on involvement, in 2004 only 40 per cent felt involved in workplace decision making, down from 50 per cent in 1996;

▮ on fairness, 40 per cent of employees felt that they were not fairly rewarded for the work they carry out and 31 per cent felt they were unfairly paid compared to others in their organization; and

▮ in respect of delivering on its promises, only 45 per cent of employees feel that their organization has fully delivered the promised employment and reward deal, while less than half reported they were regularly motivated by their manager and just 37 per cent said their manager helps to improve their performance.

Other studies support this general conclusion of a lack of meaningful and rewarding involvement and engagement of staff, underneath the welter of top-down communication they are receiving on business and reward matters. In the appropriately titled *Reconnecting with Employees*, Towers Perrin (2005) found that just 14 per cent of the thousands of UK employees they surveyed were highly engaged at work. Staff engagement scores correlated positively with employer revenue growth and declining costs, as well as significantly lower employee attrition.

Interestingly, the study also revealed that while financial rewards such as competitive base pay and benefits were the most important factors in attracting new recruits, perceived fairness of pay and particularly non-financial rewards such as career development, leadership and challenging work were the most significant determinants of retention and engagement.

Similarly, Hay Group's Insight database reveals that less than half of UK employees are positive about the openness and honesty of communication in their organization, although two-thirds of those employed by companies in their most admired, high performing company index, feel their employer does a good job of communicating (Hubbard, 2005).

THE REWARD STRATEGY AND INVOLVEMENT GAP

Hay's data is pertinent from two other perspectives, specifically concerning reward communication. First, it indicates a dissonance between how employees want to and actually are receiving information on their rewards. The preference is for face-to-face discussion with their immediate manager, but the existing predominance of written forms leaves the informal 'grapevine' to take up the slack, however inaccurately it may perform. Secondly, a survey Hay carried out of 1,200 heads of reward found that only a third rated their rewards communication as very effective, and two-thirds thought that fewer than half of their employees actually understood their employer's reward strategy.

The CIPD's annual reward management survey (CIPD, 2005a) draws exactly the same conclusion in charting who was actually involved in the development of reward strategy in some 500 employers. As can be seen in Figure 13.3, while HR and reward professionals have very much taken on the message to get strategic by consulting and engaging with board members, less than half consulted with their line managers who actually implement most of their reward policies, and fewer than 10 per cent involved employees or their elected and trade union representatives. Hardly a recipe for subsequent understanding, appreciation and support.

Trade unions have historically been a powerful force for employee involvement in pay and employment matters in the UK, and it must be

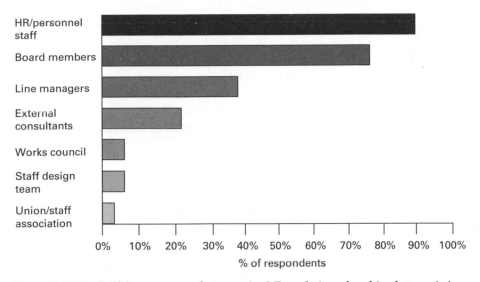

Figure 13.3 Still-born reward strategies? People involved in determining the reward strategy

said, for communicating with and educating employees on these issues. Yet despite sporadic evidence to the contrary, the proportion of employees who are unionized in this country has declined over the last 20 years to the point where fewer than one in five in the private sector are union members today. Between 1980 and 2000 the coverage of collective pay bargaining agreements fell from over three-quarters of workplaces to less than a third, with a heavy concentration in declining areas of the economy and the public sector (Emmott, 2005).

While this decline may have helped reward arrangements in UK organizations to have become more strategic in the sense of being driven more strongly and unilaterally by management and business requirements, a major concern we have highlighted in this final section of the book has been the general failure to replace these consultative channels with alternative means of employee involvement. The fifth Workshop Employee Relations Survey (Kersley *et al*, 2005) shows that a range of employee communication schemes are widespread, such as management cascades and team briefings. But the incidence of wider employee involvement mechanisms such as problem-solving groups, self-managed teams and employee share ownership schemes remain in the minority, and in some cases have declined in incidence since 1998.

There is therefore a gap, a missing link in the delivery of reward strategies and in their ability to achieve their goals of motivating and engaging employees to perform and deliver on the business strategy, as represented in Figure 13.4. On the one side employers are now providing employees

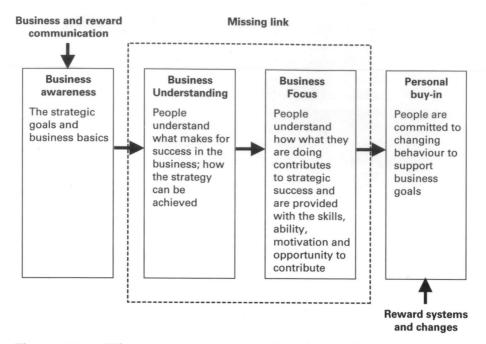

Figure 13.4 Why communication, involvement and understanding are key

routinely and often extensively with information about the business strategy and performance and to a lesser extent rewards goals and strategies. On the other side, pay and rewards schemes are being introduced to incentivize and reward staff for pursuing and achieving these performance goals.

Yet unless employees operate in a genuinely open, supportive and rewarding environment, then the connecting 'glue' of a positive psychological contract and employee engagement will not be present, and the full potential achievement of business and rewards strategies will be frustrated. Employers should not need the April 2005 regulations on information and consultation to force them to act when the business case for involvement is so clear cut.

To talk of this involvement and communication gap from a rewards perspective is doubly ironic when rewards mechanisms such as employee share schemes can themselves be powerful vehicles to promote employee ownership and participation, so as to maximize their engagement and performance. Thirty-seven per cent of organizations in the fifth Workshop Employee Relations Survey (Kersley *et al*, 2005) gave profit-related bonuses or payments, while a fifth operated employee share schemes.

An extensive review of the literature on employee participation and company performance carried out for the Joseph Rowntree Foundation

(Summers and Hyman, 2005) concluded that 'a combination of financial and work-related participative measures can have a positive impact on company performance'. Professor Andrew Pendleton, at a recent e-reward/CIPD seminar, similarly referred to a number of studies demonstrating associations between the use of employee share schemes and company performance. Employee involvement and engagement pays.

COMMUNICATING, INVOLVING, ENGAGING

Communication is not defined in the *Oxford English Dictionary* as a one-way passage of information, as an order or instruction. It is rather a two-way exchange, to promote and achieve understanding. In our modern economy and workplaces, over-centralized and hierarchical structures, top-down communication and tight management control methods are as outdated and ineffective as over-simplistic, financial carrot-and-stick strategies for motivation and reward.

In this chapter we have seen considerable attention being devoted by UK organizations to communicating the attractiveness, value and meaning of their total package, their brand of rewards, through a wide variety of increasingly creative and professional methods. Both Barclays and GAP, for example, achieved high levels of understanding of their new retirement provisions by avoiding the word 'pensions' altogether. But until this creative communication is complemented with genuinely two-way processes and wider employee involvement, then our well-thought out and designed reward strategies will never achieve their full potential in the workplace to generate high employee engagement and performance.

So finally, what are some of the ways in which organizations can increase the effectiveness of their reward strategies and initiatives through a more broadly based approach to communication and involvement? In the last sections of this chapter we draw out some key conclusions and illustrate them with further case examples. Many of the points made in previous chapters, on the need to engage with line managers and to plan and deliver reward strategies on a long-term, evolutionary basis, are also pertinent in regard to communication, where 'little and often' is a principle many successful organizations stick to. Specifically on staff communication and involvement, we draw the following conclusions.

Talking with employees

First, talk often and regularly with employees about the 'goods' and 'bads', likes and dislikes in their rewards package. We continue to be surprised at the reticence of some UK executives to consult with their staff on these issues, particularly in advance of making changes to them. The fact that research evidence shows that the simple act of consulting with employees in advance has a major impact on the success of whatever reward change is being made (see Brown and Armstrong, 1999) seems to escape them, in the face of concerns about setting expectations or fears running wild.

Consultation increases understanding of the reasons behind changes, builds support and trust in rewards, and can result in suggestions for design improvements. It has to be a more successful approach than trying to foist changes on to people unannounced at the time of implementation, however extensive and sophisticated the communication onslaught that is then launched. As Bowey (1982) put it in a study for the Department of Employment assessing the effectiveness of performance pay schemes, 'the degree of communication and involvement was more important than the design'. Employee focus groups, design teams, interviews, surveys and regular updates are all ways of involving employees when existing reward changes are being reviewed and changes considered.

Listening to staff

Second, employee surveys are an effective means of assessing staff views on their rewards and general levels of satisfaction and engagement. They are now used by around half of UK employers. Figures 13.5 and 13.6 illustrate some of the reward findings from an annual attitude survey in two employers.

The first survey in a large private sector employer revealed a level of support for changes to existing pay arrangements which surprised the management team. The second, from a public sector employer considering the introduction of variable pay, showed clear divisions in the organization on the basis of age, with younger employees strongly supporting the move, but older and longer-serving staff more suspicious. Levels of understanding and support also varied considerably between departments. This helped to shape the design of the organization-wide bonus subsequently introduced and to target the communication so as to allay any staff group concerns.

However, as a Mercer HR Consulting (2005) study, *Why Employee Surveys Fail*, points out, many surveys don't result in improvements in employee communication and engagement, primarily because no follow-up action is taken in response. This simply generates employee demotivation and cynicism. Two examples follow which illustrate the benefits of genuinely listening and responding to employee opinions.

	Mean	
We should reward effective teamwork here	4.09	
We should make greater use of bonus schemes here	3.70	
I understand how to make XYZ successful	3.68	Agree
I enjoy working for XYZ	3.68	
Individual performance should influence the size of my pay increase	3.64	
I am clear about the definition of my job, my objectives and the performance which is expected of me	3.53	
All things considered, pay, benefits and conditions are generally good here	3.48	
The performance of the organization should determine my bonus	3.30	
I get all the training I need to do my job effectively	3.26	
I have regular performance discussions with my manager/supervisor	3.23	
I fully understand our current pay arrangements, benefits and terms and conditions	3.20	
I am highly motivated in my present job	3.19	

I am fairly paid in relation to similar jobs in XYZ	3.04	
Good work here is generally recognized	2.70	
I think I will be looking to work somewhere else in the next six months	2.66	
I have found competencies helpful to focus my learning and development activities	2.63	
There are plenty of opportunities to develop and advance my career here	2.58	
The performance appraisal helps me do my job better	2.55	
We communicate well on pay matters within the organization	2.53	
I am motivated by the bonus for all staff to help XYZ succeed	2.45	
I am involved in any decisions that affect my work and rewards	2.44	
My pay level is competitive with that of similar jobs in other organizations	2.37	Disagree
The annual pay review is managed in an effective manner	2.29	
My pay progresses at a rate that reflects the growth in my skills	2.05	
There is no need to make changes to the current performance appraisal and reward arrangements	1.97	

Figure 13.5 Communication: ask your staff what they think – an example

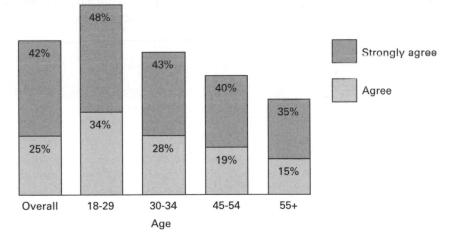

Figure 13.6 Ask your staff: views on bonus schemes in response to the statement: 'We should make greater use of bonus schemes around here'

Kwik-Fit Financial Services

Kwik-Fit Financial Services (KFS) won the CIPD's annual People Management Award in 2005 for a long-term approach to delivering performance improvement through employee involvement. In 2002 the business faced ruinous competition and staff turnover was high. Only 40 per cent of employees bothered to complete the annual opinion survey that year.

Following the sale of the business to CVC venture capitalists, the management decided that the only way forward was to engage the staff and make KFS a fantastic place to work. Thirty-two workshops were held with staff, resulting in over 6,500 ideas to improve performance and make the place fantastic. Led by the HR Director, project teams were then formed around six key areas, including facilities, working hours, customer service and pay and bonuses.

Three years later, the business performance and working environment are transformed, with major improvements in sales conversion rates, customer retention and just about every key business measure. Profits are up by over 60 per cent.

For employees, improvements to the workplace have included an on-site concierge, chill-out room and a staff crèche. In 2005 a comprehensive new flexible benefits package and pension plan were introduced. Collaborative teamworking and management styles have been adopted, and the appraisal system revamped. As a result, staff turnover and absence have fallen significantly. The number of staff recommending KFS as a great place to work has gone up from 64 per cent to 84 per cent, with almost half of all new recruits resulting from internal referrals, and the company moved up to number 15 in the *Sunday Times* best companies list in 2005.

Telewest

At Telewest a survey of employees by MORI revealed 47 per cent of the company's workforce to be disengaged. As Employee Relations Manager Kieran Scott explains, this and the impending legislation on consultation led the company to set up forums of elected employee representatives, called TIME (Telewest involving me). Some cynicism amongst the new representatives was evident at first, while other barriers to be overcome were the potential opposition of trade union officials and middle managers.

Yet helped by a clearly defined and agreed consultation agenda, and the training of employee representatives, the forums are now operating well and a number of successes are already evident. Scott cited the example of representatives' input into a suggested company bonus plan design, which led to the design being amended and an additional £5 million payment being made to employees as a result (Emmott *et al*, 2005).

Genuine involvement

Third, whatever your views on trade unions and collective bargaining, as at Telewest ensure that you have effective, extensive and varied channels of communication and involvement in your organization, to genuinely engage with staff on reward and employment issues. As the Joseph Rowntree study illustrated, these have to be tailored to suit the needs and character of each organization and its workforce, but they need to be in place.

Group HR Director Philippa Hird explains the triple-track approach to employee relations and engagement at ITV (Emmott *et al*, 2005), involving:

▌ formal negotiations with trade unions that represent 50 per cent of the workforce, though only 15 per cent of employees are union members;

▌ consultation in regular meetings with 250 elected employee representatives on 15 communication groups;

▌ direct communication and engagement with individual employees, ranging from a daily online update on the company's 'Watercooler' intranet, to involving thousands of employees in group discussions to help develop the new company branding.

Hird has found collective bargaining to be a highly effective way of agreeing the major restructuring necessitated by industry changes and the emergence of digital channels, with significant staff reductions having been made with no industrial action or protest resulting. However, she believes the one-to-one manager/employee relationship, supported by effective communication and reward policies, is key to delivering employee engagement.

Most publicity tends to be attracted to the somewhat wacky and informal involvement styles and methods employed in companies such as Google and advertising agency St Lukes, where staff have a say in who gets what share of the total annual bonus payment pot. Rachel Dobson, Head of HR at fast-growing law firm Pannone and Partners, told a recent DTI conference (2005) how the firm goes overboard on communication and recognition, with considerable quantities of cream cakes and company social events for staff in evidence. In a demanding and time-pressured environment, extra holidays are an extremely effective method of recognizing high performance, although 86 per cent of staff report that they have fun at work.

Yet the collective ethic and staff involvement are also evident in pay arrangements. In place of the partner-only individual profit sharing that exists in most of its competitors, there is an all-employee bonus scheme that pays out a common percentage of salary each year to all 600 staff.

Pannone was fourth in the 2005 *Sunday Times* best companies list, first in its employees' ratings of the fairness of their pay, second in terms of how few people reported suffering from stress at work, and fourth for employees feeling that senior managers really listened to them. This is a genuinely rewarding and engaging, high performing workplace.

WHEN THINGS GO WRONG

Yet in another sense, the ultimate test of the strength of employment relationships comes when things aren't going so well and particularly when reward schemes need to be changed as a result, as illustrated in the two cases that follow.

BAE Systems

Declining equity markets and increasing longevity left BAE Systems with a massive deficit on its main final salary pension scheme (CIPD, 2004d). Following an external valuation in 2002, the company announced that it was reviewing the scheme. A specialist communication team was set up, including the pensions and communication directors. They gained the support of senior management to core principles underpinning the review, including the need to have widespread and open communication with employees, rather than hide the problem from them.

All key stakeholders were involved in the consultation. An initial leaflet was sent to all employees' homes and a helpline set up. Further communications followed at regular intervals, including a questionnaire completed by employees, which 5,000 of them returned within 48 hours.

As a result of this communication strategy, a mutually acceptable outcome for employees, their representatives and the company's directors and investors was achieved, with the main scheme preserved and both employer and employee contributions into it increased. No members opted out of the scheme as a result of the changes, and only 250 chose to retain their existing rate of contributions in return for reduced benefits. Employee understanding of the scheme also improved markedly.

According to HR Director, Employee Communications and Involvement, Stephen Windsor-Lewis, the success of the programme was down to the fact that it was undertaken slowly, to take the emotional heat out of the situation, with regular communication to develop understanding and trust.

Barclays Bank

Barclays Bank had a bad pay dispute and strike over the introduction of performance-related pay in 1997, resulting in an ongoing climate of poor employee relations. In 2000 the bank established a new partnership agreement with trade union Unifi. Union officials and staff are elected on a 50:50 basis onto the new group and are consulted over policy changes at an early stage. The core principles of its reward strategy were agreed by the Partnership. It has also worked on setting up the bank's policies on flexible working and career breaks, supporting the goal of becoming an employer of choice (Holbeche, 2005).

A long-term approach

An even longer-term, persistent approach is evident in the recent history of Volvo's car plant in Ghent in Belgium, as related at the DTI's EU conference (2005) by director of HR, Hans Bogaert. A series of conflicts culminated in a long strike in 1978. The 'new vision' adopted in 1981 aimed to improve performance through high levels of employee involvement and motivation, and personal recognition.

This was no short-term, 'flavour of the month' HR initiative. Teamworking and job enrichment programmes in the 1980s were followed by self-steering and managed teams in the 1990s, all supported by regular staff meetings and consultation, and annual staff surveys. Numerous jobs on fixed pay rates were replaced by three pay bands, with progression related to skills and career development.

It took 22 years for the plant to produce its one-millionth car, yet the second millionth was achieved in the last four years alone. Quality, cost and delivery performance have all consistently improved over that time. There have been associated improvements in employee opinions, including levels of commitment and satisfaction with rewards. The numbers employed have almost doubled over that period to over 5,000. The very survival of the plant in such a high cost location with 100 per cent union membership is testament to the success of a high involvement approach.

THE FINAL MESSAGE

The final message in this book, therefore, is that effective reward strategies and their communication are not and never have been a 'quick win' or 'quick fix'. But the greater sense of realism that we have described as emerging in the application of the concept in the UK – with greater attention paid to the implementation and process aspects of strategy, including employee communication, involvement and engagement, and to ensuring adaptability and long-term effectiveness – means that the full potential of reward arrangements to reinforce high performing and sustainably successful organizations is far more likely to be realized in many more of our workplaces.

Conclusions

What conclusions have we reached on completing this book? Researching and writing it has certainly reinforced our belief that strategic reward is ultimately a way of thinking that you can apply to any reward issue arising in your organization, to see how you can create value from it. It has also confirmed our view that reward strategy has a vital role to play as a key element in an organization's HR strategy as long as we recognize the need to shift from planning to process, from intent to implementation. Having strategic reward goals is one thing, practising them quite another. The UK reward scene today is characterized by diversity, empiricism and, to a degree, conservatism. A number of organizations 'burnt their fingers' and experienced problems following popular and well-publicized approaches, most notably individual performance-related pay.

Aldous Huxley, the author of the well-known science fiction novel *Brave New World*, once remarked that the British are an island race that, 'dream in a pragmatic way'. Most UK organizations have now adopted the US-originated concept of a reward strategy, a dream if you like of how they want their reward arrangements to operate. They have thankfully moved a long way from their traditional, history-driven, administratively focused pay and benefits practices.

At the same time, there has more recently been a shift back from some of the rhetoric and grand claims that were initially associated with the concept, accompanied by a more realistic and pragmatic assessment of the role of reward strategy as a long-term contributor to organizational success. We have profiled the common issues experienced by UK reward professionals in trying to deliver on their reward strategies, and how by tailoring approaches to the local environment, borrowing and melding methods to suit their needs, and adopting a persistent and long-term, evolutionary perspective, they are coming closer to realizing their strategic dreams. We have also commented on the need to take a painstaking approach – there are no quick fixes. We call this approach 'the new realism'.

A reward manager responded to the question in the CIPD annual rewards survey asking him to identify the biggest strategic reward challenge he faced by listing, 'introducing a new, more flexible pay structure, appraisal system and flexible benefits, all without increasing the pay bill'. His next answer as to how he was addressing this challenge was, appropriately, 'slowly and carefully'.

We have also noted that reward management is no longer an isolated discipline practised by people living in a world of their own behind closed doors. Instead, it has become a complex process that involves addressing the alignment with business strategy, and also means taking into account the broader economic context and legislative environment, as well as in a 'sellers' labour market, the needs and motivations of an increasingly diverse workforce. Balancing these requirements in an appropriate future direction for practice is perhaps the touchstone of successful contemporary reward strategies.

In its conclusions on their findings from their 2005 survey, the CIPD commented that:

> While approaches to reward are becoming more strategic, integrated and flexible, our research also shows that they are becoming more holistic. Nearly three in ten organizations have adopted a 'total reward' approach to the financial and non-financial elements of what makes a rewarding place to work. (CIPD, 2005a)

The CIPD also commented that:

> When it comes to base pay and recruiting, retaining and engaging staff, employers have adopted a wide variety of approaches to organizing salaries and pay progression, levels and awards indicating that there is no 'one best way' to do this. Instead, organizations need to assess which approach is most likely to work given their particular circumstances and then tailor their approach accordingly. Again, what counts is not just design but delivery. (CIPD, 2005a)

A final word

> You cannot succeed without focusing on business goals and understanding what these mean for your core people goals. Shareholder value was our ultimate objective. But we unbundled this objective and examined how we would

generate shareholder value through our reward strategy. We wanted to recruit, retain and engage good people. You might do that in the short term by throwing more money at people, but we wanted a long-term solution that really focussed on the individual and their contribution within the business. Meeting individual needs by providing flexibility within a framework has enabled us to generate significant value for both employees and the company alike. (Tim Fevyer, Senior Manager, Compensation and Benefits, Lloyds TSB)

References

Alderfer, C (1972) *Existence, Relatedness and Growth,* The Free Press, New York

Arkin, A (2005) Eyes on the prize, *People Management,* 10 February, pp 29–35

Armstrong, M and Baron, A (1995) *The Job Evaluation Handbook,* IPD, London

Armstrong, M and Murlis, H (2004) *Reward Management,* 5th edn, Kogan Page, London

Audit Commission (2002) *Recruitment and Retention: A public service workforce for the twenty-first century,* Public Sector National Report, London

Barney, J (1991) Firm resources and sustained competitive advantage, *Journal of Management,* **17,** pp 99–120

Beaumont, P and Martin, G (2003) *Branding and People Management: What's in a name?,* CIPD, London

Berry, M (2005) Defining era for HR, *Personnel Today,* 9 August, p 1

Bevan, S (2005) Reward strategy, e-reward/CIPD Reward Symposium (unpublished)

Bevan, S, Barber, L and Robinson, D (1997) *Keeping the Best: A practical guide to retaining key employees,* Institute for Employment Studies, Brighton

Bissel, P (2005) Using HR metrics at Nationwide, e-reward/CIPD Reward Symposium (unpublished)

Bloom, M and Milkovich, G T (1998) Rethinking international compensation, *Compensation and Benefits Review,* April, pp 17–27

Bolger, A (2005) How Aegon's chief came of age, *Financial Times FM supplement,* 5 September, p 4

Bowey, A (1982) *The Effects of Incentive Pay Systems,* Department of Employment Research Paper, Number 36, London

Boxall, P and Purcell, J (2003) *Strategic Human Resource Management,* Palgrave Macmillan, Basingstoke

Brett, S (2005) *Reward and Diversity: Making fair pay add up to business advantage,* CIPD, London

Bronson, P (1999) *The Nudist on the Late Shift and Other Tales of Silicon Valley,* Secker and Warburg, London

Brown, D (2001) *Reward Strategies; From intent to impact*, CIPD, London

Brown, D and Armstrong, M (1999) *Paying for Contribution: Real performance-related pay strategies*, Kogan Page, London

Brumbach, G B (1988) Some ideas, issues and prejudices about performance management, *Public Personnel Management*, Winter, pp 387–402

Burns, B (1992) *Managing Change*, Pitman, London

Cendant Mobility (2002) Worldwide *Benchmark Study: New approaches to global mobility* (contact: marketing@cendantmobility.com)

CIPD (2003a) *The Change Agenda: The challenge of the age*, CIPD, London

CIPD (2003b) *HR Survey: Where we are, where we are heading*, CIPD, London

CIPD (2004a) *How to Develop a Reward Strategy*, CIPD, London

CIPD (2004b) *Business Partnering: A new direction for HR*, CIPD, London

CIPD (2004c) *Reorganising for Success: A survey of HR's role in change*, CIPD, London

CIPD (2004d) Pensions *Communications: Realising the value: a guide*, CIPD, London

CIPD (2005a) *Annual Survey Report: Reward management*, CIPD, London

CIPD (2005b) *Annual Survey Report: Recruitment, retention and turnover*, CIPD, London

CIPD (2005c) *Flexible Working: Impact and implementation, an employer survey*, CIPD, London

CIPD (2005d) *Guide to Human Capital Reporting: an internal perspective*, London, CIPD

CIPD (2005e) *Survey of Careers in HR*, CIPD, London

CIPD (2005f) *Effect of organizational change on pay systems, e-reward*, CIPD Reward Symposium (unpublished)

Cohen, D J (2005) Human resource education: a career-long commitment, in ed M Losey *et al*, *The Future of HRM*, John Wiley, New Jersey

Corporate Leadership Council (2002) *Performance Management Survey*, CLC, London

Coyle, D (2001) Power to the people, in ed N Page, *The Future of Reward*, CIPD, London

Cox, A and Purcell, J (1998) Searching for leverage: pay systems, trust, motivation and commitment in SMEs, in ed S J Perkins and St John Sandringham, *Trust, Motivation and Commitment*; A Reader, Strategic Remuneration Research Centre, Faringdon

DDI (2005) *The Leadership Forecast 2005/6: Best practice for tomorrow's global leaders*, Development Dimensions International UK, Bucks

Dennis, S (2005) Rejecting pay hierarchy: broad-banding at Britannia, *IRS Employment Review*, No 828, 29 July, pp 33–6

Dobbs, C (2005) *Patterns of Pay*, available from the UK Office of National Statistics website at www.statistics.gov.uk/downloads

DTI EU Presidency Conference (2005) High performance workplaces – because people mean business, details on the DTI website, www.dti.gov.uk, 15 September

Emmott, M *et al* (2005) *Employee Information and Consultation: Regulation, reform or revolution?* Messages from a one-day conference organised by CIPD, London School of Economics and London Metropolitan University, available on the CIPD website, www.cipd.co.uk

e-reward (2003) *Survey of Job Evaluation*, e-reward, Stockport

e-reward (2004a) *Survey of Grade and Pay Structures*, e-reward, Stockport

e-reward (2004b) *Survey of Contingent Pay*, e-reward, Stockport

e-reward (2005) *Survey of Performance Management*, e-reward, Stockport

Florida, R (2005) A dire global imbalance in creativity, *The Financial Times*, 20 July

French, W L, Kast, F E and Rosenzweig, J E (1985) *Understanding Human Behaviour in Organizations*, Harper & Row, New York

Galbraith, J R and Kazanjian, R K (1987) *Strategic Implementation: Structure, systems and process*, West Publishing, San Francisco

Gratton, L and Hailey, V H (1999) The rhetoric and reality of new careers, in eds L Gratton, V H Hailey, P Stiles and C Truss, *Strategic Human Resource Management*, Oxford University Press, Oxford

Guest, D (2000) Academic focus, *People Management*, 29 September

Guest, D (2004) *Employee Well-being and the Psychological Contract*, CIPD, London

Gupta, N and Shaw, J (1998) Financial incentives are effective, *Compensation and Benefits Review*, **28** (2), pp 28–32

Hadaway, L (2005) Sweet or sour?, *Employee Benefits*, October, pp 42–9

Hamel, G and Prahalad, C K (1989) Strategic intent, *Harvard Business Review*, May–June, pp 63–76

Herzberg, F W (1968) One more time: how do you motivate employees?, *Harvard Business Review*, January–February, pp 109–20

Herzberg, F W, Mausner, B and Snyderman, B (1957) *The Motivation to Work*, Wiley, New York

Holbeche, L (2005), *The High Performance Organisation*, Butterworth-Heinemann, Oxford

Hubbard, B (2005) The need to communicate, *People Torque, Hay Group Newsletter*, September, London

Hutchinson, S and Purcell, J (2003) *Bringing Policies to Life: The vital role of front line managers in people management*, CIPD, London

Incomes Data Services (IDS) (2004) cited by D Turner, Pay rates reflect action on the national minimum wage, *The Financial Times*, 27 September

IDS (2005a) *IDS Pay Report*, **933**, July, pp 8–9

IDS (2005b) Organisation practice on pay progression, unpublished scoping study for the Office of Manpower Economics and the CIPD, May

IDS (2005c) Job market: compensation and benefits specialists, *IDS Review*, **294**, August, pp 17–20

Jaques, E (1961) *Equitable Payment*, Heinemann, London

Johnstone, R (2004) Towards a better understanding of service excellence, *Managing Service Quality*, **14** (2–3), pp 129–33

Kanter, R M (1984) *The Change Masters*, Allen & Unwin, London

Kay, J (1999) Strategy and the illusions of grand designs, *Mastering Strategy*, Financial Times, London

Kearns, P (2003) *Human Resource Strategy: Business focused, individually centred*, Butterworth-Heinemann, Oxford

Kersley, B et al (2005) *Inside the Workplace: First findings from the 2004 Workplace Employee Relations Survey*, DTI, London

Kidder, T (1981) *The Soul of a New Machine*, Avon Books, New York

Kochan, T A and Dyer, L (1993) Managing transformational change: the role of human resource professionals, *International Journal of Human Resource Management*, **4** (3), pp 569–90

Kohn, A (1993) Why incentive plans cannot work, *Harvard Business Review*, September–October, pp 54–63

Koning, J (1993) Three other Rs: recognition, reward and resentment, *Research Technology Management*, **36** (4), pp 19–30

Lascelles, D (2005) *Other People's Money: The revolution in high street banking*, Institute of Financial Services, London

Lawler, E E III (1969) Job design and employee motivation, *Personnel Psychology*, **22**, pp 426–35

Lawler, E E III (1990) *Strategic Pay: Aligning organisational strategies and pay systems*, Jossey-Bass, San Francisco

Lawler, E E III (2000) Pay strategy: new thinking for the new millennium, *Compensation and Benefits Review*, **32** (1), pp 7–12

Lawler, E E III (2002) Pay strategies for the next economy: lessons from the dot com era, *World at Work Journal*, **11** (1), pp 6–10

Lawler E E III (2003) *Treat People Right! How organisations and individuals can propel each other into a virtuous spiral of success*, Jossey-Bass, San Francisco

Leary-Joyce, J (2004) *Becoming an Employer of Choice*, CIPD, London

Leonard, N *et al* (1999) Work motivation: the incorporation of self-concept-base processes, *Human Relations*, **52** (6), pp 969–98

Lovewell, D (2005a) Exploring new fields, *Employee Benefits*, August, pp 38–41

Lovewell, D (2005b) Recruit unifying tactics, *Employee Benefits*, September, pp 62– 66

Lovewell, D (2005c) Searching for talent, *Employee Benefits*, October, pp 66–70

Manus, T M and Graham, M D (2003) *Creating a Total Rewards Strategy*, American Management Association, New York

Mayo, E (1933) *The Human Problems of an Industrial Civilisation*, Macmillan, London

Mercer Human Resource Consulting (2005) *Why Employee Surveys Fail...and how to achieve success*, Mercer Human Resource Consulting, London

Merchants (2005) *The Merchants Global Contact Centre Benchmarking Report*, Dimension Data, London

Mintzberg, H (1987) Crafting strategy, *Harvard Business Review*, July–August, pp 66–74

Mintzberg, H, Quinn, J B and James, R M (1988) *The Strategy Process: Concepts, contexts and cases*, Prentice-Hall, Englewood Cliffs, NJ

Murlis, H (1996) *Pay at the Crossroads*, IPD, London

Murlis, H (2005) Diverse engagement factors, e-reward/CIPD Reward Symposium, (unpublished)

New Lanark Conservation Trust (2004) *The Story of New Lanark*, Lanark, p 18

O'Neal, S (1998) The phenomenon of total rewards, *ACA Journal*, **7** (3), pp 8–14

Patten, C (2005) Scientific excellence will secure Europe's future, *The Financial Times*, 18 July

Pearce, J A and Robinson, R B (1988) *Strategic Management: Strategy formulation and implementation*, Irwin, Georgetown, Ontario

Perkins, S (2006) *Guide to International Reward and Recognition*, CIPD, London

Personnel Today (2005) Vertex customer management, 6 September, p 20

Pfeffer, J (1998) *The Human Equation: Building profits by putting people first*, Harvard Business School Press, Boston

Porter, L W and Lawler, E E (1968) *Managerial Attitudes and Performance*, Irwin-Dorsey, Homewood, IL

Porter, M (1980) *Competitive Strategy*, Free Press, New York

Porter, M and Ketels, H M (2003) *Competitiveness: Moving to the next stage*, Economics Paper, No 3, Department of Trade and Industry, London

Purcell, J (1999) Best practice or best fit: chimera or cul-de-sac, *Human Resource Management Journal*, **9** (3), pp 26–41

Purcell, J (2001) The meaning of strategy in human resource management, in ed J Storey, *Human Resource Management: A critical text*, Thompson Learning, London

Purcell, J (2005) HRM and organisational effectiveness, e-reward/CIPD Reward Symposium (unpublished)

Purcell, J, Kinnie, K, Hutchinson, S, Rayton, B and Swart, J (2003) *Understanding the People and Performance Link: Unlocking the black box*, CIPD, London

Quinn, J B (1980) *Strategies for Change: Logical incrementalism*, Irwin, Georgetown, Ontario

Reed, A (2001) *Innovation in Human Resource Management*, CIPD, London

Rees, D (2005) Pay structures, in ed P Suff, *CIPD Reward Management Manual*, CIPD, London

Reeves, R and Knell, J (2001) All of these futures are yours, in ed N Page, *The Future of Reward*, CIPD, London

Reich, R (2004) *Reason: Why Liberals will Win the Battle for America*, Alfred Knopf, New York

Reilly, P (2005) What do knowledge workers really want?, *IRS Employment Review*, Number 826, 24 June, p 8

Reynolds, J (2004) *Helping People Learn*, CIPD, London

Risher, H (2002) Planning a next generation salary system, *Compensation and Benefits Review*, **34** (6), pp 13–23

Robertson, I T and Smith, M (1985) *Motivation and Job Design*, IPM, London

Robertson, J (2005) How you sell flex, *Flexible benefits research supplement, Employee Benefits*, September, pp 8–11

Robinson, D (2005) Employee engagement, e-Reward/CIPD Reward Symposium (unpublished)

Ryan, R *et al* (1983) The relation of reward contingency and interpersonal context to intrinsic motivation, *The Journal of Personality and Social Psychology*, **45** (4), pp 56–71

Scarborough, H (2003) *Change Agenda: Human capital external reporting framework*, CIPD, London

Schuster, J R and Zingheim, P K (1992) *The New Pay*, Lexington Books, New York

Schuster, J R and Zingheim, P K (2000) *Pay People Right! Pay strategies for the new economy*, Jossey-Bass, San Francisco

Scott-Jackson, W (2005) *HR Outsourcing: the key decisions*, CIPD, London

Sloman, M (2003) *Training in the Age of the Learner*, CIPD, London

Sloman, M (2005) *Change Agenda: Training to learning*, CIPD, London

Sloman, M and Philpott, J (2005) Training and learning in the knowledge and service economy, paper presented at the University Forum for HRD Conference, 27 May, available from m.sloman@cipd.co.uk

Sparrow, P *et al* (2004) *Globalising Human Resource Management*, Routledge, London

Stanton Marris (2005) *Holding on and Letting Go*, issue 7 of 'Energising the Organisation', Stanton Marris, London

Stevens, J (1998) *High-performance Working is for Everyone*, IPD, London

Stewart, T A (1996) Taking on the last bureaucracy, *Fortune Magazine*, 15 January

Stibbe, M (2005) Getting to Grips, *Flexible benefits research supplement, Employee Benefits*, April, pp 25–6

Summers, J and Hyman, J (2005) *Employee Participation and Company Performance: A literature review*, The Joseph Rowntree Foundation, York

Swart, J and Kinnie, N (2004) *Managing the Careers of Professional Knowledge Workers*, CIPD, London

Swart, J *et al* (2003) *People and Performance in Knowledge-intensive Firms*, CIPD, London

Thompson, A A and Strickland, A J (1990) *Strategic Management: Concepts and cases*, Irwin, Georgetown, Ontario

Thompson, M (1998) Trust and reward, in ed S J Perkins and St John Sandringham, *Trust, Motivation and Commitment: A reader*, Strategic Remuneration Research Centre, Faringdon, pp 66–71

Thompson, P (2002) *Total Reward*, CIPD, London

Thurley, K (1979) *Supervision: A reappraisal*, Heinemann, Oxford

Tomkins, R (2005) Digitisation makes monkeys of us all, *The Financial Times*, 19 July

Towers Perrin (2005) *Reconnecting with Employees: Quantifying the value of engaging your workforce*, Towers Perrin, London

TUC (2001) *It's your Call,* Trade Union Congress, London

Tyrrell, P (2005) Smart companies take on the intrapreneurial spirit, *The Financial Times,* 25 July, p 11

Tyson, S (1997) Human resource strategy: a process for managing the contribution of HRM to organizational performance, *The International Journal of Human Resource Management,* **8** (3), pp 277–90

Ulrich, D (1997) *Human Resource Champions,* Harvard Business School Press, Boston

Ulrich, D and Brockbank, W (2005a) *The HR Value Proposition,* Harvard Business School Press, Boston

Ulrich, D and Brockbank, W (2005b) Role call, *People Management,* 16 June, pp 24–8

West, M *et al* (2002) The link between management of employees and patient mortality in acute hospitals, *International Journal of Human Resource Management,* **13** (8), pp 1299–1310

West, M *et al* (2005) *Rewarding Customer Service? Using reward and recognition to deliver your customer service strategy,* CIPD, London

WorldatWork (2000) *Total Rewards: From strategy to implementation,* WorldatWork, Scottsdale, AZ

Wright, C (2005) Reward strategy in context in *CIPD Reward Management Manual,* CIPD, London

Zingheim, P K and Schuster, J R (2002) Pay changes going forward, *Compensation and Benefits Review,* **34** (4), pp 48–53

Subject index

Author index